Poisonous Pandas

APARC
STANFORD
IIS

THE WALTER H. SHORENSTEIN
ASIA-PACIFIC RESEARCH CENTER

Studies of the Walter H. Shorenstein Asia-Pacific Research Center

Andrew G. Walder, General Editor

The Walter H. Shorenstein Asia-Pacific Research Center in the Freeman Spogli Institute for International Studies at Stanford University sponsors interdisciplinary research on the politics, economies, and societies of contemporary Asia. This monograph series features academic and policy-oriented research by Stanford faculty and other scholars associated with the Center.

Poisonous Pandas

CHINESE CIGARETTE MANUFACTURING
IN CRITICAL HISTORICAL PERSPECTIVES

*Edited by Matthew Kohrman, Gan Quan,
Liu Wennan, and Robert N. Proctor*

Stanford University Press

Stanford, California

Stanford University Press
Stanford, California

Printed in the United States of America on acid-free, archival-quality paper

Library of Congress Cataloging-in-Publication Data

Names: Kohrman, Matthew, editor. | Gan, Quan, Dr., editor. | Liu,
    Wennan, editor. | Proctor, Robert, editor.
Title: Poisonous pandas : Chinese cigarette manufacturing in critical
    historical perspectives / edited by Matthew Kohrman, Gan Quan, Liu Wennan,
    and Robert N. Proctor.
Description: Stanford, California : Stanford University Press, 2018. |
    Series: Studies of the Walter H. Shorenstein Asia-Pacific Research Center
    | Includes bibliographical references and index.
Identifiers: LCCN 2017046984 (print) | LCCN 2017048149 (ebook) |
    ISBN 9781503604568 (e-book) | ISBN 9781503602069 (cloth : alk. paper) |
    ISBN 9781503604476 (pbk : alk. paper)
Subjects: LCSH: Cigarette industry--China--History.
Classification: LCC HD9149.C43 (ebook) | LCC HD9149.C43 P65 2018 (print) |
    DDC 338.4/7679730951--dc23
LC record available at https://lccn.loc.gov/2017046984

Cover design by Christian Fuenfhausen
Typeset by Bruce Lundquist in 11/14 Adobe Garamond

Table of Contents

Preface

China has become the world's cigarette superpower. By 2014, factories there were already cranking out almost half the world's cigarettes—an astonishing 2.6 trillion sticks per annum. Each stick is about 85 mm in length, which means that China has reached the point where it is producing some 220 million kilometers of cigarettes in any given year. That's enough to circle the globe more than 5,500 times, or to make a continuous chain from Earth to the sun, with enough left over for most of the return trip home.

Managing this production is one of the most lucrative state monopolies in human history: the China National Tobacco Corporation (CNTC). China is renowned for doing things on a grand scale, and here too in the cigarette realm we are talking about, annually, hundreds of thousands of hectares devoted to growing tobacco, millions of trees felled for flue-curing finished leaf, trainloads of natural and synthetic chemicals injected as additives, and a workforce of millions making and selling product. Curing barns, factories, storehouses, and shops link together a supply chain, delivering a torrent of cigarettes, charmingly packaged under a multitude of brands. A favorite figure for designers of these brands since the 1960s has been the panda. From Shanxi to Yunnan, from Shanghai to Sichuan, manufacturing arms of the CNTC have used images of pandas to market their cigarettes, trafficking in the animal's symbolism of nationalism, gentleness, and ecological ethics. One of the most recognizable and profitable labels today in China Tobacco's vast portfolio of brands is Panda Cigarettes, produced by the Shanghai Tobacco Group and sold in airports duty-free around the world.

Enormity is not the only striking characteristic of the CNTC, though. Also remarkable is the hauntingly familiar damage wrought by its expansion. Whatever their country of fabrication cigarettes kill, and they kill at a predictable rate: for every million sticks smoked this will cause one death, thirty years or so down the road. They kill at this all-too-predictable rate because, as physical (and pathological) objects, cigarettes are extraordinarily homogeneous worldwide. All deliver the same witches' brew of toxic agents, ranging from gases like hydrogen cyanide and carbon monoxide to cancer-causing metals like nickel, cadmium, and lead, along with radioactive isotopes like polonium-210. There is a time delay between cause and effect, which is why most of the world's cigarette catastrophe lies in the future.

Understanding this mounting catastrophe in China is imperative, and so too is untangling its origins. Tobacco is a relative newcomer in East Asia, given that civilization there has a written record spanning some four thousand years. People have been growing and using tobacco in China only since the sixteenth century, when seeds were first imported by merchants and missionaries. Factory-made cigarettes are even more recent for the Chinese mainland: they began to be sold in large quantities only at the dawn of the twentieth century, when the world's first multinational tobacco companies arrived. Legend has it that, roughly a hundred and thirty years ago, Buck Duke opened an atlas of the world and pointed to China: "Here is where we're going to sell cigarettes."

Duke and his British American Tobacco Company could not have chosen a more tumultuous land onto which to project that dream. Twentieth-century China would become a cauldron of cataclysmic events for most of its residents, who suffered decades of war, famine, and revolution. Despite such adversity and, to a certain extent, profiting from it, the world's largest cigarette industry emerged triumphant. First hatched by the likes of Duke and a collection of Chinese capitalists, then seized and coddled by a Communist Party chaired by Mao Zedong, the Chinese cigarette industry overcame unprecedented political storms, arriving at the threshold of the twenty-first century bigger, richer, and more deadly than anything Duke could have imagined. Scarcely studied by scholars is how this Pyrrhic victory was achieved. How did the Chinese Communist Party nurture an embryonic cluster of enterprises into a modern-day industrial juggernaut?

In writing this volume, our hope has been to provoke a critical historiography of cigarette manufacturing in China, a country where currently most people are exposed to toxic cigarette smoke daily. Our starting point is that cigarettes are industrial and pathological creations. Cigarettes are addictive killers, the speartips of complex manufacturing systems, possessing rich (and enriching) histories that have by and large escaped scholarly scrutiny. Our historiography challenges the optic—commonplace in the academy and public health worldwide—that sees cigarettes merely as objects of consumption, rather than as objects of production. Our goal is to challenge the reference point of consumer sovereignty dominant in discussions of the cigarette—where "cessation" is imagined as a burden only for the consumer ("Just quit!"), while everything that goes into cigarette-making is left unexamined. As if malaria were to be fought with attention to the mosquito, while ignoring the swamp. The cigarette is a symbolically saturated object in China, one produced by sprawling, state-owned industrial enterprises with enormous financial resources and political power. Industries like these are good at making themselves opaque, but with the right kind of light, their opacity can be defied.

Writing history involves unraveling—and reweaving—how the worlds that people occupy came into being. Writing history illuminates that the world into which we are born is not the world we have to leave behind. History can be empowering in that sense, helping us to understand what must be done, and what must be undone. The cigarette has become a big and perilous part of how we live and die, but the future does not have to imitate the past. A thousand years from now, people may well look back and wonder how such a small and deadly device could capture the hearts and lungs of so many millions—and what kinds of knowledge enabled people to liberate themselves from the world's most perfect engine of addiction. Hopefully this book will provide some answers.

Robert N. Proctor

Acknowledgments

This book project has been supported financially by the Hewlett Endowment Fund for International Studies and Research, the Shorenstein Asia-Pacific Research Center at Stanford University, and the American Cancer Society. Special thanks to Karen Eggleston, Gi-Wook Shin, Andrew Walder, Tom Glynn, and Lisa Lee for backing the early stages of this project. Some amazing undergraduate researchers helped out along the way, most notably Linda Shin. Many of the strengths and none of the wrinkles to be found in this book owe to our anonymous reviewers and the steadfast support of Kate Wahl, Jenny Gavacs, Geoffrey Burn, Marcela Maxfield, Olivia Bartz, and Alan Harvey at Stanford University Press.

Poisonous Pandas

Introduction

Matthew Kohrman

The purpose of this book is to throw open a critical portal onto the production of cigarettes, challenging orthodoxies within tobacco-control research that have long prioritized consumption. Instead, we offer a historiography that unravels decades of accumulated veiling that has covered, protected, and nurtured the cigarette industry in the most populous country in the world. As a gateway into a long-ignored area of study, this book is a provocation to others to take up shovels of their own, to dig into the past of cigarette manufacturing and marketing in China, and to uncover new policy-pertinent knowledge about the greatest health calamity of our day, how it has come to exist, and how it may be quashed.

. . .

On a sweltering Raleigh summer day in 2013, an eerie event occurred in the office of North Carolina's Department of Agriculture. With the department's life-sized wooden Indian standing nearby, officials announced amidst smiles the signing of a contract that made it easier for local farmers to sell a crop to a faraway client.

Nowhere in the press release for the event was it acknowledged that the farmers' product, flue-cured tobacco, is both addictive and toxic when consumed.[1] Nor was there any mention that the new contract is facilitating a human annihilation, perhaps the largest in recorded history.

Farmers in North America are not alone in selling to this buyer. In East Africa, South America, and sizable swaths of Asia today, there are farmers who are also growing and curing leaf for the client, an agro-commercial leviathan of the People's Republic of China (PRC). The leviathan goes by two interchangeable monikers: the State Tobacco Monopoly Administration (STMA) and the China National Tobacco Corporation (otherwise called "China Tobacco").

The dual naming convention betrays the conflation of government and big business that underlies the commercial tobacco sector in contemporary China and in much of the world. It also conveys something of the centripetal trajectory of STMA/China Tobacco manufacturing: using leaf bought around the world, its factories produce cigarettes that are almost all sold in the PRC. What the double naming communicates poorly, however, is any sense of China Tobacco's enormity. This corporation has become far larger, by nearly all measures, than its closest global peers, even though its manufacturing and sales are mostly limited to one country. Responsible for two out of every five cigarettes rolled, packed, and shipped worldwide today, China Tobacco produces more cigarettes now than the world's four largest publically traded tobacco companies combined: Philip Morris International, British American Tobacco, Japan Tobacco International, and Imperial Tobacco.[2]

A common mythology is that, owing to public health interventions, the cigarette epidemic is something of the distant past. Public health campaigns, to be sure, have succeeded in bringing down the prevalence of smoking, particularly among the well-educated, in a number of countries. In China, college educated residents are less likely to smoke today than they were a decade ago, and the total number of cigarettes sold nationwide during 2015 and 2016 retreated for the first time in decades.[3] Anyone who suggests, however, that Big Tobacco is on the verge of collapse, whether in China or worldwide, is gravely misguided. The cigarette business, born on the eve of the nineteenth century, has continued to generate huge profits in the twenty-first century, and, based on current trends, the number of daily cigarette smokers around the world is projected to continue climbing, especially in low- and middle-income countries.[4] More cigarettes will be produced and sold worldwide in the year of this book's publication than in 1990, and three times as many cigarettes in the year 2020 will be rolled and smoked than there were worldwide in the middle of the twentieth century.[5] Indeed, far from crumbling, the cigarette business in many regions of the world has continued to be a money-making machine.[6] China Tobacco has certainly been cashing in. It reported double-digit growth in annual profits during the initial three and a half decades after its founding in 1982. Over a twelve-year period alone, from 2000 to 2012, its profits jumped 800 percent, making China Tobacco one of the world's thirty largest companies in sales for any industry.[7] By 2010, it was churning out more profit than the entire worldwide operations of Walmart.[8]

To make this leviathan ever more lucrative, the factories that manufacture cigarettes across China hunger for unlimited access to tobacco that is better in quality and lower in price. How to satiate such a demand, though? In 1982, a founding mission of China Tobacco was the overhaul of domestic leaf production, involving heavy-handed investments in rural management and infrastructure. This overhaul has been a mixed blessing for villagers. Whereas farmers in the post-Mao era have otherwise become free to choose what they want to grow and to sell crops to the highest bidder, when it comes to cultivating tobacco today, they are regularly micromanaged by local cadres and required to sell leaf below market value to agents of China Tobacco at prices preset by Beijing. For cigarette factories, though, the overhaul of leaf production has been a bonanza. Domestic tobacco harvests tripled in volume between the early 1980s and the early 2010s. China now leads the world in tobacco tonnage, producing more leaf than that of the next nine largest tobacco-growing countries combined.[9]

The overhaul was so bountiful that by 2012, leaders within China Tobacco began worrying about oversupply and they tapped on the brakes, reducing the country's output of flue-cured leaf some 17 percent in the ensuing three years.[10] But a seeming scarcity of "high quality" leaf persisted, so the corporation extended a program of lapping up leaf of specific types wherever it could worldwide. This scarcity can be attributed to technical shortcomings out in the fields of China, but even more so to shrewd decisions made in boardrooms of the country's biggest tobacco enterprises, decisions to increasingly market cigarettes rolled with "superior" tobacco as being, at once, safer and more socially respectable. Especially coveted now by a mounting clientele across China are cigarette brands filled with tobacco meeting the highest criteria set by industry graders. Regions like Yunnan and Guangxi have become renowned for cultivating large quantities of leaf meeting those criteria, yet their harvests are simply not enough. As a result, in locales as distant as Brazil and Zimbabwe, executives of China Tobacco have been signing contracts and building logistics centers in order to ease their factories' access to top-grade leaf.[11] Ms. Liang Zhanhua is one such executive. It was she who in June 2013 stood in the office of North Carolina's Agricultural Commissioner and triumphantly announced an agreement to open China Tobacco's first North American leaf-buying facility—in the heart of America's traditional tobacco belt. The only somber face in the room, at least the only one visible in the photo released by the Department of Agriculture, was that of the office's wooden Indian mascot.

·   ·   ·

Native Americans were first mistaken for "Indians" in the fifteenth century. Soon after, the business of producing and selling tobacco became entangled with the rise of nation-states. Born at the intersection of Europe and North America, the political novelty that was the nation-state facilitated growing dependencies between *Nicotiana tabacum* and "the people."[12] So significant had such dependencies become by the mid-twentieth century that nations not only frequently extended locally owned cigarette-making enterprises preferential credit and subsidies, but they had created specially empowered government offices to monitor, assist, and even invest in such enterprises. The twentieth century also saw many nations building their own field-to-factory tobacco monopolies. State ownership of cigarette manufacturing declined somewhat after the end of the Cold War, but alliances between government and cigarette producers remain strong today worldwide. These alliances, of course, have had everything to do with money and tobacco's addictive elixir, nicotine. Since the Age of Discovery, profits and taxes generated from tobacco's unique capacity to hook people quickly on nicotine have been tantalizing, ostensibly inescapable financial resources for nation-states.

Some readers might be hoping for this book to provide theoretical ballast to a question of economics. After James Bonsack patented the first automated cigarette rolling machine in 1880, how did so many nation-states, flying under different political economic colors, come to not just nurture the buying and selling of tobacco leaf, but also invest in the highly mechanized business of producing cigarettes? Was there a single formula for what Allan Brandt has called the "cigarette century," transcending localized economic structures (capitalist, communist, or other)?[13] Was it, for instance, the adoption of applied economic principles born at the dawn of the Industrial Revolution, originally championed by statesmen like Alexander

Hamilton and Henry Clay under the monikers of the "American school" and the "national system" and more recently disseminated under designations like "import substitution industrialization"?[14] Was it the prescriptions of Hamilton and Clay—namely, extracting capital from increasingly efficient agriculture, reinvesting that capital in large infrastructural projects, establishing high tariffs, and championing specialty exports—that was the special sauce which came to nurture nation-state/cigarette manufacturing assemblages in the twentieth century up and down the Americas, across Asia, throughout Europe, and into parts of Africa?

A problem with such a line of inquiry is it could all too easily drop us into a rabbit warren of theory too narrow for the empirical material covered by this book and requiring too much in the way of comparative evidence from other countries. It would also distract from questions and themes that this volume's contributors see as being far more important for the study of cigarette manufacturing in China. *Poisonous Pandas* brings together a group of formidable thinkers from a variety of disciplines: sociology, history, anthropology, public health, economics, and political science. We have joined forces out of a common curiosity about contemporary China, frustration with a gaping hole in scholarly research, and a conviction that interdisciplinarity can catalyze needed antidotes to a pressing social problem. Whereas China's pre-1949 tobacco industry has received substantial scholarly attention,[15] the same cannot be said about the industry from the mid-twentieth century forward.[16] In assembling this volume, our main goal is to begin redressing that lacuna, offering a foundation for a new area of research: critical historical studies of the PRC's cigarette industry. This historiography will be an indispensable springboard, we hope, for future research and policy making that tackle the contemporary tobacco endemic at its very source.

Like others at the top of a newly formed Chinese Communist Party (CCP), Mao Zedong came to be an avid reader of history, a heavy cigarette smoker, and big proponent of cigarette industrialization. How did experiments with cigarette manufacturing by the CCP before "liberation" augur the governance of cigarette supply chains in a nascent People's Republic as being something tantamount to "serving the people"? In the early 1950s, what did it take to convince regional authorities to nationalize a war-torn privately owned cigarette industry and prioritize it during ensuing waves of Communist Party upheaval? How did social, symbolic, and financial processes of Maoification lay the groundwork for a massive expansion of both cigarette manufacturing and cigarette consumption? Beyond profits and white sticks, what else did the newly nationalized industry "produce," enabling it to transmogrify cigarette making and smoking, especially among men, into performances of citizenship? During the final years of the twentieth century, as new medical discourses about tobacco's toxicity increasingly circulated worldwide, what prompted Beijing to double down as a hub of tobacco governance, such that in 1982 it became the home of the newly created China National Tobacco Corporation/State Tobacco Monopoly Administration? Since then, how have different regions within China's vast network of cigarette manufacturing adapted to contradictory forces such as post-socialist decentralization, a unified management system under China Tobacco, and the rise of global tobacco control as promoted by agencies like the World Health Organization, funders such as the Gates Foundation, and networks of public health activists?

In addressing these questions, this book prioritizes three themes.

Normalization

"Cigarette normalization" is the first theme. By that phrase, we mean more than simply how the behavior of cigarette smoking has become perceived as normal. After all, for many people in and outside of China today, the behavior of lighting and smoking a cigarette is something to avoid and disdain. Our aim, instead, is to shed light on how the cigarette's widespread availability as a consumer product has come to be viewed as unremarkable, expected, and commonplace. Cigarettes have become canonical elements of consumerism around the globe, despite resistance to tobacco smoking dating back as early as King James I (1566–1625) and Emperor Chongzhen (1611–1644) and despite intensifying public health campaigns during the last fifty years. Today, from cafés to pharmacies, and from grocery stores to petrol stations, cigarettes are widely available for purchase in nearly all countries, often prominently displayed in close proximity to candy, snacks, and beauty products. How did the cigarette become so commonplace?

No doubt, part of the answer lies is the rapid development of mechanical production. Machine makers enabled cigarettes to become widely available over a relatively short historical span, no less so in China. In 1880, about ten billion cigarettes were produced worldwide,[17] and most of those were made entirely by hand. By 1949, at the time of the PRC's founding, some eighty billion cigarettes were being produced annually in China alone, nearly all machine-rolled. By 1976, Chinese domestic production of cigarettes had increased sixfold to 491 billion per annum, even after all the chaos of the Great Leap Forward (1958–1961) and the Cultural Revolution (1966–1976). Furthermore, by 2010, using freshly imported machinery—purchased from companies like Germany's Hauni Corporation, Italy's GD, and England's Molins—China Tobacco was reporting that its factories were generating over two trillion sticks annually, under more than a hundred different Chinese brands, comprising over 95 percent of the PRC's cigarette sales.[18]

All the while, nicotine has become one of the most heavily consumed psychoactive drugs on the planet.[19] A billion people in the world are now hooked on nicotine, burning through some six trillion sticks a year, modulating moods, food cravings, and cognitive focus. It was first during the early twentieth century that cigarettes became regularly available for sale in China, at least in cities. This was also a period during which the opium trade was being eradicated, a timeline that has prompted several scholars to suggest that the cigarette's initial success in China might be attributed to it having been a legally convenient psychoactive salve for a population undergoing chemical withdrawal.[20]

The century-long normalization of the cigarette in China, like elsewhere, must be viewed as more than a process of simply chemical addiction. In other cultural contexts, it is well understood that machine-rolled tubes of finely cut tobacco leaf are not just nicotine-delivery devices.[21] So too in the People's Republic, for years the cigarette has been as much a psychotropic conduit as a symbolic "semaphore" and as much a mood modulator as a cultural patois of self and society-making.[22] Across China, the symbolic signaling that is the cigarette has become so significant that a situation now exists where smokers and nonsmokers alike often have little choice but to engage in that signaling as they go about their daily activities of work, social interaction, status differentiation, and choreographies of belonging and exclusion. *I hate how this space stinks of cheap cigarettes. Here, have one of mine . . . No, no, try one of mine, they're much better. Wow, you can afford those cigarettes? It still makes me feel uncomfortable being with a woman who is smoking in public. No, thanks, I don't smoke. I quit, on my willpower alone. Children shouldn't smoke. Smoking is so dangerous. Come on, have one. My family is from XX province so we like to smoke cigarettes made there. Folks who smoke are usually of lower quality. I wish my husband would try quitting again. Real men smoke. How pathetic, you're still buying that brand; it's time to move up; those are for country bumpkins.* These are just a few of the many cigarette-related refrains one regularly hears in the PRC.

Perhaps even more than wine in France and automobiles in the United States,[23] for folks residing across China, the if, what, when, how, where, and with whom you smoke has taken on tremendous cultural significance, all of it dependent on the unquestioned expectation that cigarettes are readily manufactured, sold, and lit. Interpersonal relations, social valuation, and material success have all become contingent, in varying degrees, upon one's ability, indeed necessity, to navigate contacts with cigarettes. Managing those contacts has become all the more complicated in recent years with the proliferation of public health warnings and smoke-free regulations.

By what means did the cigarette become such a complicated, yet expected, even normal, part of daily experience in China, helping to define self, space, and status? And how has the country's sprawling tobacco industry contributed to this cultural assemblage beyond simply making a multitude of highly addictive products?

What we know is that, as the twentieth century began, early entrants to the machine-rolled cigarette business in China struggled to sell product. Initially, people showed little interest in this commercial category. If tobacco was to be bought, the favored forms at the dawn of the 1900s were snuff and loose leaf for pipes. To create market footholds, cigarette manufacturers such as British American Tobacco and Nanyang Brothers began underwriting the development of new cultural media, such as packaging, advertising, and film, blanketing large tracts of the country with positive cigarette messaging.[24] This messaging emphasized the cigarette, not as any opiate substitute, but rather as a means to define oneself along various continuums, from traditional to modern, male to female, local to national, provincial to cosmopolitan, self-made to life-of-the-party. What we also know is that cigarette companies, in their early messaging, often tried to embed cigarette symbolism into ideas about Chinese essence and national origins. Much of this was done through brand development and product placement; innumerable cigarette labels like New China, Big China, and Nationalism (*Xin Zhongguo, Da Zhongguo, Aiguo*) were introduced and heavily promoted. Something worked, because, by the middle of the twentieth century, cigarette smoking had become a common habit and form of personal expression, especially among the well-heeled, well-educated, and politically prominent.

How did patterns of change and continuity regarding cigarettes as a symbolic semaphore relate to the ways the country's tobacco industry was reorganized and expanded under the Chinese Communist Party? And how did CCP activity ahead of its victory in 1949 lay the groundwork for those patterns?

To whet your appetite for chapters of this book, let me offer a brief answer to those questions by staying with the relationship between cigarette normalization and branding. Cigarette makers experimented heavily with brand names in the middle of the twentieth century. They generated a legion of new labels, hundreds of them, and they regularly redesigned the packaging of successful brands as many as several times a year. Some of the symbolic gambits that they first introduced have remained remarkably consistent over the years, from the 1930s all the way up to the present. For instance, the industry has held fast to uses of iconography significant to national consciousness. Some prominent examples of this genre today are the labels Xiongmao (panda), Chunghwa (a metonym for China), and Zhongnanhai (a former imperial garden in Beijing and current leadership compound for the Chinese Communist Party).

Looking back at the last half century, one can also spot sizable symbolic changes in branding—some apparently short-term and tactical, some more long-term and strategic. In general, cigarette marketers in the young People's Republic steered away from imagery and meanings smacking of bourgeois, capitalist production; spurned were many of the overtly "foreign" motifs that had been used by outfits like British American Tobacco in the 1920s and 1930s. Designers dutifully embraced themes befitting the revolutionary spirit of the age and the many political campaigns that accompanied Maoist nation building. Some of their templates were cigarette brands initially introduced by cottage factories run by divisions of the People's Liberation Army in their pre-1949 base camps. Examples of the many new cigarette brands introduced in the 1950s include Liberation, Land Reform, Anti-American (a Korean War–era innovation), Manual Labor, Bumper Harvest, and Great Leap.[25]

Especially important to mention at the outset of this book is that locality and gender were two other shifts in the symbolism of branding after 1949. Many cities in the newly founded PRC became namesakes for cigarettes. Labels like Beijing, Shanghai, Wuhan, and Tianjin, often with an iconic image of an esteemed city landmark, appeared in bold lettering on packs. By contrast, a swift erasure regarding gender occurred. What had been scores of pre-revolutionary brands overtly catering to women, like Beautiful Woman, Little Sweetheart, Flying Woman, and Rich Girl (*Meinü, Qingren, Feinü, Funü*), quickly disappeared after 1949, and only a few brands touting female themes would appear over the next fifty years (Female Soldier and New Woman, for example). In late imperial China, both men and women had used tobacco, often snorting from small containers of snuff or puffing on pipes filled with chopped leaf.[26] What's more, during the first half of the twentieth century, marketers regularly promoted cigarette brands with equal vigor, whether they catered to notions of masculinity or femininity. However, codes of conduct had changed noticeably by the 1950s, particularly for women. Whereas possessing cigarettes was deemed all the more salubrious for masculine self-identification in post-1949 China, as a mark of successful Communist manhood, it was redefined in ways far more problematic for women. Maoist propagandists, striving to teach a young nation how to identify evils, both domestic and foreign, regularly portrayed women who consumed cigarettes as frivolous bourgeois "modern girls" or even as prostitutes and traitors.[27]

The reorganization of industry sweeping across China after the Communist takeover in 1949 greatly influenced many aspects of cigarette normalization—that is a theme that unites most chapters of this book. Branding again provides a purchase to consider these processes. As was the case for many commercial sectors, Beijing dictated that cigarette companies across China during the 1950s were to be gradually nationalized, merged, and placed under the administrative thumb of provincial and municipal party authorities. During this transformation, local party officials used the cigarette pack as something of a megaphone to trumpet their ability to build local goodwill and to fulfill Beijing's mandate of industrial reorganization. Local officialdom did this by emblazoning packs with provenance information: large text on each pack stating the name of the local cigarette factory in which the sticks were produced (e.g., the Shanghai Cigarette Factory, the Wuhan Cigarette Factory). Before 1949, cigarette packs in China rarely demarcated place of manufacture. The new practice of boldly stating factory of origin on packs also allowed local officials to claim credit among their constituencies for providing the public access to both a substance long prized in China (tobacco) and a product category (the cigarette) which newspapers of the day flaunted as regularly smoked by the nation's new leaders.

It is easy today, in an age of commercial abundance, to overlook the significance of access to something like cigarettes in the early years of the People's Republic. For most citizens, the 1950s and 1960s were decades textured by comparative scarcity. Even what we might consider the most inexpensive consumer goods were regularly hard to come by. City authorities distributed their factory-demarcated cigarettes for sale to constituents via governmental shops, but also for free, a perk of city residency managed through household ration coupons. As the 1960s progressed, many cities issued ration coupons to their residents for a wide array of basic necessities. Ration coupons were again a type of megaphone for local officialdom. Cigarette coupons regularly stated that they were issued by a city's People's Government and that they were redeemable for cigarettes made by the city's recently nationalized local factory. Through these coupons, cigarette normalization took a giant leap forward, with cigarettes becoming recognized as both a basic necessity and an entitlement of city life, on par with rice, sugar, meat, cloth, and bicycles. Holding up a megaphone has its risks, however. Local city authorities needed to be especially careful that cigarettes under their supervision would not clash with tenets of the party line. After 1949, this meant rooting out any and all symbolism smacking of bourgeois excess, sex work, or anti-revolutionary sentiment. Fearing sharp disciplinary rebuke, few local party leaders overseeing cigarette manufacturing dared to permit their factories to brand packs overtly directed at women. Instead, the common move was simply to name cigarettes after the factory's host city. The practice may sound mundane, but it functioned more than adequately for many a conservative, praise-seeking, local official. Likewise, city-based branding was effective at saturating the otherwise generic cigarette in an aura of positive symbolism pertaining to belonging, value, propriety, urbanity, and government authority.

Cigarette brands changed again following Mao's death in 1976, as steady supplies became more available in village and city alike. Many cigarette labels first introduced during Mao's reign disappeared. Packs with names like Leap, Open Hearted, Big Star, Contribute, Resilience, and countless others were dropped. Coupon schemes likewise disappeared, and so too went most labels named after cities. Today, the total number of domestic cigarette brands sold in China is well below Mao-era numbers, despite the industry's accelerating production of the last three decades. The State Tobacco Monopoly Administration has overseen this brand reduction, acting like a gardener tending an overgrown and mismanaged orchard.[28] Such brush-clearing has been at the center of the STMA's organizational mandate: to increase efficiencies, transform scarcity into growth, and make cigarettes the centerpiece of a new consumerist era. Soon after the STMA took over many of the reins of China's cigarette businesses from local party authorities in the 1980s, it began consolidating and closing smaller cigarette factories in order to engineer economies of scale.

The STMA still permitted a small number of new brands to be introduced, including several, as one might expect, tapping into symbols evoking decidedly pre- and post-Maoist ethics. In the 1990s, we saw new brands like Nobility, West, and E Times. However, the STMA has been steadfast when it comes to gender norms. Relatively few brands generated today by a China Tobacco subsidiary cater overtly to female smokers. Claiming that symbols dictate behavior is always risky, yet academic and everyday observers continue to widely credit the strongly negative meanings, which were first attached to female cigarette usage during the mid-twentieth century, as a primary reason smoking rates have remained so lopsided between men and women. How lopsided? National surveys indicate that roughly 60 percent of men, ages twenty-five to sixty-four, have been daily cigarette smokers during the last two decades. These same surveys consistently show that among women, less than 3 percent have been lighting up.[29]

Of course, branding and pack design are not the only means by which the tobacco industry in China has come to define and redefine normative relationships between cigarettes and consumer experience. What other mechanisms have been pivotal? And, in particular, how has the industry blended engineering innovations, public relations, popular media, and class and psychographic marketing? We take up both of these questions in this volume.

To better appreciate the significance of the second question, regarding blending, consider a prominent trend for cigarettes in China over the last decade: price expansion. In the 1990s, the STMA did away with Mao-era price caps, allowing tobacco marketers to shrewdly capitalize on a society undergoing dramatic post-socialist socioeconomic stratification. A steep ladder has subsequently emerged between the cheapest brands made in China (now about US$1 per pack at retail) and the most expensive (over US$35 per pack). Such price variation has been effective at transmogrifying cigarettes, as much as any other object in China today, into emblems of class and income. Status pandering is not altogether novel for the cigarette in the PRC, however. Even amidst the most ardent periods of Maoism, ambitious players in China's cigarette industry subtly positioned some of their products as status symbols, with the most premier of their labels, such as Panda brand, distributed exclusively to party elites. What's more, at least one of the brands first made for party elites, Yunyan ("Yunnan smoke"), has enjoyed meteoric market growth during the last two decades, and variants of Yunyan now command some of the highest prices of any cigarettes in China. This begs a question that many of the authors here ask: to what degree were mid-twentieth century Maoist tobacco pitchmen the prophets of the country's contemporary cigarette business?

Imperiled Life

Endangerment is the second of the three central themes animating this book. Researching how things become commonplace, how they become insinuated into everyday life as normal, is a vital line of inquiry for scholars of culture. The importance of studying the tobacco industry of the PRC, though, far exceeds simple matters of cultural insinuation. The State Tobacco Monopoly Administration/China Tobacco has become the world's largest cigarette maker. Being the largest means that this government-business leviathan owns a title of ignominy like no other. It is arguably the single largest corporate machine of death and social suffering to ever exist.

Industrial manufacturing, to be sure, has imperiled people around the world for well over a hundred years. Dangerous offerings—everything from pesticides to pharmaceuticals, alcoholic beverages to aerosol agents, cleaning compounds to knives, razors, and revolvers—have been manufactured and distributed worldwide since the dawn of the Industrial Revolution. In recent years, journalists have often shed light on defective products (milk powder, toys, medications, for example) being manufactured in China—matters that, in turn, have become of personal concern to people in Chongqing as much as in Chicago, in Guangzhou as much as in Guatemala City. Factories across China, however, have been manufacturing cigarettes in far greater numbers than anything like knives and razors or, for that matter, medications and toys. Moreover, these cigarette factories of China, by striving to reach ever higher levels of productivity, have been contributing to a global catastrophe that is unprecedented in terms of scale and intensity.

This global catastrophe is already taking its toll. Although it is expected to grow much larger, it has been unfolding around the world for quite some time and is wreaking havoc now. Worldwide, the catastrophe has been the single greatest cause of premature death for more than a decade, even for people in countries as far apart as the United States and New Zealand, where smoking rates have declined significantly since the 1970s.[30] Over ten years ago, John Seffrin, CEO of the usually restrained American Cancer Society, categorized the cigarette as being "the most effective killing machine mankind has ever invented."[31] Seffrin went on in 2008 to label the cigarette "the world's greatest weapon of mass destruction," testifying that, if the cigarette continues to be consumed at current rates, "it will kill more than 600 million people alive today."[32]

Already bearing much of the burden of this global annihilation is China. With over half of its residents today regularly exposed to cigarette smoke (first- and second-hand), and with those fumes being more significant contributors to indoor air pollution than smog in even notoriously congested cities like Beijing, the global cigarette catastrophe is bursting out across the PRC.[33] At present, more than a million people per year die from contact with cigarette smoke in the People's Republic, more than thirty times the number of deaths annually caused by HIV-AIDS.[34] Furthermore, assuming that current rates of cigarette smoke exposure persist, morbidity is slated to surge dramatically in the next twenty years, tripling to 3.5 million annual deaths by 2030.[35] Conventional thinking attributes this surging death toll to people having "chosen" to smoke. However, we find that explanation inadequate. It is inadequate not simply because it ignores how much, over the last century, the industry and its allies have fostered cigarette smoking as a normative aspect of everyday life. It is inadequate not simply because it ignores that nicotine is one of the most addictive of all pharmacological substances. It is also woefully inadequate because it ignores supply. Statisticians tell us that per capita smoking rates have gone up in China since the 1950s, based on surveys they have conducted on the country's prototypical smoker, the adult male. Average male smoker consumption grew from a mean of just one cigarette per day in the early 1950s to four cigarettes per day in the early 1970s. That figure rose further to ten cigarettes per day by 1992 and to fifteen cigarettes per day by 1999.[36] This was a meteoric rise. However, to primarily attribute this fifteen-fold increase to lifestyle decisions is to fundamentally obfuscate the industry's own triumphalism regarding manufacturing. It is to obfuscate that a gigantic supply-chain investment made by government authorities, central and provincial, supercharged the surge in per capita smoking. This investment, after all, enabled cigarette production during the same period to jump some twenty-fold (see Figure I.1).

The rise of this manufacturing juggernaut challenges how the relationship between supply and demand is commonly understood. When it comes to cigarette exposure in the People's Republic, has it been unmet demand getting joyfully sated or, rather, has it been enormous overproduction creating conditions requiring disposal of huge surpluses?

Certainly, given surging torrents of cigarettes across the country, it is little wonder that citizens seeking treatment for all manner of tobacco-induced illnesses have inundated hospitals for some years now. Departments of respiratory medicine, cardiology, and cardio-thoracic surgery have become

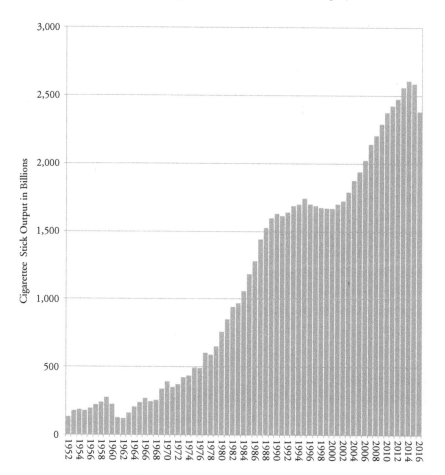

FIGURE I.I.
Cigarette production in China, 1952–2016. National Bureau of Statistics of China, http://data.stats.gov.cn/search.htm?s=卷烟产量.

particularly swamped, facing growing throngs of people pursuing treatment for malignant tumors, emphysema, heart attacks, and other life-threatening ailments. Death brought on by lung cancer alone has soared 400 percent in China during the past three decades.[37] Epidemiologists attached to China's Ministry of Health are quite matter-of-fact regarding causation, attributing nearly all of the country's lung cancer to first- and second-hand cigarette smoke exposure.[38]

Perhaps because of China's capaciousness, death across the country is all too often represented through the lens of statistics. It must be remembered, though, that lives lost cannot be measured in terms of numbers alone. Anyone dying from tobacco is not just a data point. She is a sister, a mother, an aunt, a former classmate. He is a brother, a father, an uncle, a neighbor. And with their lives deeply embedded in webs of social and affective significance, men and women who die from cigarettes in China tear at the very fabric of human experience, not just of their own, but also of innumerable others. Their death invariably subjects family, friends, and attendant social intimates to protracted periods of suffering, involving grinding emotional, moral, psychological, and financial dissolution.[39]

Today, the manifold forces of tobacco-induced death have left few in China untouched, and fewer still will remain untouched a decade from now. This rising tide of devastation demands an ethical response from all sectors, including the academy. Looking back is vital for looking forward, the authors of this volume assert. Looking back is vital for nurturing a new ethics and, thus, a new politics about the future. At minimum, to foster popular momentum against the surge of tobacco in China, people spanning numerous social domains need better information about how actors and allies of the cigarette industry have shaped current circumstances in the People's Republic.

Politicization of Smoking and Depoliticization of the Cigarette Industry

In order to shake the PRC free from its painful role as protagonist and victim in the global cigarette catastrophe much more must be learned about how production works there. Two questions in particular must be answered. First, how have manufacturing units of STMA/China Tobacco come to enjoy so much latitude as to imperil people by inundating them with an item which, if used exactly as intended, kills half of its regular users?

Next, what has been done to stem the cigarette endemic in recent years, and how has China Tobacco coordinated with regional manufacturers to thwart those efforts? Both of these lines of inquiry, in their own ways, engage the third of this book's three themes: politicization and depoliticization.

With those terms, we mean processes by which something is framed as either political, and thus needing human struggle, or nonpolitical—say, "purely" aesthetic or technical—and thus undeserving of contestation. Such framing almost always involves knowledge, but so too affect and history. To clarify all this, consider an example outside of the tobacco realm from East Asia's past, something that has undergone intense politicization recently. In 1937, during a six-week period, members of the Imperial Japanese Army killed hundreds of thousands of Chinese civilians and soldiers and perpetrated wide-scale rape and looting in the Chinese city of Nanjing. Several of the perpetrators were subsequently tried and found guilty. Despite their ferocity, these events were largely ignored by Chinese media outlets during the Maoist era (1949–1976), a time when internal class struggle was a political priority. Then, in the 1980s, as Beijing's reformers started to need new ways to energize the nation, what is now known as the Nanjing Massacre or the Rape of Nanking began to be framed as profoundly political. This framing has transpired through a prolonged multimedia barrage including film, novels, and scholarship. Through this framing, Chinese citizens are encouraged today to experience the Nanjing Massacre as a festering sore on the heart of the nation. And via this framing, China's leadership is expected to posture aggressively toward the Japanese government and carry out costly military maneuvers to signal that the PRC will never allow Japan to enact such an atrocity on Chinese soil again.

Juxtapose that to the massacre the PRC's domestic cigarette industry has been visiting upon the country. How is it that an industry first introduced into China by foreigners can currently flood the PRC with a tsunami of toxic products (that are now generating annually three times as many deaths as that wrought by the Nanjing Massacre), yet elicit a popular outcry that is highly circumscribed? In other words, how is cigarette-induced death in China today typically politicized and depoliticized?

One answer is differential problematization. Whereas cigarette *smoking* has come to be treated as a problem, the *industry* has not. Much of this began after Mao's death in 1976, when international tobacco-control discourse began to flow into the country under Deng Xiaoping's Open Door policies. Since then, a growing stream of health advocates, policy makers, and experts from numerous fields have invoked tobacco-related morbidity statistics and pressed the party-state to better instruct the public about tobacco's toxicity and to implement anti-smoking measures. Most of these tobacco-control specialists have adopted an approach of top-down regulatory intervention designed to condition citizens to avoid making risky decisions regarding smoking. The approach problematizes the behavior of "smoking," while largely ignoring both the industry and its products. The World Health Organization's Framework Convention on Tobacco Control (FCTC), the world's first public health treaty, has provided impetus, institutional legitimacy, and codes of conduct for this unbalanced approach. The FCTC offers largely a demand-side methodology to resolve a complex public health issue. Much of what it mandates from countries is intervention on behalf of their populations in ways that empower citizens to make better decisions on how to manage the risks posed by smoking cigarettes. Comparatively few FCTC protocols are designed to curtail the worldwide industry's freedom to produce highly addictive products. No FCTC protocols mandate that manufacturers disclose how their products are made. No protocols mandate that cigarette manufacturers make changes to their products (such as reducing nicotine levels) to make them less addictive. And none actively encourage governments to nurture political consciousness among people—not just about smoking, but also about the industry.

Against this international regulatory backdrop, problematization of cigarette smoking has occurred on several levels since Beijing signed on to the FCTC in 2005. Here are a few examples: The party-state has restricted people's exposure to commercial speech, implementing a series of ever-tighter bans on cigarette advertising. It has required people to learn a new choreography of locales where smoking is prohibited, implementing smoke-free rules for public spaces. It has required that a small increase in text-based warning labels regarding "smoking" be attached to cigarette packaging. And through the allocation of small sums of money, it has encouraged the flow of knowledge about the dangers posed by cigarette use, increased epidemiological surveillance of consumption, promoted the creation of smoking-cessation clinics in major cities, and funded school-based programs to dissuade youth from taking up the habit. I encourage you to read through these examples again. All emphasize the behavior of smoking and, through indirection, deemphasize the import of the industry.

This trend is not unique to China, of course. It is a global phenomenon, one that has been thinly studied in almost all contexts. Currently, statisticians attribute half a million premature deaths a year in the United States to cigarettes. Yet even in the United States, where tobacco regulators have enjoyed relative success, few people today challenge cigarette manufacturers in any direct way other than plaintiffs enlisted by lawyers. Perhaps this is because, as is the case in China, tobacco control in the United States has done little to nurture a victimology except one of smoker self-blame. Tobacco-control programming in North America over the last fifty years has championed empowering people to make healthy decisions (read: those who do not are negligent), but rarely has it reached out to survivors or their families, let alone encouraged them to mobilize against an industrial offender. There has been popular backing and grassroots activism in the United States during recent decades for numerous social movements, replete with pink and red ribbons, aimed at changing the political economy of breast cancer and HIV/AIDS. However, lung cancer and its principal causal chain are objects of essentially no political activism, even though far more women in North America die annually from lung cancer than from breast cancer, and ten times more Americans die from lung cancer than from HIV/AIDS.[40] In other words, China possesses no proprietary claim to the depoliticization of the tobacco industry. Yet, being by far the world's largest producer of cigarettes, the PRC is arguably the most important setting in which to investigate this phenomenon.

This then brings us to the question: How has China's cigarette industry worked to avoid being problematized?

Of primary importance has been the ways the industry nuances its status within both government and everyday life. In an era when so many forms of commercial activity have been heavily privatized, manufacturing and sale of cigarettes has remained a governmental fiefdom. State control of a supply chain, particularly in a single-party authoritarian system such as China, inescapably confers a certain respectability on an industry and its signature product. Also, that much of the supply chain remains locally embedded, especially as experienced by citizens, makes this respectability all the stronger. STMA/China Tobacco officials based in Beijing indeed oversee the country's sprawling cigarette industry today. However, much of what people experience when they reach for a pack of cigarettes is something regional, a product manufactured by a "local" factory entwined in webs of provincial and city-based associations. Domestically produced cigarette packs today still almost never state "manufactured by China Tobacco," but instead typically state on their side that either one of the country's older city-based factories (e.g., Changsha Cigarette Factory), post-Mao enterprises (e.g., Guizhou Tobacco Industrial Corporation), or one of the new large "tobacco groups" (e.g., Shanghai Tobacco Group, Hongta Yuxi Tobacco Group) have manufactured the product. Inasmuch as STMA/China Tobacco has been coaxing consolidation of the industry, trying to push factories into "groups," all manufacturing units carry in their names and emphasize in marketing copy easily recognized identifiers of province- and city-based locales. This betrays the degree to which regionalism continues to define the industry, particularly at the provincial level. Local party officials and the media outlets under their authority regularly encourage people to smoke local brands as a way of taking pride in their community and supporting its economy. Smoke local, the message runs, and everyone nearby will benefit from the profits.

But of course, the money generated by China's vast cigarette manufacturing infrastructure does not all stay local, as Beijing extracts much of it away. The tobacco industry in the People's Republic today is as much a Beijing-run state monopoly as it is a set of regionalized public cartels, run along the lines of what Jean Oi has called "local state corporatism."[41] It is a hybrid governmental-industrial assemblage, one in flux, with many internal tensions and regional stakeholders. Through complex webs of personal ties, regulations, and laws, this assemblage uses the powers of the central government to impede both foreign competitors and uncertified counterfeiters. At the same time, it struggles to keep regionally based cigarette enterprises in line with all of Beijing's edicts and party priorities. For example, China Tobacco manages the inflow of leaf across national and provincial borders, but has struggled to break regional barriers that protectionist local enterprises and provincial party bosses have erected to maximize local cigarette sales. This same tension exists in terms of how many cigarettes are produced in the People's Republic each year. China Tobacco annually assigns a production quota/cap on cigarette factories, dictating the total number of sticks the factory should manufacture. However, because the local enterprises that manage these factories compete fiercely for market share, a process encouraged by government leaders eager to showcase local GDP growth, enterprises press Beijing for higher quotas, as well as the right to absorb other enterprises during this era of consolidation.

Most citizens are unlikely aware of such organizational gambits, especially given how much they are encouraged to think insularly and clannishly about cigarettes. China Tobacco has been around for over thirty years, and all domestic cigarette enterprises are its subsidiaries, but they are still named in ways conveying not so much central government ownership as local rootedness. Inasmuch as most cigarettes in China today are homogenous tubes of paper-rolled tobacco grouped twenty to a pack, they are diversified under many different labels and flavor profiles, most of which by name, insignia, and fragrance hark back to particular geographic localities and city-based enterprises that were first created during the 1950s. What most Chinese are conditioned to see when they look at a pack of cigarettes is neither industrial machination nor endangerment, but rather, government-endorsed branding saturated by positive homegrown meanings. What they are conditioned to see is a sociopolitically celebrated opportunity to demonstrate pride of place and regional allegiance.

This brings us to another way the industry avoids problematization: its representation of profits. Many residents of the PRC today are well aware that cigarettes are moneymakers for the state, but they know little else about industry finances, whether it is in terms of how revenue gets generated or distributed.[42] Before the 1980s, tobacco revenues were treated like most government matters: as state secrets. In the early 1980s, this seemed to change when agencies overseeing tobacco and its taxation began releasing annual and, more recently, quarterly reports to the public. The purpose of these reports, however, has been not so much transparency as self-serving political theater. Each report generally states very little, yet is always issued with great fanfare, touting that its findings reaffirm that tobacco is a "pillar" industry for the nation and for the party, contributing as much as, if not more than, any other industry to the government's mandate to "serve the people." What else is to be learned from the content of these reports is that, in general, government revenue from cigarettes, nationwide, as well as within many provinces, has been growing rapidly over the last three decades. According to one such report, in 1981, the tobacco industry generated some 7.5 billion yuan in "income and taxes."[43] By 2012, that figure had grown more than a hundredfold, reaching 864 billion yuan (US$140 billion).[44] The reports also allow for a general appreciation of how much cigarette-related taxes have come to make up a sizable portion of all government revenue collected in China. In 2010, for example, the country's cigarette-related taxes equaled one out of every fourteen yuan of revenue collected by the central government.[45]

If little information has been available regarding industry earnings besides a few eye-popping statistics wrapped in political theater, even less transparent has been the expenditure of the money generated by cigarette manufacturing and sales. How has this vast influx of money been applied to governmental budgets across the country, and what has it bought? Regarding depoliticization, we might assume that being such a cash cow for the state, and one growing fatter by the decade, the country's cigarette industry has been able to curry favor and dampen dissatisfaction within the highest corridors of the Communist Party. Likewise, we might assume that party leaders, especially those based in the tobacco heartlands of China—like Yunnan, where the tobacco industry was generating almost 80 percent of provincial government revenues in the late 1990s—have been susceptible to industry co-optation, if not outright corruption, and, in turn, themselves actively lobbied supervisors in Beijing for pro-tobacco policies. Finally, we might presume that the industry has, sometimes stealthily and sometimes with flourish, spent money over the years to divert public attention from its responsibility for the hazards posed by its products. Simply presuming that industry income and taxes have been so deployed, however, is insufficient. We must also ask and document: By what means has tobacco money been actively directed in ways generative of depoliticization? And we must ask and document: What roles have industry actors and their proxies played in using corporate largesse to depoliticize the disease and death created by the cigarette business?

These questions are more difficult to answer when it comes to China Tobacco and its subsidiaries than to other large cigarette producers in the world today. Anyone with Internet connectivity today has easy access to tens of millions of pages of internal corporate documents from the likes of Philip Morris, Imperial Tobacco, RJ Reynolds, British American Tobacco, and Lorillard, dating back to the early years of the twentieth century. Most of these are documents that have entered the public domain through lawsuits in North America, and they are now viewable for free at the Truth Tobacco Industry Documents website. Based on this huge archive, historians have revealed myriad ways cigarette manufacturers active outside of China have budgeted large sums of money over the years for efforts to defuse, distract, and dupe the public.[46]

Such revelations beg inquiry into transpacific mimesis. In what ways have subsidiaries of China Tobacco been replicating the spending priorities of their foreign competitors, diverting some of their cash flow to wrap themselves in a cloak of distortions? In what ways have the subsidiaries been devising novel techniques? My own research—notably numerous interviews carried out over the last decade and time spent in the library of the Yunnan Academy of Tobacco Scientific Research, one of China's largest industry-funded quasi-scientific public relations institutions—has illuminated for me that at least since the founding of the STMA in 1982, Chinese cigarette manufacturers have closely studied how foreign companies have defused public opinion about the dangers posed by cigarettes. What's more, a small but growing body of knowledge, comprising journalistic reporting and preliminary academic inquiry, suggests that China Tobacco subsidiaries have gone well beyond study. STMA subsidiaries, it would seem, have adopted an armory of familiar techniques of obfuscation, misdirection, disinformation, and denialism, all designed to divert public attention and policy makers from seriously addressing the tobacco endemic, while simultaneously portraying the industry as responsible and ethical.[47] These techniques seem to include, but are not limited to, the following:

- Encouraging the public to adopt a perspective of individual responsibility, rather than one of corporate liability, in response to risks posed by tobacco;
- Introducing purportedly "low-tar" products sometimes designated as "light," which are then marketed as safer alternatives (when in fact they are just as deadly);
- Thwarting initiatives requiring cigarette packs to carry effective warning labels;
- Generating misleading "scientific" knowledge about cigarettes, smoking, and secondhand smoke;
- Blocking tax reforms designed to lower cigarette consumption;
- Trumpeting philanthropic whitewashing, as when tobacco enterprises give away funds to bolster non-tobacco-related causes like poverty alleviation, rural educational advancement, and natural disaster relief.[48]

The publication of *Poisonous Pandas* comes at an especially timely moment for exposing the inner workings of disinformation campaigns like these. Environmental protest has become increasingly common across the

PRC during the last decade. Outfitted with new knowledge, villagers and urbanites alike have become intolerant, litigious, and even rebellious when menaced by industrial polluters, including state and private enterprises. China Tobacco and its subsidiaries have avoided any such collective defiance so far, in part because of their success in managing popular appreciation of endangerment. Any casual observer in China has witnessed an upswing in tobacco-control knowledge during the last three decades. Multiple channels—the media, schools, and popular culture—communicate information about dangers inherent to cigarette smoking. This is borne out by survey data. By 2010, most Chinese adults, as high as 80 percent, were "aware" that tobacco smoke causes "disease."[49] In addition, by 2010, twice as many adults (77 percent) were aware that "smoking" causes lung cancer than had been the case just four years earlier (39 percent). All this appears to be good news for public health. The bad news is that, owing in part to industry activity, tremendous gaps remain in popular knowledge about tobacco's toxicity and the forty-odd life-threatening diseases caused by exposure to its smoke. Consider three of the leading causes of death in China today: heart disease, stroke, and lung cancer. As of 2010, 80 percent of adults were unaware that cigarettes cause all three conditions. Meanwhile, most adults remained poorly informed about the health effects of secondhand smoke. Four out of five did not know that secondhand smoke causes both lung disease among children and life-threatening heart and lung conditions among adults.[50]

One of the most important channels through which the industry has been conditioning what the public knows (and doesn't know) has been warning labels. Cigarette packs in China have carried warnings for over a decade. The State Tobacco Monopoly Administration, however, has consistently blocked all efforts to expand the form and content of warnings. At present, warnings are abjectly innocuous, deploying the most tepid language to describe a risky behavior (but not a dangerous product). Labels state in small print that "smoking is harmful to health, quitting can reduce health risks." This wording could not be better for the industry. The phrasing affords industry advocates grounds to claim that they have acted ethically—cautioning citizens and encouraging them to behave responsibly—while, in fact, leaving the public largely ignorant of the depths of endangerment at work.

Equally insidious has been industry marketing that toxins inherent to tobacco can be easily limited by smoking "safer cigarettes." Recently, small e-cigarette enterprises have contributed to this outlook. However, more significantly, conventional cigarette enterprises in China have transmitted decades of "light" messaging. In a recent national survey, 86 percent of respondents were unaware that the term "low tar" does not mean "less harmful." The industry's "low-tar cigarettes are safer" rhetoric, it should be noted, has not taken root simply among the general public. Half of college-educated citizens nationwide, including 54 percent of medical professionals, now accept as truth the industry's low-tar cigarette/safe cigarette canard.[51]

. . .

So, here's how the chapters of this book are laid out. In Part One, we detail how the early Communist leadership embraced cigarette manufacturing and how that embrace sowed the seeds of normalization, depoliticization, and endangerment present today. Liu Wennan describes what is probably the first instance of the Chinese Communist Party managing the business of cigarettes. This occurred during the Anti-Japanese War (1937–1945) in a rustic region of northwestern China that was an important base for the incubation of the CCP. Sha Qingqing explores tense debates among party leaders and cigarette manufacturers during the early 1950s regarding how nationalization of the industry would proceed. He focuses on the country's first National Cigarette Industry Conference, held in Shanghai, a city in which over a hundred tobacco companies were manufacturing products at the start of 1949. Huangfu and Kohrman examine cigarette production during one of the most tragic periods of the Maoist era, the Great Leap Forward. They conclude that the campaign's turmoil helped foster and normalize a number of characteristics typifying China's twenty-first-century cigarette sector. These include mass consumption, governmental stewardship of commercial logistics, localization of production, cigarette content as object of innovation, and prioritization of industrial minutia over human harm.

In Part Two, we describe various ways that the industry has benefited from visual culture and historical representation in its efforts to normalize cigarettes and depoliticize their harm. Carol Benedict surveys Chinese images of smoking in advertisements, cartoons, and propaganda posters from the 1920s to the 1970s. She shows that these illustrations vividly inscribed Maoist ideals of smoking and masculinity at the same time that they telegraphed improprieties of female smoking that had emerged in the 1930s and were carried over after 1949. Matthew Kohrman turns from visual media to historical discourse. Taking us on a stroll through a newly built museum devoted exclusively to the cigarette, he shows how the industry has come to use historical representation in an effort to inoculate its employees against rebuke and instill in them a proud sense of vocational ethics.

In Part Three, we consider two offshoots of the PRC's tobacco industry—taxes and corruption—that have been indispensable for normalization and differential politicization. Kohrman, Gan, and Hu offer one of the most detailed descriptions to date of evolving policies regarding tobacco revenue in the PRC. They reveal that, in recent years, although cigarette-related taxes have been mostly garnered by the central government, the country's complex web of tax policies has incentivized local cigarette manufactures and provincial leaders to expand production. Cheng Li maps dynamics among elite politics, local governments, and tobacco industry interest groups. Focusing on Yunnan Province in the early post-Mao era, he reveals key features of tobacco governance, including how provincial leaders have coordinated with factories to lobby leaders in Beijing and how tobacco-related corruption has penetrated many levels of the party-state.

In Part Four, we delve more fully into ways the industry has tried to depoliticize tobacco in the age of the World Health Organization's Framework Convention treaty. Kohrman, Sun, Proctor, and Yang take up the history of "light cigarettes" in China, outlining how filter-tipped cigarettes were first piloted in 1959 to fête government leaders. Then, to boost government revenue, a number of enterprises switched over to filter-tipped cigarette production during the early stages of the Deng era (1976–1997), marketing them as more modern and higher quality. In the late Deng years, the rhetoric of "light cigarettes" was ramped up, supervised in the 2000s by a STMA-orchestrated "low-tar, less-harm" public relations campaign. Gan Quan and Stanton Glantz interrogate relationships that have grown over the last fifty years between the tobacco industry and China's academic institutions. They demonstrate that, in the 1990s, during a time when the public was growing increasingly concerned about dangers posed by smoking, the industry turned more and more to academic scientists to participate in tobacco research and increasingly used them in efforts to counter public health messaging. Wu Yiqun and her colleagues analyze two Chinese-language books about the FCTC written by industry researchers that were published in the last ten years and which touted themselves as being "scientific achievements" safeguarding the interests of consumers and the nation. Released by a reputable Beijing press, these books are industry manifestos, unabashed handbooks in public health interference, each laying out a set of "best practices" for thwarting tobacco-control policies.

In his Afterword, Robert Proctor provides us with some closing thoughts, bringing to bear his vast experience researching, writing, and challenging the machinations of the tobacco industry elsewhere in the world.

．　．　．

Despite a slurry of distortion and cynicism uncovered by this book, my coauthors and I remain hopeful. It was a spirit of hopefulness that initially brought us together on the grounds of Peking University in 2012 to discuss how we could open up a new area of research on tobacco. Something else brought us together as a group then and has animated us ever since. All of us believe that it is vitally important to draw on a variety of academic backgrounds to better understand how cigarettes in China are made. An upshot of our interdisciplinarity fervor is that, unlike most existing books about tobacco, this volume both considers production seriously and recognizes it as involving far more than simply making objects. Cigarette production is a wide-ranging process, we posit, one involving an interdependent mix of objects, webs of meaning, social relationships, government regulation, scientific research, systems of labor, spatial and class differentiation, embodied dispositions, and competing ethics.

Why go so big and broad on production? At issue is simultaneously a central plank in public health and all those people who are regularly imperiled by tobacco smoke worldwide. More to the point, at issue is whether tobacco prevention continues to inch along shackled by ill design.[52] Tobacco prevention in China and elsewhere can easily continue to focus narrowly and often fecklessly on control of consumers and their behavior. It can easily continue to pose the problem at hand as mostly one of how to help people avoid making misguided decisions to smoke. Or tobacco prevention in the twenty-first century can become more substantial and consequential. It can expand its aperture and start to abrade actively the filaments of production that engulf the world annually with trillions of freshly rolled cigarettes.[53] The chapters of this book are designed to examine existing patterns and break homogenous notions of what has been and what could be. We advocate an approach supportive of smokers' desires to quit, to be sure, but one that probes more fervently into all that's involved in producing cigarettes themselves. Ours is a call for a new history and ultimately a new political approach toward tobacco. What is needed, what this book strives to kindle, is an open-ended historical appraisal of tobacco manufacturing, a roomy reckoning of all manner of remnants: whether its corporate reports, newspaper images, tax codes, recollections of bureaucratic wrangles, discarded packaging, or even museum galleries.

Directing the bright light of historical reckoning on little-studied remnants carries the promise of conjuring new consciousness and hitherto unimagined social action.[54] The time has come for cigarette production in the People's Republic to feel that light.

Notes

1. "China Tobacco International Opens Company in N.C.," North Carolina Department of Agriculture and Consumer Services, June 27, 2013, http://www .southeastfarmpress.com/tobacco/china-tobacco-international-open-north-caro lina-office.

2. "Tobacco 2016: New Insights and System Refresher," Euromonitor International, 2016, retrieved from Euromonitor Passport database.

3. Paul McClean and Lucy Hornby, "China Tobacco Sales Fall for First Time in Two Decades," *Financial Times*, June 20, 2016.

4. Ver Bilano et al., "Global Trends and Projections for Tobacco Use, 1990–2025: An Analysis of Smoking Indicators from the WHO Comprehensive Information Systems for Tobacco Control," *Lancet* 385, no. 9972 (2015): 966–76.

5. Michael Eriksen, Hana Ross, and Judith Mackay, *The Tobacco Atlas*, 4th ed. (Atlanta: American Cancer Society, 2012), 28; "Market Sizes, Historical/Forecast," Euromonitor International, retrieved from Euromonitor Passport database.

6. Gary A. Giovino et al., "Tobacco Use in 3 Billion Individuals from 16 Countries: An Analysis of Nationally Representative Cross-Sectional Household Surveys," *Lancet* 380, no. 9842 (2012): 668–79.

7. China Tobacco, *Specifying Two Aims, Strictly Controlling Total Production: Improving the Industry's Control Over Production of Cigarettes and Tobacco Leaf* (规范两端 严控总量—行业加强卷烟和烟叶生产总量控制) (Beijing, 2013), http:// www.tobacco.gov.cn/history_filesystem/2013yckz/jd8.htm.

8. Daryl Loo, "China's Tobacco Monopoly Bigger by Profit Than HSBC, Walmart," *Bloomberg News*, March 6, 2012.

9. Eriksen et al., *Tobacco Atlas*, 52.

10. National Bureau of Statistics of China, http://data.stats.gov.cn/search.htm?s=烟叶产量.

11. "Brazilian States of Alagoas and Bahia to Export Tobacco to China," Macauhub, 2012, https://macauhub.com.mo/2012/08/29/brazilian-states-of-alagoas-and-bahia-to-export-tobacco-to-china/; Andrew Meldrum, "Zimbabwe's Tobacco Making a Comeback," *Global Post*, May 10, 2012, https://www.pri.org/stories/2012-05-10/zimbabwes-tobacco-making-comeback; and "China Tobacco International Opens Company in N.C."

12. Iain Gately, *Tobacco: A Cultural History of How an Exotic Plant Seduced Civilization* (London: Simon & Schuster, 2001).

13. Allan M. Brandt, *The Cigarette Century: The Rise, Fall, and Deadly Persistence of the Product That Defined America* (New York: Basic Books, 2007).

14. For a discussion of the rise of the American school of applied economics in China, how it was initially formulated by the likes of Hamilton and Clay, how it was exported to Bismarck's Germany by Friedrich List, and then transmitted into Asia via Japan, see James Fallows, *Looking at the Sun: The Rise of the New East Asian Economic and Political System* (New York: Vintage, 1994); Arthur Kroeber, *China's Economy: What Everyone Needs to Know* (Oxford: Oxford University Press, 2016); and Joe Studwell, *How Asia Works: Success and Failure in the World's Most Dynamic Region* (London: Profile Books, 2014).

15. Sherman Cochran, *Big Business in China: Sino-Foreign Rivalry in the Cigarette Industry 1890–1930* (Cambridge, MA: Harvard University Press, 1980); Wennan Liu, *"No Smoking" for the Nation: Anti-Cigarette Campaigns in Modern China, 1910–1935* (Berkeley: University of California Press, 2009); and Carol Benedict, *Golden-Silk Smoke: A History of Tobacco in China, 1550–2010* (Berkeley: University of California Press, 2011).

16. Some Chinese-language literature exists regarding the mainland tobacco industry from the mid-twentieth century to the present, but much of it is far from empirically rigorous. Having been funded by one or another China Tobacco subsidiary, these texts have usually been designed to do little more than celebrate the commercial achievements of their sponsor subsidiary.

17. Judith Mackay and Michael P. Eriksen, *The Tobacco Atlas* (Geneva: World Health Organization, 2002), 30.

18. Liu Tienan and Xiong Bilin, *Yancao jingji yu yancao kongzhi* (Tobacco economy and tobacco control) (Beijing: Economic Science Press, 2004), 141–42; Hong Wang, "Tobacco Control in China: The Dilemma between Economic Development and Health Improvement," *Salud Publica de Mexico* 48, Supplement 1 (2006): 140–47; "The Chinese Tobacco Market and Industry Profile," Campaign for Tobacco-Free Kids, 2012, http://global.tobaccofreekids.org/files/pdfs/en/TI_

Profile_China.pdf; and Cheng Li, *The Political Mapping of China's Tobacco Industry and Anti-Smoking Campaign* (Washington, DC: Brookings Institution, 2012), 18.

19. World Health Organization, *Neuroscience of Psychoactive Substance Use and Dependence* (Geneva: World Health Organization, 2004), http://www.who.int/substance_abuse/publications/en/Neuroscience_E.pdf.

20. Frank Dikötter, Lars Laamann, and Zhou Xun, *Narcotic Culture: A History of Drugs in China* (London: C. Hurst, 2004), 201–2.

21. Richard Klein, *Cigarettes Are Sublime* (Durham, NC: Duke University Press, 1993).

22. On the cigarette as "semaphore," see Peter Hessler, *Country Driving: A Journey through China from Farm to Factory* (New York: Harper, 2010), 233.

23. Pierre Bourdieu, *Distinction: A Social Critique of the Judgement of Taste* (Cambridge, MA: Harvard University Press, 1984).

24. Cochran, *Big Business in China*.

25. Wang Tianpei, "Ingenious Character, Yunnan Tobacco Advertising" (独具特色的云南烟草广告), *Hongyun Honghe* 34, no. 4 (2012): 46–51.

26. Timothy Brook, "Smoking in Imperial China," in *Smoke: A Global History of Smoking*, ed. Sander L. Gilman and Zhou Xun (London: Reaktion Books, 2004), 84–91.

27. Benedict, *Golden-Silk Smoke*, 199–239.

28. Between 2001 and 2014, the total number of brands nationwide decreased from 1,183 to 89. It should also be noted that, during this same period, manufacturers increased the number of variants within brand families. Just as Philip Morris sells several variants of Marlboros in most parts of the word today—e.g., Reds, Golds, 72's Edge, Smooths—Chinese cigarette manufacturers today sell variants of most of their brands, packaging them in distinctive ways and pricing them at different levels. By 2015, the total number of variants of Chinese cigarettes had grown to over 870. See Steve Shaowei Xu et al., "Trends in Cigarette Brand Switching among Urban Chinese Smokers: Findings from ITC China Survey," paper presented at the 11th Asia Pacific Conference on Tobacco or Health, Beijing, 2016.

29. This is among adults twenty-five to sixty-four years of age surveyed between 1996 and 2010. Gonghuan Yang et al., *Smoking and Health in China: 1996 National Prevalence Survey of Smoking Patterns* (Beijing: China Science and Technology Press, 1997); and Qiang Li, Jason Hsia, and Gonghuan Yang, "Prevalence of Smoking in China in 2010," *New England Journal of Medicine* 364, no. 25 (2011): 2469–70.

30. World Health Organization, *Report on the Global Tobacco Epidemic, 2009: the MPOWER Package* (Geneva: World Health Organization, 2009); "Health Effects: How Does Smoking Harm Us and What's in a Cigarette?," Health Promotion Agency, 2010, http://www.smokefree.org.nz/smoking-its-effects/health-effects; and "Tobacco Statistical Snapshot," National Cancer Institute, 2012.

31. John Seffrin, "National Conference on Tobacco or Health/Tobacco—Greatest Weapon of Mass Destruction," *San Francisco Chronicle*, November 20, 2002.

32. Adam Gorlick, "Tobacco Companies Compared to al-Qaida," *Stanford Report*, Stanford University News Service, May 21, 2008, http://news.stanford.edu/news/2008/may21/tobacco-052108.html.

33. "Second-Hand Smoke Greatest Source of Indoor Pollution in Beijing: Study," Xinhua, September 12, 2012, http://www.china.org.cn/environment/2012-09/21/content_26601998.htm; World Health Organization, "Tobacco in China," 2013, http://www.wpro.who.int/china/mediacentre/factsheets/tobacco/en/.

34. *2012 China AIDS Response Progress Report*, Ministry of Health of the People's Republic of China, 2012, http://files.unaids.org/en/dataanalysis/knowyourresponse/countryprogressreports/2012countries/ce_CN_Narrative_Report[1].pdf; and World Health Organization, "Tobacco in China."

35. "Experts Raise Estimates of Deaths Caused by Tobacco-Related Illness in China," Xinhua, January 6, 2011, http://infoweb.newsbank.com/resources/doc/nb/news/1349C000EB2808E0?p=AWNB.

36. Richard Peto, Zheng-Ming Chen, and Jillian Boreham, "Tobacco: The Growing Epidemic in China," *CVD Prevention and Control* 4, no. 1 (2009): 61–70.

37. Jun She et al., "Lung Cancer in China: Challenges and Interventions," *Chest* 143, no. 4 (2013): 1117–26.

38. Ministry of Health, *Report on Smoking and Health in China: Tobacco Control and Lung Cancer Prevention, 2006* (2006 nian Zhongguo xiyan yu jiankang baogao: Kongyan yu feiai fangzhi) (Beijing: Ministry of Health, 2006).

39. Li Xiaoliang, *The Loss Is Not Just Health* (Shiqu de bu zhi shi jiankang) (Kunming: Yunnan Publishing Group, 2013).

40. "Lung Cancer Fact Sheet," American Lung Association, 2012, http://www.lung.org/lung-disease/lung-cancer/resources/facts-figures/lung-cancer-fact-sheet.html (accessed August 2013); and "HIV in the United States: At a Glance," Center for Disease Control and Prevention, 2013, http://www.cdc.gov/hiv/pdf/statistics_basics_factsheet.pdf (accessed August 2013).

41. As Divakara Babu Chennupati and Rajasekhara Mouly Potluri, "A Viewpoint on Cartels: An Indian Perspective," *International Journal of Law and Management* 53, no. 4 (2011): 252–61, explain: "A cartel is a formal (explicit) agreement among competing firms. It is a formal organization of producers and manufacturers that agree to fix prices, marketing and production. Cartels usually occur in an oligopolistic industry, where there are a small number of sellers and usually involve homogeneous products. Cartel members may agree on matters such as price fixing, total industry output, market shares, allocation of customers' allocation of territories, bid rigging, establishment of common sales agencies and the division of prof-

its, or [a] combination of these. The aim of such collusion is to increase individual members' profits by reducing competition. One can distinguish private cartels from public cartels. In the public cartel, a government is involved to enforce the cartel agreement, and the government's sovereignty shields such cartels from legal actions" (253). Jean Oi, "Fiscal Reform and the Economic Foundations of Local State Corporatism in China," *World Politics* 45, no. 1 (1992): 99–126, describes "local state corporatism" as follows: "Fiscal reform has assigned local governments property rights over increased income and has created strong incentives for local officials to pursue local economic development. In the process local governments have taken on many characteristics of a business corporation, with officials acting as the equivalent of a board of directors. This merger of state and economy characterizes a new institutional development that I label local state corporatism. I want to make clear that 'corporatism' as used here differs from its use in previous studies. By local state corporatism I refer to the workings of a local government that coordinates economic enterprises in its territory as if it were a diversified business corporation" (100–101). Also see Barry Naughton, "Implications of the State Monopoly over Industry and Its Relaxation," *Modern China* 18, no. 1 (1992): 14.

42. Hu Dewei [Teh-wei Hu], ed., *China Tobacco Tax: Historical Changes, Current Situation and Reforms* (中国烟草税收: 历史沿革, 现状及改革) (Beijing: China Taxation Press, 2009).

43. Li, *Political Mapping of China's Tobacco Industry*, 91.

44. "Tobacco Industry Pays to the Nation's Finance System 716 Billion Yuan, a Rise of 19%" (烟草行业2012年上交国家财政7166亿 同比增19%), Xinhua, January 17, 2013, http://business.sohu.com/20130117/n363764597.shtml.

45. "Our Country's 2010 National Tobacco Industry's Taxes and Profits are 604 Billion Yuan" (2010年我国烟草行业实现工商税利6045.52亿元), Central People's Government, January 18, 2011, http://www.gov.cn/jrzg/2011-01/18/content_1787549.htm; and National Bureau of Statistics, *2011 China Statistical Yearbook* (Beijing: China Statistics Press, 2011), 277.

46. Brandt, *The Cigarette Century*; and Robert Proctor, *Golden Holocaust: Origins of the Cigarette Catastrophe and the Case for Abolition* (Berkeley: University of California Press, 2012).

47. Matthew Kohrman, "Smoking among Doctors: Governmentality, Embodiment, and the Diversion of Blame in Contemporary China," *Medical Anthropology* 27, no. 1 (2008): 9–42; Matthew Kohrman, "New Steps for Tobacco Control in and outside of China," *Asia Pacific Journal of Public Health* 22, no. 3 Suppl (2010): 189S–196S.

48. Zhou Ruizeng and Cheng Yongzhao, ed., *Research for Countermeasures to Handling the Influence of the WHO Framework Convention for Tobacco Control* (WHO《烟草控制框架公约》对案及对中国烟草影响对策研究) (Beijing:

Economic Science Press, 2006); Yuanjin Ni, "Xinhua Insight: WHO Official Urges China to Print Graphic Warning Labels on Cigarette Packs," Xinhua, July 15, 2011, http://infoweb.newsbank.com/resources/doc/nb/news/13885BE5A8A30 BB0?p=AWNB; John Garnaut, "Losing the Battle in a Country Where Tobacco Sponsors Schools," *Sydney Morning Herald*, August 26, 2012; Xie Guangrong, "Agency of the Guizhou Provincial People's Political Consultative Conference, Guizhou Tobacco, Donates Rice and Water to Xifeng Drought Area" (贵州省政协机关, 贵州中烟向息烽旱区捐赠矿泉水, 大米), 2013, http://www.tobacco.gov.cn/html/30/3005/4537882_n.html (accessed September 2013); and Gonghuan Yang, "Marketing 'Less Harmful, Low-Tar' Cigarettes Is a Key Strategy of the Industry to Counter Tobacco Control in China," *Tobacco Control* 23, no. 2 (2013): 167–72.

49. Yan Yang et al., "Awareness of Tobacco-Related Health Hazards among Adults in China," *Biomedical and Environmental Sciences* 23, no. 6 (2010): 437–44.

50. Ibid.

51. Yang, "Marketing 'Less Harmful, Low-Tar' Cigarettes."

52. Matthew Kohrman and Peter Benson, "Tobacco," *Annual Review of Anthropology* 40 (2011): 329–44.

53. Zhang Xiliu, "Smoking Control Should Start from Control over Tobacco Companies" (控烟应从控烟企开始), *Fazhi wanbao* (Legal Evening News), May 25, 2015, http://dzb.fawan.com/html/2015-05/25/content_553942.htm (accessed September 2015).

54. Walter Benjamin, "Theses on the Philosophy of History," *Illuminations* (New York: Houghton Mifflin Harcourt, 1968).

PART ONE

Industrial Change across Revolutionary Borders

CHAPTER ONE

Experimentation
Cigarettes in the Communist Base Areas during World War II

Liu Wennan

> When hosting guests, I boil water, but don't offer tobacco;
> I use my clothes and bedding for three years;
> I use one mu of land for cultivating tobacco as my contribution to the
>   public;
> And I pay for a few pickles with my own income.
>   *"Ode to Austerity," by Lin Boqu,*
>   *chairman of the Shaan-Gan-Ning Border Region government, 1944*

A few years before the start of the Second Sino-Japanese War (1937–1945), Mao Zedong and his Communist troops were in full retreat. Chiang Kai-shek's Nationalist soldiers had forced the Communists to flee, driving them on the Long March from southern locales to remote regions in the center of China. Where the Red Army took refuge became known as the Communist base areas. There, for over a decade, Mao's troops regrouped and launched guerilla attacks, while the Chinese Communist Party (CCP) tested new forms of governance and economic self-reliance. The most important base area, the Shaan-Gan-Ning Border Region, stretched across three different provinces (Shaanxi, Gansu, and Ningxia) and was centered on the town of Yan'an. The reader should keep in mind that this border region was barren and drought-ridden, with little in the way of modern infrastructure. Most people lived under rudimentary conditions; even Mao himself, like several of his lieutenants, slept in a cave-style dwelling. (The region became first known to a wide English-language audience through Edgar Snow's book *Red Star over China* and Agnes Smedley's *China Fights Back: An American Woman with the Eighth Route Army*). It was in Yan'an that the CCP set up its wartime capital; it was also in that setting that the CCP first experimented with the production and regulation of cigarettes.[1]

This chapter chronicles cigarette manufacturing and management in Yan'an and its environs in these crucial years after the Long March. Why did the CCP strive to supervise cigarette-making and trade in such an inhospitable locale? How did base area authorities integrate the making and regulation of cigarettes into new forms of governance? What lasting knowledge was gained, and what principles of nation building were defined by the party through these experiments?

.   .   .

Before the Communists' arrival in Yan'an, the smoking of loose-leaf tobacco was already a part of everyday life for many locals in the Shaan-Gan-Ning Border Region (SGNBR). At the outbreak of war with Japan in 1937, the SGNBR economy was heavily dependent on the Guomindang government, insofar as many of its resources had to be imported from areas controlled by Nationalist armies. In the wake of the 1941 Wannan Incident, which shattered a brief and tenuous Communist-Nationalist anti-Japanese alliance, the Guomindang imposed a strict economic blockade on the SGNBR, which led to severe financial and economic hardship for the CCP's new headquarters. In response, the Communist government adopted a policy of economic self-reliance, which included the funding and management of factories to fabricate various types of goods.

Yan'an's Communist authorities underwent a paradigm shift regarding cigarettes during World War II. Originally, they had often criticized cigarettes as an unnecessary extravagance and a drain on the regional economy. Gradually, however, the party came to view cigarettes as a vital economic tool. The promise was that local cigarette production would provide a crucial economic boost, allowing the party to generate revenue and quash inflation. This paradigm shift helped normalize cigarette smoking as a respected Communist activity, respect that would spread throughout China once the People's Republic was founded.

The health effects of tobacco were rarely if ever questioned in the base areas, with smoking instead imagined as a psychic salve for war-torn nerves, a reward to be savored, a relaxation tool and hoped-for feature of the good life to come once a new China was built. Tobacco products in general and cigarettes in particular concerned the SGNBR government only insofar as they influenced the economy, a view that endures to a large extent to this day. All policies regarding cigarettes in the SGNBR—taxation schemes, bans on exogenous brands, and promotion of government-owned and -directed cigarette manufacturing—were centered on this perception of the cigarette as an economic good, a good that could impede or enhance the goals of Communist economic self-reliance.

Making and Smoking Tobacco in the SGNBR

During the Anti-Japanese War, the CCP controlled the northcentral portion of the agricultural plateau, a region comprising northern Shaanxi, eastern Gansu, and southeastern Ningxia formed by wind-blown soil deposits. By 1939, the area under the CCP's control encompassed 99,000 square kilometers, with a total population of 1.5 million.[2] Geographically speaking, the region was vast, sparsely populated, and inaccessible. Agriculture was the economic mainstay, but farming technology was backward and the soil was poor. Before the Anti-Japanese War, the region had practically no modern industry, and even Yan'an, the largest city in the region, could only boast a smattering of handicraft industries. Consequently, "the entire regional economy was impoverished and sealed off from the outside world."[3]

After the CCP established its political base in the SGNBR, it used political campaigns and land reform to promote agricultural production. At the same time, it gradually experimented with industries such as textiles, chemicals, military equipment, machinery, and paper manufacturing, aided by technically skilled émigrés and intellectuals who had escaped from enemy-occupied territory. In spite of these efforts, the economic picture changed little: traditional agriculture continued to dominate with industry lagging behind. As a result, Communist authorities in the SGNBR were extremely dependent on the outside world, and had to trade salt, furs, licorice, and other local produce for textiles, medicines, and other necessities. Trade between the SGNBR and the outside world led to what economists call an urban-rural price scissors problem: low-value raw materials and agricultural products were exported in exchange for high-value industrial goods, causing a flow of wealth from the countryside to the cities. In 1941, cooperation between the Guomindang and the CCP ended with the Wannan Incident— when armed conflict between Nationalist and Communist forces broke the united front against Japanese occupation—and the Guomindang imposed an economic blockade on Communist base areas. This caused a severe shortage of industrial products in the SGNBR, but it also caused its trade deficit to grow uncontrollably.[4] It is only by considering this economic backdrop that we can understand the production, consumption, and management of tobacco in regions controlled by the young Chinese Communist government.

As in much of rural China, in the SGNBR the most widely smoked form of tobacco before the Anti-Japanese War was shag, also known as rolling tobacco. Shag could be produced as a supplement to mainstream agricultural activities: one could easily satisfy one's own tobacco needs by growing a little on the edge of one's fields for example.[5] In addition to shag, the middle and upper levels of SGNBR society often grew water-pipe tobacco. After the outbreak of war in 1937, the demand for cigarettes rose dramatically in the Communist base areas, as outsiders poured in, bringing their more cosmopolitan tastes with them. Intellectuals, military officials, and refugees from the more prosperous coastal regions of China formed a new cadre of cigarette smokers in the SGNBR.[6]

Shag tobacco, water-pipe tobacco, and cigarettes were seen as reflections of the cultural background and social status of their consumers. Shag tobacco, usually made from sun-dried homegrown leaves, had a pungent taste but was cheap and easy to produce, even at home. It was popular among lower-middle-class farmers. By contrast, water-pipe tobacco was more arduous to produce (involving destemming, perfuming, and curing), making it more expensive. To smoke water-pipe tobacco, one has to regularly rinse the tobacco pot, and the process of loading and lighting is more elaborate than with a normal pipe. The upper-middle classes in Late-Imperial China tended to prefer using the water-pipe.

Cigarettes were introduced to China at the end of the nineteenth century, and within a few decades they had become a fashionable way to consume tobacco in major coastal cities. Unlike shag and water-pipe tobacco, cigarettes were viewed as modern industrial artifacts. Cigarettes are often made from Virginia tobacco, which is flue-cured to reduce the harsh sting from the nicotine, making it easier especially for novices to inhale the resulting smoke. Cigarette paper is also machine-made, allowing cigarettes to be wrapped tightly and uniformly with little smoke released upon burning. Cigarette rolling machines dramatically improved production speed and efficiency, but they also increased cigarette consistency, turning cigarettes into an affordable mass-market product. From a consumer perspective, cigarettes were easy to carry and to light, and provided milder smoke than other forms of tobacco. Cigarettes became integral to a fashionable lifestyle, a notion conveyed by the energetic promotion of manufacturers. Cigarettes quickly cut a swathe among the young and people with a bit of money in urban centers.

From 1937 to 1939, the SGNBR was a place of pilgrimage for patriotic youth, as swarms of urban intellectuals made the journey to Yan'an. Many of these youths were smokers, as were many of the senior leaders of the CCP, who had acquired the habit when they lived in cities—Mao Zedong is perhaps the most famous example. These people formed the primary cigarette market within the SGNBR. Prior to the Guomindang's imposition of an economic blockade, the region had obtained most of its cigarettes from neighboring Guomindang-controlled areas, though some had been obtained from Japanese-occupied territories. According to a survey conducted in Yan'an in December 1941, the biggest sellers were lower-end Virginia-style domestic brands like Daxihu, Huashan, and Siling.[7]

The SGNBR's backward, preindustrial economy was largely dependent on external connections. Cigarettes, the style of tobacco preferred by government workers, patriotic youth, and war refugees, could only be obtained via trade with the outside world, aggravating the already serious trade deficit. As the Guomindang tightened its economic blockade of the SGNBR during 1941, the cost of imported goods soared. Between 1938 and 1941, the price of cigarettes brought in from cities skyrocketed from 0.1 yuan per pack to an average of 4 yuan per pack. A pack of ten Daxihu or Huashan cigarettes went for 5 yuan in 1941, while a pack of Siling went for 2 yuan. This contrasts with the cost of local cut rolling tobacco, which remained steady at around 0.35 to 0.4 yuan per 50 grams, roughly the weight of leaf in two or three packs of machine-rolled cigarettes.[8] It was within this context that the SGNBR Trade Bureau decided to ban the import of cigarettes, a step taken on December 15, 1941.

Prohibition of Cigarette Imports

Prior to banning cigarette imports, the SGNBR government had tried to stifle them with high taxes. On September 29, 1941, the government raised the sales tax on non-SGNBR tobacco products to 40 percent for cigarettes and 20 percent for water-pipe tobacco and other styles of prepared tobacco.[9] The high tax rate evidently did not produce the desired effect, as cigarette imports still exceeded ten million yuan in 1941.[10] As the Nationalists continued tightening the economic blockade, the SGNBR Trade Bureau began to swap surplus rural products for essential or irreplaceable items and to restrict the import of objects used in religious ceremonies (such as incense and candles). But "luxuries" such as cigarettes, alcohol, and soap were also on the hit list.[11] At its third administrative meeting toward the end of 1941, SGNBR leaders accepted a Trade Bureau proposal to outlaw the import of cigarettes. New government guidelines not only criminalized the import of cigarettes, but also barred shops from selling them. Shopkeepers found in violation would have their cigarettes confiscated and could be fined up to five times the value of the tobacco. What is interesting about these regulations is that they targeted only cigarettes from outside the SGNBR, while water-pipe tobacco, shag, and locally produced and processed leaf were not prohibited.[12] This demonstrates that leaders did not intend to outlaw tobacco use; rather, they aimed to alter its method of consumption, by promoting local tobacco products as a replacement for imported machine-made cigarettes.

At first, the ban on the sale of cigarettes was poorly enforced. Some shops continued selling cigarettes, prompting the Yan'an City Tax Bureau to launch an inspection of over a hundred stores in March 1942, resulting in the confiscation of 2,289 cartons of cigarettes (a "carton" at that time was 500 cigarettes). An unnamed "state-run shop" was found to have hoarded the largest quantity of unregistered cigarettes, accounting for more than 90 percent of the total.[13] State-run shops were income-generating schemes begun after 1940 by the army, public schools, and other government organs. That they flouted the ban on cigarette imports and sales illustrates how different branches of government pursuing their own financial interest can hinder policy implementation. An even more glaring example involves the SGNBR's Department for the Management of the Import-Export of Goods and Materials. Well after the ban began, the agency continued to surreptitiously traffic in cigarettes, even down to the subdistrict level. The agency's abuse explains why this initial ban was ultimately a failure, and illustrates how easily gatekeeping prerogatives can upend prohibition.[14] Nonetheless, at least publicly, the government championed the ban during the early 1940s, as we see in a call to arms published in the *Liberation Daily* during April 1942. Penned by the bureaus of Trade, Public Security, and Taxation, the article applauds the ban for having raised the street price of cigarettes.[15] It emphasizes the ban's economic importance, and orders all merchants to hand in their remaining stock by April 10.[16]

After the article's publication, the ban seems to have been strengthened, probably due to enhanced involvement of the Pubic Security Bureau. Or perhaps this only seems to be true in retrospect, given that the archives offer few reports about black market cigarettes during this period.

What we certainly find is a mixture of government bromides and self-serving pronouncements by individual leaders of their personal sacrifice. On January 15, 1943, the General Office of the CCP Central Committee issued an edict that "all state-run shops and state employees in the SGNBR should boycott imported cigarettes in favor of selling and consuming locally produced cigarettes."[17] The chairman of the SGNBR government, Lin Boqu, set the tone in his belt-tightening plan, published as the lead article on the front page of *Liberation Daily* on January 28. His plan included the statement that "from January 25, 1944, I will abstain from smoking imported cigarettes." He even penned a poem to encourage belt-tightening: "When hosting guests, I boil water, but don't offer tobacco; I use my clothes and bedding for three years; I use one mu of land for cultivating tobacco as my contribution to the public; and I pay for a few pickles with my own income."[18] Gao Gang, CCP party secretary for the Northwest Bureau and speaker of the SGNBR Senate, published his own austerity plan in *Liberation Daily* on February 5. The plan also included a line about "smoking shag tobacco instead of cigarettes in the future."[19]

But these testimonials could not stanch the ongoing supply of and demand for imported cigarettes. The Tax Bureau was powerless to control smuggling by profit-seeking government departments. And without any strong regulations regarding smuggling, there was nothing to quash demand from the market, which tended to push prices up as supply diminished, which in turn increased the lure of black marketeering. This was arguably the main reason why this Communist ban on cigarettes was short lived.

However ineffective the ban, it is worth reemphasizing the terms of its promulgation. The goal was not to protect health, even though evidence suggests that at least some of the SGNBR's leaders knew something even then of cigarettes' pathogenic effects. Rather, the ban's logic was entirely economic:

> Cigarettes are not essential for life, and are of no beneficial effect to the individual's health; in fact they are a tremendous waste of money. . . . At a time when the Anti-Japanese War is entering its most difficult stage, and the entire nation is economizing to save itself from destruction, the patriotic, democratic

SGNBR must immediately abolish the import of cigarettes in order to curtail futile expenses, to balance the trade deficit, to control financial difficulties brought about by the Anti-Japanese War, and to strengthen ourselves for the struggle.[20]

On the same page as this announcement, the *Liberation Daily* published an article titled "End the Cash Draining-Cigarettes—18 million." This was an appeal to the public to modify its behavior. Readers were not, however, urged to stop smoking. Instead they were simply encouraged to switch from cigarettes to pipes, and from imported to local tobacco.[21] Tobacco smoking was treated as normal, even desirable.

When considering the involvement of Communist base areas in normalizing tobacco use, it is important to keep in mind that, given the dire straits of the SGNBR economy at this time, few people had enough cash to buy cigarettes with any frequency. Soldiers and peasants did not earn much money, so they usually could only afford locally grown shag. Rank-and-file party cadres, thanks to their cash subsidies, were bigger buyers of cigarettes. And of course, many a SGNBR leader smoked cigarettes. Mao Zedong was a big cigarette smoker, but so too were Lin Boqu, the chairman of the SGNBR government, and Gao Gang, the speaker of the Senate.[22]

In other words, if you were well-heeled or powerful, you likely smoked not just tobacco but some of the imported cigarette offerings readily available, making cigarette consumption all the more a mark of special privilege in the base areas. Arguably the regulatory rhetoric at the time—the proscription of imports in particular and the affirmation of smoking more generally—only served to reinforce the cachet of cigarettes.

From Prohibitive Taxation to Total Prohibition—and Monopoly

In June 1943, the SGNBR government changed course again in its experimentation with tobacco management. Leaders dropped the ban on imported cigarettes and issued a new set of regulations. These regulations were designed to suppress consumption of imported cigarettes through heavy taxation. Rescinding the ban was an acknowledgment that prohibition had reduced tax revenue while also fueling a black market. The about-face may also have reflected an acknowledgment of the improving market conditions during early 1943. Campaigns to promote production of various goods were beginning to pay off.

As Table 1.1 shows, SGNBR's authorities were especially interested in cigarettes. By June 1943, in fact, the SGNBR had started to produce its own cigarettes. And to encourage success, SGNBR cigarettes were taxed at a lower rate than imported brands. So eager were leaders to promote local cigarette manufacturing that they set relevant taxes roughly on par with levies on shag and water-pipe tobacco.

It was around this time that the SGNBR tried to establish a monopoly over two profitable products of a recreational nature: tobacco and alcohol. The aim was to create a system incorporating the entire supply chain, from sourcing raw materials to manufacture and sale.

The design of the monopoly, at least in terms of tobacco, was riddled with flaws from the start. One flaw involved ownership structure. Although labeled a monopoly, the system issued stock, with a capital value of eight million yuan divided into eight thousand shares, each of which had a face value of one thousand yuan. The SGNBR Finance Department was responsible for buying half of these shares, while the other half could be purchased by other government units or individual SGNBR citizens. If insufficient shares were sold, the Finance Department would be tasked with purchasing the rest. Provisional Regulations for the SGNBR Alcohol and Tobacco Monopoly stipulated that shareholders should be able to withdraw half their dividends by installments during a certain period of time, and that 40 percent of the total revenue should be turned over to the government's Finance Department as income.[23]

Although superficially resembling a modern corporation, the state-run monopoly was expected to operate with little regard for market logic. One

TABLE 1.1.

Tax rates for entry, transit, and production of tobacco products in the SGNBR, June 1943

	Roll-your-own "shag" tobacco	Water-pipe tobacco	Blended pipe tobacco	Cigars and cigarillos	Cigarettes
Intra-SGNBR production tax	—	—	—	—	10%
Transit tax	5%	10%	10%	15%	20%
Import tax	10%	20%	20%	30%	40%

SOURCE: "Shaan-Gan-Ning bianqu yanlei zhengshui zhanxing tiaoli" [SGNBR Provisional Regulations for Tobacco-Based Products] (June 12, 1943), in *Shaan-Gan-Ning geming genjudi gongshang shuishou shiliao xuanbian* [Collection of historical documents on taxation of industry and trade in the SGNBR], ed. Shaan-Gan-Ning geming genjudi gongshang shuishou shi bianxiezuo [Writing group of the history of taxation of industry and trade in SGNBR] and Shaanxi sheng dang'an'guan [Shaanxi provincial archives] (Xi'an: Shaanxi renmin chubanshe, 1986), vol. 4, 149.

can see this again in the monopoly's Provisional Regulations. In an effort to guarantee profits, the regulations authorized the government to dictate manufacturing targets, to fix retail prices (at 20 percent over the wholesale price), and to ensure shareholders huge annual dividends.[24] By failing to consider factors such as product quality and market demand, and by making unrealistic plans on the basis of guaranteed profits and dividends, the monopoly immediately foundered in the face of rampant cigarette smuggling carried out by army personnel and public employees.

Another flaw from the outset was a lack of capital investment. The nascent SGNBR cigarette industry could only produce tiny volumes, most of which were manufactured by hand. Moreover, the monopoly used tobacco leaves and wrapping papers of poor quality. Overall, SGNBR-manufactured cigarettes had little chance of competing against cigarettes made by manufacturers outside the region.

This experimental monopoly system had an even harder time after the SGNBR's ban on imported cigarettes was lifted in June 1943. Even with tax policies designed to protect the local industry, there was no way to stem the influx of better-made cigarettes from elsewhere. According to Tax Department figures, the SGNBR imported 6.5 billion yuan worth of goods in 1943, including tobacco and alcohol valued at 350 million yuan, which made up over five percent of total imports, a contribution exceeded only by clothing, cotton and wool products, and sundry goods.[25]

A further flaw of the monopoly pertained to taxation. Whereas most smuggled cigarettes went untaxed, the Provisional Regulations directed the government to create a stifling taxation hydra that would in effect ensnarl the monopoly. All levels of the SGNBR's tax bureaucracy were instructed to set up their own tobacco and alcohol monopoly offices. These offices were charged with monitoring the flow of monopoly products within the SGNBR and across its borders. The tax offices were also required to supervise production at each cigarette factory.

Given all these problems, the monopoly system was never extended beyond the core area of the SGNBR and was short lived. It only operated in Yan'an for a few months in 1943 and then again briefly in March 1944.

On February 8, 1944, the pendulum swung back in the direction of prohibition, as SGNBR authorities announced another ban on imports. Stocks of imported cigarettes had to be sold off before March 20, following which the Goods and Materials Bureau would swoop in and purchase all remaining cigarettes and sell them outside the SGNBR. In at least one respect this new policy was even more far-reaching than the previous ban. Not only was importing cigarettes banned, but so too was cross-border transit of cigars and water-pipe tobacco.[26] The announced purpose of this strict gatekeeping was "to facilitate the smooth implementation of cross-border and internal trade, promote a trade surplus, and safeguard production in the SGNBR."[27]

Like the 1942 embargo, the 1944 ban was linked to fiscal belt tightening. By the end of 1943, austerity had again become the SGNBR's mantra. As a nonessential consumer good that generated a substantial outflow of cash, the imported cigarette became one of the first targets of new austerity policies. No doubt, one calculus here was also to help local cigarette manufacturers. Agricultural, industrial, and handicraft capacity in the SGNBR had all improved since the preceding year, which meant that additional resources were available for developing the local cigarette industry.

Other Aspects of SGNBR
Government-Owned Cigarette Production

Large-scale cultivation of tobacco had never been attempted in this part of China, though the region was certainly suitable, given that locals had long been planting leaf for personal consumption. When it became a political entity in 1939, the SGNBR government began pushing tobacco cultivation as an income generator, but it also began experimenting with different varietals—Virginia tobacco acquired from Shanxi and Sichuan provinces, for example. Perhaps to avoid undermining grain production, or perhaps to keep an economic grip on a cash crop, SGNBR authorities insisted that Virginia tobacco cultivation should remain firmly in the hands of the government.[28]

Promotion of tobacco leaf cultivation jumped after the Wannan Incident in spring 1941, with the push toward autarchy. Under the banner of "self-reliance," authorities encouraged all government departments, schools, and army units to take part in all manner of agricultural production, so that they could each cover a certain portion of their own daily needs. Perhaps the most famous example was the 359th Brigade, praised by Mao in December 1942. The brigade opened up wasteland in Nanniwan, growing grain, vegetables, hemp, and (especially) tobacco on twenty-five thousand mu of land (one mu is about a sixth of an acre).[29] As a cash crop, tobacco at the time was worth much more than grain. Thus, as soon as the population's supply of grain, cotton and flax, and other essential items had been assured, government bureaus, army units, and peasants all began to push further into tobacco cultivation.

Government departments set up facilities for making hand-rolled cigarettes, leveraging increases in local tobacco output. By 1943, the Finance Bureau had set up the Northwestern Cigarette Factory, and the Party School of the CCP Central Committee had set up the Yufeng Cigarette Factory. The 1944 ban on cigarette imports supercharged the creation of such factories, urged by the shift to self-reliance. Most of these were small, privately run workshops employing between two and fifteen people; in some instances, a workshop consisted of only a single person, who made cigarettes by hand during his or her spare time.[30] Government-owned cigarette factories were generally larger. In 1944, there were seven government-owned factories with a total of 150 employees altogether. By 1945 there were thirty such factories, with the largest being the Huafeng Factory (with 80 employees), the Yufeng Factory (60–70 employees), the Northwestern Factory (40-plus employees), and the Tuanjie Factory (more than 50 employees), the last of which was affiliated with the Central Administrative Bureau of the CCP.[31] All told, large and small, by the spring of 1945 there were more than *two hundred* of these facilities, with an estimated annual production reaching over seven hundred thousand cartons (with five hundred cigarettes per carton).[32] This was something of the Wild West of cigarette manufacturing in China.

Not surprisingly, quality was often slipshod. With limited access to machinery, most cigarettes were rolled by hand using a wooden rolling device, which yielded irregular shapes and sizes. And although the SGNBR had introduced the cultivation of high-quality Virginia tobacco, much of what was grown was useless because curing processes were faulty. "In most cases cured tobacco was over-dried, resulting in substandard taste and appearance."[33] Another problem had to do with the papers used. Most manufacturers only had access to low-quality stock that they brushed with a mixture of plaster, alum, and water, and then left to dry overnight to ensure it was airtight. Adhesive was typically made from common, food-grade flour.[34] Highlighting how chaotic production must have been in this context, during the summer of 1945 SGNBR authorities announced that factories were barred from using "toxic materials in their cigarettes."[35] Apparently, in a frenzied attempt to compete in taste, feel, and freshness with cigarettes smuggled in from outside, local factories were resorting to all manner of chemical additives and adulterants.

Management methods also impaired product quality and yield. Under government ownership, cigarette factory managers' main responsibility was little more than meeting production targets set by higher-level administrators. Managers were not accountable for costs, distribution methods, or product quality, and were routinely reimbursed for expenses according to a fixed ratio. Administrators "provided or reimbursed raw materials and expenses on the basis of a quota decided by the SGNBR government, and received the finished product in return."[36] Because factories were not expected to consider market demand or the cost of raw materials when making products, they regularly racked up big losses, with investors left holding the bag. During 1943–1944, for example, the Northwestern Local Products Company suffered a loss of nearly three hundred million yuan from its investment in cigarette production.[37] Furthermore, when a factory happened to turn a profit, the impulse of the investing institution was to cash in quickly rather than make further investments in equipment. This was the case with the then relatively large Yufeng Cigarette Factory. The Central Party School extracted profits from the factory but rarely reinvested in equipment to improve product quality.[38]

Pervasive smuggling facilitated by army units and their governmental allies fostered this grab-and-run outlook. According to a report submitted by the Tax Bureau in May 1945, in three counties near Yan'an alone, two hundred thousand cartons of black market cigarettes had been traded during the month of April, with an estimated value of at least four hundred billion SGNBR yuan. Most of this smuggling, investigators found, was carried out "by army and government units, with perhaps some ordinary citizens, mostly sheltered by government agents or the army, also holding a stake."[39] Investigators further noted that one reason the army was inclined to smuggle cigarettes was the politics of "self-sufficiency" in the SGNBR. Army units resorted to smuggling to demonstrate that, like any other government unit, they had generated "income," fulfilling budgetary targets.[40] Of course, the army's trafficking of exogenous cigarettes slowed sales of locally produced brands, causing prices to tumble and reducing the revenue of the Tax Bureau.

This brings us back to a basic conclusion of this chapter: government experiments pertaining to cigarettes within the SGNBR were, on balance, managerial fiascos. Central authorities there failed in their efforts to control the market and to make money. In some of the CCP's other base areas, cigarette policies were more successful. To be sure, all the base areas experienced cash outflows due to the consumption of non-local cigarettes, and to combat this outflow, most adopted policies, such as prohibition, heavy tariffs, and government-controlled monopolies, to stem the trade in illicit cigarettes (and to support the local economy). However, several base areas differed significantly from the SGNBR when it came to efforts at manufacturing cigarettes.

Cigarette Production in Other Communist-Controlled Regions

Two significant differences between the SGNBR and these other regions pertain to their degree of militarization and distance from economically advanced areas. Because the SGNBR was far from the front lines, it had relatively few soldiers. Apart from some skirmishes with the Guomindang in 1940, the region saw no fighting during the Anti-Japanese War. By contrast, other CCP base areas tangled with the Japanese army and were full of battle-tested (and sometimes battle-weary) soldiers—this included the Eighth Route Army in the Shanxi-Hebei-Shandong-Henan Base and the New Fourth Army in the Jiangsu-Anhui Base. Irrespective of locale, however, soldiers during the twentieth century were significant consumers of cigarettes—even more so outside of China. Armies in both Europe and the United States, for example, were given cigarettes as part of daily rations, considered vital for calming frayed nerves and shoring up morale.[41] The Japanese army also had a standard allocation of forty cigarettes per person per week.[42] But unlike the Japanese army, the armies of the Chinese Communist Party controlled few cities with cigarette manufacturing facilities. Thus the party encouraged its army commanders to guarantee a steady supply whenever necessary by organizing mobile tobacco production units.

Frontline army units often found it easier to manufacture cigarettes than did units back in the SGNBR. Frontliners were regularly in areas controlled by the enemy, where it was relatively easy to acquire cigarette papers, rolling machines, and technical personnel familiar with manufacturing. The Chinese Communist Shanxi-Hebei-Shandong-Henan and Jiangsu-Anhui base areas lacked access to advanced machinery, but they were close to well-established plantations growing Virginia tobacco. Therefore, as long as they had suitable paper, it was possible for these army units to crank out cigarettes with hand-rolling techniques. Other army units, however, produced more machine-rolled cigarettes than they could consume and cashed in on the surplus. Sometimes, they even developed broad brand recognition. The New Fourth Army's Flying Horse brand, for example, produced in its factory in Xinqun, became a favorite even in enemy-occupied areas.

The Xinqun factory deserves further consideration because of how it handled profits. This factory, by 1944, had over two hundred employees and was making a profit of more than ten thousand yuan.[43] However, it did not allow tax collectors or other entities to siphon off all these earnings. Instead, it continued to update its machines, smuggling in new ones from Shanghai. It sought out skilled technicians, including personnel who had originally trained with the British American Tobacco Company. It also sought out better-cured tobacco from Anhui, on the other side of the enemy's blockade. In other words, Xinqun was successful not only because it was close to the enemy and had lots of soldiers, but also because it strived to improve product quality, as opposed to the SGNBR approach.

Final Thoughts

Mark Selden, in his assessment of early Communist economic policies, lavishes praise on modes of production in the SGNBR. He suggests that these modes of production helped stabilize the base areas in a period of great precariousness for the CCP.[44] In our examination, a different image emerges. Governmental experimentation with cigarette manufacturing in the Yan'an region was riddled with problems. Illogical plans led to failures in manufacturing and sales; top-down production pressures induced cutting corners; shortsighted investment precluded capital improvements; and incomplete efforts at prohibition fueled smuggling and other forms of misconduct. In some instances, base areas in other parts of China met with notable success when it came to cigarette manufacturing, but this was rarely so in the SGNBR.

Chronicling all this experimentation is significant for understanding tobacco in China from the mid-twentieth century forward. In February 1949 the CCP launched a new effort to create a state monopoly apparatus covering alcohol and tobacco. This time, however, monopoly building was not limited to just any one base area. It covered what had become the newly named Northeast China Liberated Zone.[45] Unlike the party's modus operandi in the SGNBR, in the Northeast the nascent monopoly would come to involve heavy investment in local factories, strict limits on imported cigarettes, mechanized production, bans on handmade cigarettes, and anti-smuggling measures. Through these efforts, regional cigarette production in the Northeast climbed quickly, generating profits for the regime. All this became an important model for CCP planners as they began configuring cigarette manufacturing nationwide after 1949, as Sha Qingqing elaborates in the next chapter. It remains unclear how much party leaders, when designing their Northeastern monopoly in the late 1940s, actively contemplated the mistakes made earlier in the SGNBR. What is clear is that they took a different approach than had typified Yan'an and environs.

From the late 1930s to the late 1940s, what was consistently at the heart of CCP experimentation with cigarettes? Certainly profits. Cigarette manufacturing held the great promise of high financial returns for the party. At the heart of all this experimentation, however, were also discourses that would carry over into the post-1949 era. Base area experimentation elicited managerial discussions aplenty, pertaining to raw-material sourcing, quantity, quality, taxation, and smuggling. Out of these discussions, a number of notions would become deeply rooted in the psyche of the People's Republic. Of these, two became especially normalized in the latter half of the twentieth century. The first is that producing cigarettes is a responsibility of CCP governance. The second is that, within the party-state, impediments to cigarette manufacturing and sources of slipshod production need to be overcome.

Mao Zedong quietly codified these notions not long after the founding of the People's Republic. In 1953, when the Ministry of Health was planning its early rounds of programming, it proposed making abstention from tobacco a pillar of its public health outreach. Mao and others atop the CCP would have none of it. He and the CCP Central Committee swiftly endorsed the position of China's southern provinces that health campaigns against tobacco were forbidden because, as Mao personally penned, they would "harm production."[46] Basic principles for a young polity were thus set. Health-related branches of government were to stay out of the way so that a newly nationalized tobacco industry could devise better means to cultivate leaf, manufacture cigarettes, and sell smoke.

Notes

1. To be sure, local policy experimentation in the base areas was not limited to the realm of tobacco governance. For a discussion of how and why the CCP

was so prone to experimentation in the base areas and how policy experimentation there subsequently became a template for how the party would devise new national policies of many types running all the way up to the present day, see Sebastian Heilmann, "From Local Experiments to National Policy: The Origins of China's Distinctive Policy Process," *China Journal*, no. 59 (January 2008): 1–30. For a discussion of Maoist notions of self-reliance and science, see Sigrid Schmalzer, "Self-Reliant Science: The Impact of the Cold War on Science in Socialist China," in Naomi Oreskes and John Krige, eds., *Science and Technology in the Global Cold War* (Cambridge, MA: MIT Press, 2014).

2. Yan Yan, *Shaan-Gan-Ning bianqu jingji fazhan yu chanye buju yanjiu (1937–1950)* [Research on economic development and the distribution of industries in the Shaan-Gan-Ning Border Region, 1937–1950] (Beijing: China Social Sciences Press, 2007), 23–25.

3. Zhongguo kangri zhanzheng shi xuehui [Chinese Association of Historical Study of the Anti-Japanese War] and Zhongguo renmin kangri zhanzheng jinianguan [Chinese People's Anti-Japanese War Memorial Hall], eds., *Kangzhan shiqi de Shaan-Gan-Ning bianqu* [The Shaan-Gan-Ning Border Region during the war] (Beijing: Beijing Press, 1995), 435.

4. In 1943, the SGNBR had 6.47 billion yuan of imports and 5.36 billion yuan of exports, of which 68 percent were "special local products." See Shaan-Gan-Ning bianqu caizheng jingji shi bianxie zu [Financial and Economic History of the Shaan-Gan-Ning Border Region Writing Group] and Shaanxi sheng dang'anguan [Shaanxi Provincial Archives], eds., *Kangri zhanzheng shiqi Shaan-Gan-Ning bianqu caizheng jingji shiliao zhaibian* [Selected extracts from historical materials pertaining to finances and economics in the Shaan-Gan-Ning Border Region during the Anti-Japanese War] (Xi'an: Shaanxi People's Press, 1981), vol. 4, 50. According to research by Chen Yung-fa, the "special local product" was, in fact, opium. In other words, the SGNBR had no choice but to rely on the secret trade in opium in order to maintain a trade balance, and even this was not sufficient to reverse an overall trade deficit. See Chen Yung-fa's "Hong taiyang xia de yingsuhua: yapian maoyi yu Yan'an moshi" [Poppies under the red sun: The opium trade and the Yan'an model], *Xin shixue* [New History], vol. 1, no. 4 (December 1990): 41–117.

5. Regarding tobacco consumption habits in rural China during the Republic of China, see Carol Benedict, *Golden-Silk Smoke: A History of Tobacco in China, 1150–2000* (Berkeley: University of California Press, 2011), 171–77, 185–98.

6. *Shaanxi sheng zhi: Yancao zhi* [Shaanxi provincial gazetteer: Tobacco] (Xi'an: Shaanxi renmin chubanshe, 2006), 5.

7. *Jiefang ribao* [Liberation Daily], December 24, 1941, 4.

8. Ibid.

9. Shaanxi sheng dang'an'guan [Shaanxi Provincial Archives] and Shaanxi sheng

shehui kexue yuan [Shaanxi Provincial Academy of Social Sciences], eds., *Shaan-Gan-Ning bianqu zhengfu wenjian xuanbian* [Selected documents of the Shaan-Gan-Ning Border Region government] (Beijing: Dang'an chubanshe, 1988), vol. 4, 218.

10. Ibid., 407.

11. *Kangri zhanzheng shiqi Shaan-Gan-Ning bianqu caizheng jingji shiliao zhaibian*, vol. 4, 111.

12. *Jiefang ribao*, January 17, 1942, 4. Among the foreign cigarette brands mentioned in the sales ban, Xiandao (8 yuan per 10 cigarettes), Qianmen, and Paotai were all manufactured by the Yee Tsoong Cigarette Company, and Fengche was manufactured by the Eastern Tobacco Company in Yingkou. Yee Tsoong and the Eastern Tobacco Company were both Chinese firms belonging to the tobacco giant British American Tobacco.

13. *Jiefang ribao*, March 10, 1942, 4.

14. *Shaanxi sheng zhi*, 542.

15. *Jiefang ribao*, April 12, 1942, 2.

16. Ibid.

17. *Shaanxi sheng zhi*, 542.

18. *Jiefang ribao*, January 28, 1944, 1.

19. Ibid., February 5, 1944, 1.

20. *Kangri zhanzheng shiqi Shaan-Gan-Ning bianqu caizheng jingji shiliao zhaibian*, vol. 4, 156–64.

21. *Jiefang ribao*, December 24, 1941, 4.

22. It is reasonable to assume that the SGNBR Department for the Management of the Import-Export of Goods and Materials granted a "special license" in order to satisfy the cigarette cravings of these leaders. *Shaanxi sheng zhi*, 542.

23. *Kangri zhanzheng shiqi Shaan-Gan-Ning bianqu caizheng jingji shiliao zhaibian*, vol. 4, 158–61.

24. Ibid., 161–62.

25. Ibid., 50.

26. Ibid., 579–81.

27. *Shaan-Gan-Ning geming genjudi gongshang shuishou shiliao xuanbian* [Selected documents on industrial and commercial taxation in the Shaan-Gan-Ning Revolutionary Base Area] (Xi'an: Shaanxi renmin chubanshe, 1986), vol. 5, 263.

28. *Shaanxi sheng zhi*, 527.

29. *Mao Zedong xuanji* [Selected Works of Mao Zedong] (Harbin: Dongbei shudian, 1948), 830.

30. *Shaanxi sheng zhi*, 532.

31. Ibid.

32. *Shaan-Gan-Ning geming genjudi gongshang shuishou shiliao xuanbian*, vol. 5, 470.

33. *Shaanxi sheng zhi*, 539.

34. Ibid., 533.

35. *Kangri zhanzheng shiqi Shaan-Gan-Ning bianqu caizheng jingji shiliao zhaibian*, vol. 5, 474.

36. *Shaanxi sheng zhi*, 540.

37. Ibid.

38. Zhang Guozhen, "Huiyi Yan'an zhongyang dangxiao de yufeng juanyan chang" [Memories of the Yufeng cigarette factory affiliated with the Central Party School in Yan'an], in *Yan'an zhongyang dangxiao zhengfeng yundong* [The rectification movement at the Central Party School in Yan'an] (Beijing: Zhonggong zhongyang dangxiao chubanshe 1989), 240.

39. "Waiyan zousi qingkuang ji jidai chuzhi banfa de baogao" [A report on the smuggling of imported cigarettes and the urgent need to prohibit it], *Shaan-Gan-Ning geming genjudi gongshang shuishou shouliao xuanbian*, vol. 5, 464.

40. Ibid., 466.

41. See Richard Klein, *Cigarettes Are Sublime* (Durham, NC: Duke University Press, 1993), chap. 5.

42. *Jiefang ribao*, November 6, 1942, 4.

43. Liu Zhihui and Yue Xin, "Ji Xinqun yancao gongsi" [Remembering the Xinqun Tobacco Company], *Zhongguo yancao* [China Tobacco] no. 1 (1985): 1–4; Hu Biliang, "Xinsijun ershi de gongji he shengchan" [Supply and production of the New Fourth Army Second Division], *Zhongguo kangri zhanzheng shengli de yiyi he sikao—Beijing Xinsijun ji Huazhong kangri genjudi yanjiuhui jinian kangri zhanzheng shengli 60 zhounian dahui lunwenji* [The implications of and reflection on China's victory in the Anti-Japanese War: Proceedings of the conference of the Beijing New Fourth Army Anti-Japanese Base in Central China Research Society to commemorate the sixtieth anniversary of the victory in the Anti-Japanese War], vol. 4 (2005), 295–97.

44. Mark Selden, *China in Revolution: The Yen'an Way Revisited* (Armonk, NY: M.E. Sharpe, 1995), 196–208.

45. Yang Guoan, ed., *Zhongguo yan ye shi huidian* [Documents on the history of the Chinese tobacco industry] (Beijing: Guangming ribao chubanshe, 2002), 1585.

46. *Jianguo yilai Mao Zedong wen'gao* [Mao Zedong's manuscripts since the founding of the PRC] (Beijing: Zhongyang wenxian chubanshe, 1990), vol. 4, 172. I am grateful to Sha Qingqing for providing me with this reference.

CHAPTER TWO

Malformed Monopoly
How Nationalization of China's Tobacco Industry Was Shanghaied by a 1950s Cigarette Conference

Sha Qingqing

> Party and government officials should not smoke foreign cigarettes, and should avoid cigarettes produced by private companies.
>
> *Mao Zedong's annotation on Yang Lisan's Summary Report regarding the*
> *National Cigarette Conference, November 22, 1950 (China Tobacco Museum)*

Setting the Stage

In the 1930s and 1940s, Shanghai was a beehive of cigarette production. When the Communists "liberated" the city in the spring of 1949, the "Pearl of the Orient" had no fewer than 112 factories involved in churning out cigarettes, perhaps more than any other city in the world at that time. Among these factories only one, Chunghwa, was state-owned; all the rest were privately held.[1] This posed both opportunities and problems for a young Communist regime in need of tax revenue and looking to create a socialist economy. To nobody's surprise, the Communist Party wasted little time in creating a Tobacco Takeover Group to oversee the nationalization of the industry.[2]

But how was this new group to proceed? How would it convert and consolidate Shanghai's beehive of cigarette makers, let alone the country's other cigarette manufacturers, into a single-minded government apparatus?

The complexity of that task had started to emerge by the summer of 1949, when Shanghai's once-booming cigarette industry was plunged into a crisis. Summer passed and then came September, which was normally the peak season for the city's cigarette makers. But production was in a tailspin. Prices of both raw materials and commodities had risen so sharply that the costs of manufacturing cigarettes exceeded what the retail market could bear. The more Shanghai's manufacturers produced, the greater were their losses. Most felt immense pressure to cut back on production, and so they did.

This meltdown likely caught many Communist leaders off guard. As Liu Wennan recounts in this volume, before "national liberation" in 1949, the Communist Party had run its own cigarette industry in remote base areas. There, the CCP had overseen the supply of raw materials and delivered a steady stream of inexpensive cigarettes to Communist forces. Base area production proved to be a poor post-Liberation (i.e., after 1949) template, however. It had had neither the complexity nor the scale to be found in mid-century Shanghai, let alone the nation.

This brings us to the central topic of this chapter: a meeting held during the summer of 1950, one year after the Communist revolution. Representatives from China's main tobacco companies were summoned to Beijing, where they met during the third week of July in the Great Hall of the Ministry of the Food Industry. This was the First National Cigarette Industry Conference of the People's Republic, a momentous albeit conflicted event in the formation of China's current cigarette monopoly. Vice-Minister Song Yuhe kicked off the symposium with an impassioned speech, congratulating delegates for "fervently seeking to address the challenges facing today's cigarette industry." The vice-minister applauded the assembled delegates for their desire to develop a "powerful sense of solidarity" within the industry, and declared that they would all help to "pave a glorious path to the future."[3]

The conference was something of a debacle. Not only did it fail to generate a consensus, but it also exposed conflicts festering since the recent founding of the People's Republic. During the meeting, Shanghai delegates led a fierce opposition to most of the fast-paced moves that the party leaders envisioned. Facing a filibuster, symposium organizers had little choice but to concede the need for a soft approach toward cigarette industry restructuring. Indeed, perhaps the most important outcome of the meeting may have been that reformers acknowledged that Shanghai would be ground zero for devising and implementing reforms for a nascent cigarette conglomerate. Solving the riddle of how to stitch together the numerous companies in Shanghai would be key to building a nationwide monopoly.

This chapter explores this First National Cigarette Industry Conference and its aftermath, with special attention to the Shanghai manufacturing environment. Drawing on recently uncovered archival materials in the Shanghai Library, the story told here offers insights into what remains a relatively blank chapter in the history of China's tobacco industry: the initial years after the Communist takeover, when decisions were made that would lead to the formation of the world's largest cigarette corporation.[4]

.   .   .

Contributing a third of the country's GDP in the 1940s, Shanghai was China's wartime industrial heartland, and cigarette production was one barometer of the city's economic prowess. The relevant unit of analysis was a "case" of cigarettes (one case back then equaled fifty thousand sticks). Even in 1948, after more than a decade of war, Shanghai's cigarette production exceeded a million cases.[5] All this changed with the campaign to "liberate" Shanghai in May 1949, which involved fierce battles between half a million Communist and Nationalist troops. During this campaign, over a hundred thousand people, mostly Nationalist soldiers, were killed, and nearly all of Shanghai's economic activity ground to a halt. How Liberation affected the city's industries was immediately measurable in terms of cigarette production. In early 1949, during the months leading up to the Shanghai campaign, the city's cigarette manufacturers produced more than one hundred thousand cases per month.[6] During May, however, as Communist forces routed their opponents, output plummeted, dropping more than 99 percent. Although much of the city's industrial infrastructure remained unscathed, the Communist consolidation of the new regime did not quickly revive Shanghai's cigarette industry. June production amounted to only twenty-four thousand cases. Even in December, during what was supposed to be the "high season," cigarette output barely reached thirty thousand cases, a level "practically unheard of for the Shanghai cigarette industry."[7]

This collapse in Shanghai's cigarette production was felt throughout China—everywhere cigarettes were sold. After June 1949, Shanghai's share as a proportion of all cigarette sales in China fell by around 50 percent. None of this escaped the notice of the Communist Party's most important financial managers, such as Chen Yun, head of the newly formed Central Finance and Economic Commission. At a meeting in June 1949, Chen observed that "the quantity of goods coming out of Shanghai is falling, especially goods such as gauze and cigarettes." Of particular concern to the party was that Shanghai's tax revenue from cigarettes was in free fall. As an advocate of a command economy, Chen Yun did not mince words about what he saw as the remedy: "Efforts shall be made to maintain the production activities of Shanghai's main industries (textiles, printing, cigarettes, etc.)." The plan was for Shanghai's cigarette factories to "restore normal production and increase tax revenue."[8]

To fulfil Chen's demands and to alleviate the dire economic straits affecting many other parts of the economy, authorities at central and local levels, including in Shanghai, began to adopt a centralized planning approach. On March 3, 1950, the Finance and Economic Commission of the Government Administration Council issued a directive, the "Decision Regarding the Centralization of State Financial and Economic Activities," emboldening the party to take greater control of national finances, commodity management, and market liquidity.[9]

It was against this backdrop that, within months of the founding of the People's Republic, two central government offices issued an invitation to representatives of the country's major cigarette companies to attend a conference on China's tobacco industry.

Destination Beijing: The First National Cigarette Industry Conference

A total of ninety-six representatives from all across China came to Beijing to participate in this conference. They came from five different regions: East, Northeast, Southwest, Southcentral, and North China. Among the participants, the delegation from North China was the largest, with 31 representatives. East China's was next with 29 delegates. The Southcentral region sent 22, and Northeast China and the Southwest each sent 7. Of the 29 delegates sent from East China, 21 were from Shanghai; of Shanghai's 21 delegates, 5 were from the state-run sector, 14 from private enterprises, and 2 from joint ventures.[10]

The conference was held in July 1950. Notable are the institutions that convened the event: the Ministry of Food Industry and the Central Finance and Economic Commission. Their involvement reveals the importance of the symposium in the thinking of the party. So inclined were Communist leaders to see cigarettes as basic to daily living, on a par with rice and cooking oil, that party architects assigned initial responsibility of cigarette manufacturing to the Ministry of Food Industry. Commissars were clearly aware that a revival of cigarette sales could help fund other party priorities, so much so that the full weight of the Central Finance and Economic Commission was thrown behind the meeting.

The conference was formally opened on July 18, and for the next ten days representatives presented reports on local situations. Four sub-groups were also formed, with the separate tasks of tackling raw materials, manufacturing, product standards, and marketing. Each group first engaged in discussion of motions and policy proposals before reporting back to the plenary secretariat.[11] The raw materials group, the manufacturing group, and the product standards group focused on manufacturing technology, while the marketing group debated how to reform the Chinese cigarette market and its supply and sales mechanisms, a topic that would become the focus of considerable controversy at the conference.

The conference report and related archival documents suggest that a number of matters were taken up and easily resolved during the ten-day meeting. In these areas, the documents convey a process in which attendees conversed amicably, and the new party-state openly shared how it intended to fulfil its mandate to fold the industry into the socialist economy. So smooth were the deliberations in these areas that the summary report just matter-of-factly states a set of relevant decisions.

For example, the report urges the Ministry of Food Industry to establish uniform profit margins across the industry. The ministry should harmonize profit margins, the report continues, by setting prices for each stage of the cigarette distribution process, from prices at the factory door to wholesale and retail prices.[12]

Production planning was another example of apparent harmony. The report calls on the ministry to ensure that cigarette makers comply with new principles outlined concerning planned production. Enterprises were to adhere to tenets not simply of "matching supply to demand" but also pertaining to "geographic settings, public or private ownership status, and magnitude and degree of mechanization."[13]

Raw materials are yet another topic addressed in clear terms by the conference report, which stipulates that with regard to tobacco leaf, the government "will take charge of centralized planting, curing, classification and grading, and will set appropriate prices and management conditions." Moreover, "illegal activities to disrupt the market, such as hoarding and speculating and manipulating supplies of tobacco leaf, cigarette papers, and reconstituted tobacco will be prohibited."[14] And what institution was to oversee all this?

Beijing will create a new "overarching procurement agency," the conference report states. The government was to establish "an overarching body responsible for procurement and will coordinate regional bodies, which will then establish connections with regional manufacturers."[15]

Reading through the archive, it seems that China's new leaders had several aspirations for the symposium. Beijing hoped the conference would assess the status of China's regional tobacco manufacturers and generate dialogue around relevant policies. We also clearly see a hope to establish, through negotiation, a legitimate foundation for the planned socialist reforms to transform the industry, and a hope that the private enterprises in attendance would endorse the transitional institutions that would eventually be moved into a socialist economy.[16]

Some of these aspirations were easier for conferees to realize than others, however. Whereas deliberations regarding profit margins, production technology, and raw materials were relatively open and marked by consensus, discussions were bumpier when it came to taxation, monopolization (a foregone conclusion, as we shall see), and market demarcation (i.e., bans on trans-regional commerce).

Taxation was a key issue for the symposium, given the enormous potential revenues at stake—and potential harms to cigarette makers' profits. The General Bureau of Taxation sent a staff member to observe and answer delegates' questions, which at points became heated. Some of the most outspoken delegates were from Shanghai, eager to express their concerns regarding taxation. They emphasized that cigarette enterprises would find profits elusive if increased taxes were in the offing (on top of new price controls and increases in the cost of raw materials). Shanghai cigarette makers asked that business taxes in particular be cut, to maintain sales and profits. They suggested that if any levies were to go up, these should be on lower-grade cigarettes—meaning cigarettes of the sort manufactured by Shanghai's provincial competitors.[17] Shanghai delegates also expressed the hope that an independent auditing system would be adopted to assess commercial taxes. The extant system, known as "democratic appraisal," involved no audits of actual financial accounts, but rather came about from negotiations between cigarette makers and tax agents, who together would establish how much tax would have to be paid in any given year.

The new regime's General Bureau of Taxation was unmoved by these appeals. It denied the request to reduce the business tax on the grounds that "if taxation were reduced for the cigarette industry, other industries would expect the same." Regarding higher levies on low-grade cigarettes, the bureau stated that "more research and reflection would be needed before a response can be issued." On commercial taxation, it conceded that "an auditing approach is indeed far superior, but, because the Bureau of Taxation has insufficient personnel and a number of manufacturers have incomplete accounts, the democratic appraisal system is the only viable approach."[18]

Equally of concern to nearly all attendees was whether Beijing would be forming a national tobacco company. On this issue, though, unlike others, the conveners refused to permit an open dialogue. "When and how such a body should be established are questions that will be decided by the government," they declared. "This is a decision for government leaders, and cannot be discussed."[19] The conference summary report makes it clear that party leaders had already defined an approach in advance of the meeting: the report calls for the establishment of a "National Cigarette Industry Management Body," allowing "harmonization of policies, planning and operations." What's more, the report states that, before establishing this Management Body, "cigarette enterprises in all regions should create industry associations" and that "state-owned enterprises should take the lead in the management of these associations."[20]

If dialogue did not always go smoothly at the conference, nowhere was it more fraught than on the topic of the demarcation of markets, including where in the country producers based in Shanghai would be permitted to transport and sell their goods. Here the tensions have to be understood in terms of competing politics of geography and nation building.

In 1950, China's national tobacco industry was being run according to two models simultaneously. The Northeast region, which was liberated in November 1948, had already begun to implement a "market monopoly," while the rest of China was operating according to principles of free market manufacturing and trade, as exemplified by Shanghai's powerful tobacco companies.[21] In the eyes of many government leaders in Beijing, the most serious problem facing the industry at the time was its anarchic nature. Manufacturing and production under free market conditions often resulted in over-production, tax avoidance, and other problems. On the eve of the conference, Zhou Enlai had issued instructions to "intensify the work of the Central Financial and Economic Commission's Bureau of Private Enterprise," strengthening control over private enterprises and markets.[22] As a consequence, the question of how to use planning to exercise greater control over markets was firmly on the meeting's agenda. The conveners also sought to use the meeting to explore the feasibility of rolling out the Northeast region's tobacco monopoly system at a national level.

Hints of these intentions can be heard in the symposium's opening speech given by Song Yuhe, vice-minister of the Food Industry. Here, Song compared the Northeast and Shanghai cigarette industries, noting that the Northeast region had produced a monthly average of 7,678 cases of cigarettes from February to December 1949, and nearly 14,000 cases per month from January to April 1950, a 78 percent increase. By contrast, Shanghai had produced an average of 35,593 cases per month from January to April 1950, a 36 percent decrease over the same period. The vice-minister went on to summarize: "The former [increase] is the result of the transition from a semi-colonial economy to a New Democratic economy; the latter [decrease] is the consequence of a temporary drop-off during the rapid reform of a New Democratic economic system." Song added that it was therefore necessary for the government to carry out adjustments to the market and the structure of the industry.[23]

On day four of the conference, the discussion group on marketing met. A key agenda item was the question of "whether regional market areas could be demarcated,"[24] meaning a ban on distribution and sale of cigarettes across regional boundaries. Guo Ran, representing a state-run tobacco company from the Northeast region, staked out an early position, proposing the strong demarcation of regional markets. Guo's proposal received little support, despite offering no less than "ten rationales" for his stance (most of which centered on promotion of local economies). Representatives from Guangzhou and Zhengzhou in the Southcentral region, Southwest's Chongqing representative, and East China's representatives from Shandong and Shanghai were mostly opposed to demarcation, recognizing this as a threat to their market domination.

Official chroniclers of the conference make clear that the standoff was not simply one bedeviling the marketing group. The question of market demarcation quickly evolved into the "most important, most central question" of the ten-day meeting. In a nutshell, a bureaucratic battle broke out between a "Northeast model" and a "Shanghai model."[25]

In essence, the question of demarcation centered around whether regional tobacco cartels would be established, requiring that cigarettes produced within one region would be available for sale only within that region, and requiring that exports from one region to another would be barred.[26] The Northeast region had implemented just such a system in February 1949, meaning that only cigarettes manufactured in that region were for sale in that part of the country. Soon thereafter, parts of North China replicated the Northeast model. Whether an expansion of this approach would "prevent the creation of a competitive market and have impacts on production" was a question that government authorities wanted answered.[27]

During discussions on July 24, opposition to Guo Ran's pro-cartel motion was fierce. On one side were representatives from Shanghai and other traditional cigarette-producing regions wanting to retain their national market prominence. On the other side were representatives from regions where state cartels had already been created, along with regions where cigarette-manufacturing infrastructure was still rudimentary. To resolve the impasse, Guo's group offered a compromise. They watered down their original motion to read: "demarcations set out in this motion do not represent absolutely isolated markets; it is rather proposed that appropriate limits be put in place concerning the sale of cigarettes between regions. Unplanned sales will be barred, as they would disrupt planned production."[28]

Guo's opponents were unmoved. They held fast, rejecting the revised motion on the grounds that it still contravened the principle of a "free internal national market" as espoused in the Common Program, a temporary constitution approved by the Chinese People's Political Consultative Conference in September 1949. The Beijing-based representative for the North China region tried to break the impasse with new phrasing, offering a motion to establish "a regional monopoly system." But this motion went nowhere. A representative for the Shanghai region immediately pointed out that "such a motion would be equivalent to the demarcation of markets in all but name." The North China motion was voted down.[29]

On July 29, on the last day of the conference, a party official by the name of Yang Lisan delivered a summary report, declaring with regard to the question of market demarcation that "with the exception of the Northeast region, which has already instituted a monopoly system, other regions should engage in free transport and sale of tobacco based on market demand, under a contract and responsibility-based system. In line with the stipulations of the Taxation Conference, joint operations entering into other regions must obtain the authorization of the local government before engaging in business." The report also required companies "to be careful to avoid situations where supply exceeds demand, which could lead to blind competition."[30]

In other words, a compromise was struck. The Northeast did not have its system formally replicated in a honeycomb fashion across the entirety of China, and the Shanghai group failed in its effort to preserve the nation-wide market freedoms they had sought. For the time being, hard-nosed command economists lurking in the background were stymied from immediately creating a national state-owned monopoly.

Shanghai's Post-Conference Steps—and Mao's Cigarette Directive

After the National Cigarette Industry Conference, a public meeting was convened in August 1950 to share information about its results with a larger audience.[31] At the event, deliberations concerning tax regulations and regional monopolies were emphasized. Two months later, the East China Military and Administrative Commission organized an even larger task-setting event.[32] Shanghai-based enterprises were unhappy with both of these meetings, notably the meager manufacturing quotas allocated to them by central authorities. The enterprises pushed back, requesting that "the overall quotas for Shanghai be changed."[33]

One month later, however, a force with the strength of a hurricane struck China's tobacco world, sending everything toppling. In November 1950, Mao Zedong personally weighed in with a few choice words regarding cigarettes. As quoted in the epigraph of this chapter, Mao directed party and government officials not to smoke foreign cigarettes, but also not to smoke those produced by private companies. Central authorities took these words as a green light to begin a takeover of foreign-run tobacco companies. Within eighteen months, the process was well underway: Shanghai enterprises like the British-owned Etsong Company conceded to terms of transfer, and the famed Nanyang Brothers Tobacco Company shuttered its operations. Dissolution of foreign ownership set the scene for much larger changes for Shanghai's cigarette industry, especially for those many companies privately owned by Chinese nationals.

To topple Shanghai's private tobacco companies, the authorities decided to squeeze them in various ways, including via the manipulation of the cost of raw materials. Chen Yun set the tone: "Nowadays there are some capitalists who think like this. . . . 'The government takes care of raw materials and we do the manufacturing. You bear the costs and we earn the money.' Of course, that way of doing things is unacceptable."[34] Accordingly, the authorities directed the state-owned Chunghwa Tobacco Company to found the Shanghai Cigarette Industry Tobacco Leaf Joint Purchasing Bureau in December 1950. Twenty other Shanghai cigarette manufacturers, of which seventeen were privately owned, were brought into this new bureau. Chunghwa would run the bureau, but private enterprises would bear most of the costs of raw material procurement and allocation.

Soon thereafter, other steps were taken to further squeeze private enterprises. In May 1951, for example, the Ministry of Finance issued the Monopolies Regulations (Draft) and the Organizational Standards for Monopoly Companies at All Levels, which listed "cigarette paper" as a product to be monopolized. The General China Monopolies Corporation was also established, with the task of controlling the processing and manufacturing of tobacco leaf, cigarette paper, and other raw materials used in making cigarettes.[35]

The outcome of these moves was a dramatic consolidation of cigarette manufacturing. By 1952, the proportion of tobacco companies in Shanghai under private ownership had fallen to a mere 24 percent. This was all the more dramatic given that, at that time, private enterprises still accounted for 61 percent of the value of the city's overall industrial production.[36]

Meanwhile, Beijing was in the process of reorganizing its bureaucratic architecture, establishing (inter alia) the early scaffolding of what would become the nation's tobacco monopoly administration. On June 2, 1952, the Ministry of Light Industry established the China Tobacco Industry Corporation. It also renamed the Shanghai Tobacco Corporation—the new and short-lived title would be the Shanghai State Tobacco Corporation—and gave exclusive rights to sell the cigarettes it produced to the East China branch of the China General Merchandise Corporation. In October 1953, the Shanghai State Tobacco Corporation was dissolved, and all operations were transferred to the Tobacco Bureau of the Ministry of Light Industry. The factories it controlled were then put under the administration of the Ministry of Industry's East China Tobacco Industry Bureau.

On top of all of these reshufflings came the thorny political campaigns of the early 1950s, which took a decisive toll on the autonomy of private cigarette companies in Shanghai. Between late 1951 and early 1952, the Communist party launched the so-called Three Anti and Five Anti campaigns, with the intent of ridding China of capitalism and related institutions thought to

be undermining Communist nation building. The CCP incited campaign-
ers to root out everything from bribery to corruption, including wasteful
bureaucracy, theft of state property, tax evasion, cheating on government
contracts, and stealing state secrets. Following a wave of unrest caused by
these campaigns, Shanghai's state-owned tobacco enterprises launched their
own kindred campaign in June 1952, the Democratic Reform campaign.
Cigarette enterprises were pressured to set up "campaign offices" in their
factories for the purpose of exposing public vs. private and labor vs. capital
conflicts. "Exposures" of this sort prompted Shanghai's vice-mayor, Fang Yi,
to recommend enhanced supervision of cigarette companies, and by 1953
every privately owned cigarette factory in the city was required to host a
full-time municipal government representative.[37] The mandate of these municipal monitors included enhancing "the authority of the people," tightening oversight, and promoting the reform of private enterprises.

As China crossed into the mid-1950s, a half-decade of nation building
had already dramatically transformed the face of cigarette manufacturing in
Shanghai. Before Liberation, there had been a hundred or so enterprises operating across the city. By early 1954, only twenty-three remained. Whereas
Shanghai had only one single state-owned cigarette manufacturer in 1949,
by 1954 factories owned in part or in full by the party-state controlled well
over seventy percent of cigarette production. And more changes were in the
offing. By the end of that year, consolidation would bring the number of
cigarette companies in Shanghai down to fourteen, of which five were state-
run and nine were operating as joint state-private companies.[38] In other
words, by the start of 1955 the nationalization of China's cigarette industry
was largely complete. All private tobacco companies were gone, having been
acquired or dissolved by the party-state.

Despite all this consolidation, output did not decline. This could be
considered somewhat surprising given that, at the time of Liberation, the
central authorities had repeatedly criticized the country's tobacco industry
for over-concentrating cigarette manufacturing in Shanghai and allowing
factories there to dwarf the output of others elsewhere. However, as nationalization neared completion, criticism ebbed and Shanghai began to see a
surge in production. The city produced over 1,405,792 cases (about seventy
billion cigarettes) in 1954, breaking its 1948 record. This constituted almost
half of all cigarettes manufactured across China during that year. Furthermore, only 12 percent of all these Shanghai cigarettes were allocated to the

local market, with the remainder distributed nationally. Contra early calls for "demarcation," the once-criticized phenomenon of "local production, national supply" had become even more pronounced.[39]

This suggests that the true reason for the young government's erstwhile criticism of the Shanghai cigarette industry was not because of "excessive production." Rather, this charge offered a convenient rationale to target private cigarette companies immediately after Liberation. Once the industry was consolidated and nationalized, the party-state was more than happy to shore up Shanghai's manufacturing prowess, allowing the city to reclaim its mantle as China's most important cigarette production base and sales hub.

Conclusion

After decades in the wilderness, the Chinese Communist Party in 1949 needed quick cash to build a new nation. For this reason, one might have expected the party to have immediately nationalized all cigarette manufacturing. This chapter presents a slightly different narrative. What we have learned is that the CCP's approach was initially shaped by internal divisions within the industry. Central authorities viewed the cigarette industry as vitally important and wanted to achieve comprehensive takeover and control, but they initially took a cautious approach to nationalization, especially when it came to the industry's flagship city. Reform policies were selected after consultation with manufacturers, assessment of likely impacts on production, and negotiations with stakeholders.

An important crucible was the First National Cigarette Industry Conference in 1950. Deliberations there had a clear influence on the new government's understanding and handling of the industry. It was resistance by Shanghai conferees to the idea of a demarcated monopoly system that led Beijing to decide that it would begin by establishing control over supply networks for raw materials, including tobacco leaf and cigarette paper. And it was likely the resistance of Shanghai representatives that prompted Mao's November 12, 1950, pronouncement to buy only state-owned Chinese-made cigarettes. After that, the latitude for economic survival among private cigarette enterprises in Shanghai became increasingly circumscribed. Cornered, private enterprises either collapsed or conceded to buyouts and, by 1955, nearly all had vanished. In parallel, the government's criticism of the Shanghai cigarette industry declined and government investment took off.

These were pivotal moments for the normalization of cigarettes and their manufacture in the budding People's Republic. Indeed, this opening "liberation" phase of the PRC was indispensable for inaugurating systems that grew into the state-owned leviathan that is the China National Tobacco Corporation today. As such, this chapter reminds us of the prominent role that government policy and government officials can play in the normalization of mundane aspects of everyday life.

A guiding principle of this book, as set out in its introductory pages, is that we investigate history with an eye toward the future. This allows us not only to better appreciate how people created the world as we have come to know it, but also to imagine alternative futures. Thus, consider this: What if in November 1950, the pronouncement by the most important person in the land had been a few words different than the epigraph that starts this chapter? What if, in the wake of the First National Cigarette Industry Conference, that pronouncement went something like this: "Party and government officials should not smoke cigarettes, and they should do away with cigarette production"? What if instead of party authorities in the nascent People's Republic fostering cigarette manufacturing by nationalizing hundreds of cigarette enterprises across the country, consolidating them, and strategically investing in new cigarette infrastructure in cities like Shanghai and elsewhere across the country—party authorities had instead taken some very different steps, allowing the industry's trajectory to unfold in dramatically different ways than we have witnessed? What we now see as the cigarette's "normal" role in government finance, consumer culture, and how people live and die would be more properly regarded as outlandish. That is an alternative state of affairs certainly worth contemplation.

Notes

1. *Shanghai juanyan gongye gaikuang* [Overview of the Shanghai cigarette industry], state-owned Chunghwa Tobacco Company, internal publication, February 25, 1950, 1.

2. See "Shanghaishi qinggongyechu baogao" [Shanghai Light Industry Office report] (June 1949), in *Jieguan Shanghai* [The Shanghai takeover], eds. Chinese Communist Party Shanghai Municipal Committee Party History Research Office and Shanghai Municipal Archives (Beijing: China Broadcasting and Television Press, 1993), 272.

3. Song Yuhe, "Diyijie quanguo juanyan huiyi kaimuci" [Opening address at First National Cigarette Industry Conference], *Zhongguo yancao yuekan* [China Tobacco Monthly], combined issue 4 & 5 (1950): 581–82.

4. Currently, academic research on China's tobacco industry is mostly focused on two historical periods: the period between the end of the Qing dynasty and the founding of the People's Republic, and the period beginning in the 1980s, following the initiation of the process of reform and opening up. There are large quantities of research on the first of these two periods, and I will not go into further detail here. For an overview of the research, I recommend Fang Xiantang, ed., *Shanghai jindai minzu juanyan gongye* [A recent history of Shanghai's national cigarette industry] (Shanghai: Shanghai Academy of Social Sciences Press, 1989). For research on China's tobacco industry during the period of reform and opening up, see Peng Yali, "Smoke and Power: The Political Economy of Chinese Tobacco," PhD dissertation (University of Oregon, 1997); Wang Junmin, "Market-Building as State-Building in China's Tobacco Industry," PhD dissertation (New York University, 2007); and Tao Ming, "China's Tobacco Industry under Monopoly Control—Theory, Problems and Systemic Reform," PhD dissertation (Fudan University, 2005).

5. *Shanghai juanyan gongye gaikuang*, 13–14.

6. Ibid., 17. In this essay, cases (*xiang*) are referred to as units of production, with each case containing 50,000 cigarettes.

7. Ibid., 17–18.

8. Chen Yun, "Kefu caizheng jingji de yanzhong kunnan" [Overcoming serious economic difficulties], August 8, 1949, in *Selected Works of Chen Yun*, vol. 2 (Beijing: People's Publishing House, 1995), 5.

9. "Guanyu tongyi guojia caizheng jingji gongzuo de jueding" [Decision regarding the centralization of state financial and economic activities], in *Zhonghua renmin gongheguo caizheng shiliao dierji caizheng guanli tizhi (1950–1980)* [The second collection of the financial records of the People's Republic of China: Financial management systems, 1950–1980], ed. Ministry of Finance General Planning Office (Beijing: China Finance and Economy Publishing House, 1982), 31–36.

10. "Quanguo diyijie juanyan huiyi daibiao mingdan" [First National Cigarette Industry Conference participant list], in *Shanghai juanyan gongye tongyehui chuxi quanguo juanyan gongye huiyi de youguan wenshu* [Documents pertaining to the participation of the Shanghai Cigarette Industry Association in the National Cigarette Industry Conference], Shanghai Municipal Archives, S68-4-73.

11. "Yuhui xuzhi" [Notice to conference participants], in *Shanghai juanyan gongye tongyehui chuxi quanguo juanyan gongye huiyi de youguan wenshu*.

12. Yang Lisan, "Quanguo juanyan gongye huiyi zongjie baogao," in *Shanghai juanyan gongye tongyehui chuxi quanguo juanyan gongye huiyi de youguan wenshu*.

13. "Shoujie quanguo gongye huiyi de zhongdashouhuo" [Important outcomes

of the First National Cigarette Industry Conference], *Zhongguo yancao yuekan*, combined issue 4 & 5 (1950): 554.

14. Yang, "Quanguo juanyan gongye huiyi zongjie baogao."

15. Ibid.

16. Song Jicheng, "Mantan jinhou juanyan gongye jingying fangshi de gaijin" [Discussing approaches to reform in the cigarette industry: Impressions from the First National Cigarette Industry Conference], *Zhongguo yancao yuekan*, combined issue 4 & 5 (1950): 568–69.

17. "Huadong juanyan gongye tian huibian" [Compendium of proposals by the East China cigarette industry], July 10, 1950, in *Shanghai juanyan gongye tongyehui chuxi quanguo juanyan gongye huiyi de youguan wenshu*.

18. "Zhang Bajiong zai shoujie quanguo juanyan gongye huiyi chuanda dahui de baogaoci" [Zhang Bajiong's report at the First National Cigarette Industry Conference public information meeting], August 7, in *Shanghai juanyan gongye tongyehui chuxi quanguo juanyan gongye huiyi de youguan wenshu*.

19. Ibid.

20. Yang, "Quanguo juanyan gongye huiyi zongjie baogao."

21. Ministry of Food Industry's Tobacco Group, "Zhengfeng wenxian: Juanyan gongye zhi jingti" [Rectified publications: Caution in the cigarette industry], *Zhongguo yancao yuekan*, issue 3 (1950): 675.

22. "Guanyu tiaozheng gongsi guanxi jiaqiang siying qiyeju gongzuo de zhishi" [Directive on adjusting public-private relationships and strengthening the activities of the Private Enterprise Office], in Central Committee of the Communist Party Literature Research Center and Central Archives (ed.), *Jianguo yilai Zhou Enlai wen'gao* [Articles of Zhou Enlai since the founding of the PRC], vol. 3 (Beijing: Central Literature Publishing House, 2008), 43–44.

23. "Dui ruhe wanjiu muqian shijie Shanghai juanyanye mianlin shifen yan-zhong weijisheng zhong ji xu jinji caiyong de shidang yewu buzhou" [Appropriate industry measures are urgently required to deal with the serious crisis facing the Shanghai and global cigarette industries, National Cigarette Industry Meeting working report], in *Shanghai juanyan gongye tongyehui chuxi quanguo juanyan gongye huiyi de youguan wenshu*.

24. "Quanguo juanyan gongye huiyi ribao" [National Cigarette Industry Meeting working daily report], July 21, in *Shanghai juanyan gongye tongyehui chuxi quanguo juanyan gongye huiyi de youguan wenshu*.

25. "Zhang Bajiong zai shoujie quanguo juanyan gongye huiyi chuanda dahui de baogaoci."

26. "Gedi tian huibian: shier, guanyu tizao shixian juanyan fenqu zhuanmai zhidu wenti" [Compendium of regional proposals: Twelve, on rapidly creating

a regional monopoly system in the cigarette industry], *Zhongguo yancao yuekan*, combined issue 4 & 5 (1950): 628.

27. "Dongbeiqu siying daibiao Huang Shaomin fayan" [Speech by Northeast region private sector representative Huang Shaoming], in Yang Guoan (ed.), *Zhongguo yanyeshi huibian* [A history of China's tobacco industry] (Beijing: Guangming Daily Publishing House, 2002), 1693–94.

28. "Zhang Bajiong zai shoujie quanguo juanyan gongye huiyi chuanda dahui de baogaoci."

29. "Quanguo juanyan gongye huiyi ribao" [National Cigarette Industry Meeting working daily report], July 24, in *Shanghai juanyan gongye tongyehui chuxi quanguo juanyan gongye huiyi de youguan wenshu.*

30. Yang, "Quanguo juanyan gongye huiyi zongjie baogao."

31. "Shanghai juanyan gongye gonghui wei tongzhi gongshang dengji huiyi" [Notice regarding the participation of the Shanghai Cigarette Industry Association in the Trade and Industry Registration meeting], August 4, in *Shanghai juanyan gongye tongyehui chuxi quanguo juanyan gongye huiyi de youguan wenshu.*

32. Shanghai People's Government Bureau of Trade and Industry, "Wei zhunbei Huadong gongyebu han dingqi zhaokai Huadong juanyan gongyehuiyi xitui daibiao zhunbei ziliao chuxi" [Meetings to prepare the letter to the East China Department of Trade and Industry and delegate preparation materials], in *Shanghai juanyan gongye tongyehui chuxi quanguo juanyan gongye huiyi de youguan wenshu.*

33. Shanghai Cigarette Industry Association, "Qingcha fushixiao genju ji gechangjian de fenpei genju" [Verifying sales records and inter-factory allocations], September 2, 1950, in *Shanghai juanyan gongye tongyehui chuxi quanguo juanyan gongye huiyi de youguan wenshu.*

34. Chen Yun, "Yijiuwuyi nian caijing gongzuo yaodian" [Summary of finance work in 1951], April 4, 1951, in *Selected Works of Chen Yun*, vol. 2, 136.

35. "Guanyu chaofa zhuanmai shiye zanxing tiaoli caoan de tongzhi" [Notification concerning the promulgation of the Provisional Draft Monopoly Regulations], *Zhongyang shuiwu gonggao* [Central Tax Report], 11th ed., 1951, 1–3.

36. *Shanghai juanyan gongye gaikuang* [An overview of Shanghai's cigarette industry] (1954), Shanghai Municipal Archives, B163-2-389-61.

37. *Fang Yi zhuan* editorial team, *Fang Yi zhuan* [Biography of Fang Yi] (Beijing: People's Publishing House), 201–2.

38. Shanghai Tobacco Records Compilation Committee, *Shanghai yancaozhi* [Shanghai tobacco records] (Shanghai: Shanghai Academy of Social Sciences Press, 1998), 50; *Shanghaishi siying juanyan gongye hangye heying zongjie baogao* [Summary report on Shanghai private cigarette industry joint ventures], Shanghai Municipal Archives, B5-2-47-54.

39. *Shanghai juanyan gongye gaikuang.*

CHAPTER THREE

The Chinese Cigarette Industry during the "Great Leap Forward"

Huangfu Qiushi and Matthew Kohrman

On August 7, 1958, as the Great Leap Forward was unfolding, Mao Zedong visited Xuchang, Henan Province, to inspect tobacco production. Casting his eyes over abundant green fields, Mao gleefully turned to Ma Jinming, deputy party secretary of Xuchang Prefecture, and exclaimed with joy: "What a kingdom of tobacco!" As his visit concluded, the Chairman turned to local cadres, prodding them to "give it your all, and strive for the best."[1]

Few in Xuchang that August likely had any inkling that Mao's departing quip portended events that would profoundly shape the nation for decades to come. This chapter discusses the significance of the Great Leap Forward for cigarette manufacturing in China. How did the industry adapt to this now vilified political paroxysm of the late 1950s? What were the long-term influences of the campaign? We argue that the Great Leap, as cataclysmically disruptive as it was to wide swaths of the country, served to foster and normalize some of the very characteristics typifying China's twenty-first-century cigarette sector, in particular, mass consumption, governmental stewardship of logistics, cigarette content as object of innovation, localization of production, and prioritization of industrial minutia over human harm.

The Great Leap Forward eluded academic scrutiny for decades, but that is no longer the case, with detailed histories having been written in recent years.[2] In general, these histories have emphasized the immediate human catastrophes wrought by the campaign. Still obscured, though, are the complex and varied socioeconomic adaptations that the Great Leap spawned. This chapter, in focusing on the Great Leap's influence on a commercial sector, reminds us that the original rationale for the Great Leap was not human devastation but rather political-economic transformation.

The Chinese Communist regime was not the first central government in Chinese history that attempted to achieve economic transformation in a short time frame through a large-scale mobilization campaign. As Bin Wong outlines, beginning in the eighteenth century, the Qing government launched several wide-sweeping initiatives with the goal of shoring up the central government's revenues.[3] These earlier projects at socioeconomic mobilization, of course, differed from the Great Leap in numerous regards. Particularly striking for the late 1950s mobilization were the oversized roles played by Mao and his distinctive rhetoric of rapid transformation.

In October 1955, during the Sixth Plenary Session of the Seventh Central Committee of the CCP, Mao began testing this rhetoric. The central topic of that October meeting was what role communes would have in the transformation of agriculture from capitalist to socialist modes of production. Mao had become a major proponent of communes over other options under consideration for the countryside, and at the 1955 Central Committee meeting he not only trumpeted this option but urged that the development of communes be guided by the slogan: "faster, greater, better." Soon thereafter, during a meeting of the Political Bureau of the Central Committee, he expounded that "greater, faster, better" should be the tenets for all manner of "socialist construction."[4]

Already Mao's rhetoric of choice by the mid-1950s, "greater, faster, better" was not uniformly embraced across China's new leadership, including luminaries like Zhou Enlai and Chen Yun. Such resistance, as Mao viewed it, only hardened his resolve. And within three years he'd pushed away nearly all opposition. By the spring of 1958, not only had phrases like "give it your all, and strive for the best" become mainstays of newspaper editorials, but "leap" language was starting to dominate the machinery of governance. Most notably, in May 1958 the Second National Congress of the CCP deployed leap rhetoric to define how economic targets should be generated and applied to all levels of the polity. The congress declared that targets for the Second Five-Year Plan were to exemplify "give it your all, and strive for the best in the achievement of greater, better, quicker and more economical socialist construction."[5] This declaration as much as any other marks the bureaucratic beginning of the Great Leap Forward.

How did the launch of the Great Leap influence the tobacco industry? Looking back at news clippings from Mao's August 1958 visit to Henan Province it would be easy to assume that tobacco and cigarette production boomed during the Great Leap. It would also be easy to presume that an emphasis on tobacco cultivation directly contributed to the agrarian mismanagement that triggered the outbreak of famine. Neither seems to have been the case. The campaign did not lead to any short-term surge for this industrial sector. Nor did tobacco cultivation directly lead to the misadventures within the countryside that would expose yawning swaths of the Chinese population to starvation. Linkages between Great Leap policies and the cigarette industry would bring about profound and widespread human carnage, to be sure, but that carnage would not become manifest until decades later. Tobacco-related diseases, after all, take decades to incubate.

So, how then did the Great Leap shape tobacco and cigarette production? Perhaps one of its more important effects was that of reinforcing logics of governance that were already underway. These are logics that posit cigarettes as managerial problems to be solved through good governance, not problems of health per se, but rather problems of everyday economic exchange. Within these logics, it is normative to expect cigarettes being manufactured and sold; it is normative to expect them to be sources of government income. What becomes a problem then is the management of logistics: everything from avoiding scarcity and spoilage to overseeing supply chains, infrastructure, staffing, packaging, transport, distribution, and sales. By being so disruptive, the Great Leap made the governance of cigarettes' logistics that much more pressing. It encouraged managerial experiments that would affect the structure of the tobacco industry for decades to come, but it also cemented the notion that cigarette commerce was a domain of great import that participants in the Communist polity should strive to resolve.

Raw Material Shortages

One branch of the young Communist government animated by these logics during the Great Leap was the Ministry of Agriculture. One might think that the Ministry of Agriculture's primary objective would be food supply, especially during the late 1950s. But tobacco was also very much part of that ministry's portfolio. One way this became manifest was in terms of how farmland should be used. This was not altogether new in the history of agronomy in China. During the Ming and Qing dynasties, scholar-officials worried about the cultivation of tobacco undermining the production of grain in the competition for agricultural resources, and this led to episodes wherein imperial regimes tried to ban land from being used for tobacco farming.[6] Similar but more local-level disputes over land use emerged during the Great Leap, with again the loser being tobacco. This was something that the Ministry of Agriculture strived to temper. In an August 1959 report, the ministry fretted that tobacco-planting areas had shrunk dramatically with the onset of the Great Leap. Land devoted to tobacco cultivation fell well below what the ministry had originally planned for that year, with tobacco cultivation dropping 620,000 mu from 1958.[7]

The availability of fertilizer, something that tobacco cultivation requires in large quantities, was a big part of the ministry's concern. The 1959 ministry report details that, over the preceding year, fertilizer available for use on tobacco plantations in Henan, Shandong, Anhui, and Guizhou fell so precipitously that approximately half of those provinces' traditional areas of tobacco cultivation went without chemical enrichment.[8]

The Great Leap did not just intensify managerial tussles over land and fertilizer. Nor did it only create logistical fights between tobacco and grain. The Great Leap's political emphasis on certain forms of industrial production—iron and steel most notably—at the expense of all forms of agriculture intensified challenges for the management of numerous resources essential for cigarette production.

The Great Leap particularly disrupted where and especially when agricultural labor was available. This hit tobacco cultivation hard because the crop is so labor intensive. So topsy-turvy was farm labor in 1958 and 1959 that tobacco fields were commonly poorly prepared to accept fragile tobacco seedlings, with rough and inadequate tilling. The Ministry of Agriculture report outlines that, in 1958, initial planting was decidedly haphazard and that the outlook for "second-growth tobacco"—the autumn-winter season—was ominous. Because of labor disruptions, second-growth transplantation took place well behind schedule in poorly prepared fields.[9]

In 1960, the situation worsened in many parts of the country. Nationwide, the area devoted to tobacco cultivation decreased to roughly 5 million mu—more than 1.4 million mu less than had originally been planned. Neither Henan nor Guizhou received their respective requests for 3,000 tons and 700 tons of chemical fertilizer. Few tobacco farmers had any fertilizer for a second growth. Larger tobacco plantations in areas of Henan and Guizhou were likewise hard hit by labor shortages. In Guizhou alone, some 150,000 mu of late season tobacco fields went unfarmed. Disruptions to labor also meant that land planted in tobacco often went unprotected against disease. Blights like budworm ravaged tobacco plants across the country. In Xiangxian, Henan, 40 percent of the tobacco fields were ravaged by budworm.[10]

Unlike most agricultural crops, tobacco requires not just tremendous amounts of labor but also fuel. The last stages of tobacco cultivation involve the burning of fuel to dry and cure leaves. Because of the priorities and disruptions of the Great Leap, few tobacco-growing areas had access to the fuel they needed, whether straw, coal, or other combustible materials. Large quantities of perfectly grown tobacco could neither be dried nor flue cured. In 1958, because of coal shortages, 50 million catties of tobacco leaves in the Xuchang region in Henan Province were left to rot. And 1959 started off no better for Xuchang. By April, the region's tobacco industry had received just 15 percent of the 600,000 tons of coal it required for the year.[11] Without coal, many curing barns across the country were simply shuttered. This was all deeply troubling to the Ministry of Agriculture. In a 1960 report, it specified that over 80 percent of barns in Hubei, Jiangsu, Heilongjiang, and other newly established tobacco-growing areas had been shuttered, and that Henan alone suffered a shortfall of 17,000 curing barns.[12]

Further evidence that the Ministry of Agriculture was worried about tobacco cultivation can be found in party archives. Not only did the ministry generate reports filled with alerts for party elites, but it tried to use those reports to prompt key party luminaries to intervene directly. For example, Liao Luyan, the Minister of Agriculture, when submitting a 1960 report, directly lobbied Prime Minister Zhou Enlai to reallocate coal from the steel to the tobacco industry.[13]

As much as it was the Ministry of Agriculture that worried about the production of tobacco leaf, it was the Ministries of Light Industry and Commerce that fretted about the manufacture of cigarettes. In May 1958, these two ministries hosted a conference wherein the main concern was ensuring that cigarette manufacturers could access sufficient materiel, especially leaf. Vice-Minister for Light Industry Di Jingxiang reported to attendees that cigarette factories were having such a hard time getting their hands on properly prepared leaf that many would run out of stock by August.[14] Making access to tobacco leaf all the more bedeviling for cigarette enterprises were logistical factors inherent to the industry. The Communists inherited a cigarette industry that was geographically challenged, with most cigarette manufacturing concentrated in coastal regions and much of the best tobacco-growing areas sequestered inland. Consider the cities of Shanghai and Tianjin. During the First Five-Year Plan (1953–1957), those two cities generated 45 percent of the cigarettes in the People's Republic, despite being located far away from key leaf-producing areas.

This geographical legacy was something that agencies like the Ministry of Light Industry were prompted to confront during the disruptions of the Great Leap. With nationwide tobacco leaf output declining between 1957 and 1960 by nearly a third, from 250,000 tons to 186,000 tons,[15] government offices and China's newly nationalized cigarette factories had to experiment and adapt. This came in several forms.

One was infrastructural. Today, the heart of China's tobacco leaf and cigarette production is its southwestern provinces. But that was not always the case. Consider Yunnan, located just north of Myanmar, Laos, and Vietnam. Owing to early twentieth-century investments by British American Tobacco and Yunnan's World War II status as a Nationalist refuge, in 1949 the province was already producing tobacco leaf for cigarettes and had numerous small cigarette factories in its capital of Kunming, but production on both fronts was meager, heavily overshadowed by other locales, even places like Hebei, Anhui, Henan, and Shandong. Fast forward to 2007 and Yunnan was producing a third of China's flue-cured leaf and a fifth of its cigarettes. By then, Yunnan's two state-owned tobacco behemoths—the Hongta Group and the Hongyun Group—were together manufacturing 40 percent more cigarettes than any other province or municipality.[16] Yunnan's rise to cigarette preeminence came in several waves. One of the most important began during the Great Leap Forward, when the Hongta Group's first cigarette factory was set up in the small town of Yuxi, and it piloted now long-forgotten brands like Renmingongshehao (People's Communes Are Good) and Fengshou (Bumper Harvest).

The choice of the small town of Yuxi was not a regional fluke. It was part of a broader infrastructural policy. In 1958, the Ministry of Light Industry declared that the country's cigarette manufacturing hubs needed to be decentralized. Localities were encouraged to set up new provincial and prefectural cigarette manufacturing facilities. This greatly benefitted tobacco-growing areas, which no longer had to suffer under an arrangement of "finished products enter, raw materials exit."[17] But it created challenges for both erstwhile strongholds of cigarette manufacturing and provinces with no history of large-scale tobacco cultivation. Consider the inland city of Taiyuan, the capital and largest city of North China's Shanxi Province. Shanxi had no history of large-scale tobacco cultivation but in the 1950s it had a number of cigarette factories based in Taiyuan. Those factories had historically imported as much as 85 to 90 percent of the flue-cured leaf they needed, transported overland from Henan, Guizhou, the Northeast, and other regions. After the industry decentralization program was launched, cities like Taiyuan found raw materials hard to come by, so much so that by 1959 its factories ground to a halt.[18] Older factories elsewhere, including Shanghai, similarly had to suspend production and were subjected to repurposing.[19] The Shanghai facility producing famed A-grade brands Chunghwa and Double Happiness had to suspend production in 1959 after making only 3,400 of its planned 11,000 cases.[20]

Shanghai's numerous pre-1949 cigarette companies were already undergoing a process of state-managed consolidation—being folded into what today is the Shanghai Tobacco Group—well before the slogan "greater, faster, better, more economical" came into political favor. But early 1958 saw a clear intensification of consolidation, much of it facilitated by the fact that, starved for resources, most of Shanghai's cigarette factories were largely idle. Between May and August, buildings that had long been devoted to cigarette manufacturing by private enterprises were repurposed into state-run factories making toys, electronics, and various types of tools. Not long afterward, the famed Nanyang Cigarette Factory and the lesser-known Shanghai No. 3 Cigarette Factory were retrofitted into the Nanyang Engine Factory and the Shanghai Watch Factory.[21] That today Shanghai's cigarette industry is so efficiently managed out of one mega-factory in the city's central Yangpu district owes much to the Great Leap.

Adaptation did not happen only at the level of infrastructure. Change also occurred to the cigarette itself. For factories obsessed with quality, like several in Shanghai, one solution to resource scarcity was simply reducing the diameter of cigarettes to save on premium leaf.[22] A more common tack, though, involved manipulating the types of combustible materials inside the cigarette, swapping in either lower quality tobacco or non-tobacco components.[23] Some coastal cigarette factories changed their tobacco formulation more than seven times during the first three weeks of April 1959 because of shortfalls in quality tobacco leaf.[24]

Today, around the world, few cigarettes are made up of only tobacco leaf. The modern cigarette is a complex recipe of non-tobacco material like moisteners and flavorings (e.g., sugar, licorice, coffee), chemicals (most notably ammonia, used to puff up shredded tobacco leaf and to increase nicotine's "kick"), and unexpected tobacco components, including large amounts of what is now called "recon," that is reconstituted tobacco comprising stems or midribs, which early cigarette manufacturers discarded.[25]

The Great Leap forced cigarette manufacturers to become far more adept at manipulating what tobacco materiel went into cigarettes. To be sure, such manipulation was not altogether new in China. In the early twentieth century, the British American Tobacco Corporation tinkered heavily with tobacco varietals in China, trying to substitute local leaves for imported Virginia tobacco.[26] During the economic depression in the 1930s, Chinese cigarette companies used sun-dried native tobacco to replace cured leaf in order to reduce costs. But during the Great Leap, such manipulation became not simply a matter of product design but also government policy. Government agencies mandated that cigarette factories use recon in a systematic way never seen in China before. At the forefront were the Ministries of Light Industry and Commerce. After Shanghai Tobacco successfully incorporated tobacco stalk skin into its lowest grade (D) cigarette brands in 1958,[27] the Ministries of Light Industry and Commerce issued a new regulation in 1959. Called the "Joint Notice on Large-Scale Purchase of Tobacco Stems and Ribs," the document required cigarette factories to incorporate recon along a sliding scale. The country's lowest quality cigarettes, E-grade, had to use 50 percent recon; D-grade cigarettes had to use 15 percent, and C-grade brands 10 percent.[28] In 1960, the recommended proportion of tobacco stalks in E-grade cigarettes was raised further.

The high wood-fiber content (50–60 percent) in tobacco stalks meant that managers of some cigarette factories worried that recon inclusion would harm product quality and value. But this wasn't their only worry. There was insufficient steel to fabricate the additional equipment needed to process the tobacco stalks into proper recon. To overcome this challenge, the Ministry of Light Industry and the National Committee of the Light

Industry Trade Union held a six-day conference in February 1960 entitled "Experience-Sharing on Techniques for Dealing with Tobacco Stalks." Light Industry officials from nine provinces and municipalities as well as twenty-four delegates from cigarette factories descended upon Shanghai to take part in the meeting.[29]

After delegates departed, government officials and factory managers continued to fret over how to better incorporate recon. For example, a State Council document describes the factories in the city of Taiyuan as having such a hard time incorporating stalk into production while maintaining minimal quality standards that only half of their planned 41,000 cases of cigarettes for the first half of 1960 could be produced.[30] Monitors from the Ministries of Light Industry and Commerce likewise brooded that stalk incorporation at such Taiyuan factories in early 1960 only made up 14.2 percent of cigarette content, far short of the mandated amount.[31]

In light of such challenges, later in 1960 the ministries declared cigarette manufacturers had to expand adoption of substitutes beyond tobacco material. Newly authorized substitutions were diverse. The most commonly used authorized substitutes were byproducts of sugar—bagasse and sugar beet waste—processed and supplied by the Ministry of Light Industry. Also permitted were remnants of other "commonly eaten" plants, including the lotus, bean, sesame, radish, banana, mint, hops, plantain, pear, peach, cherry, apple, hazel, Mongolian oak, sunflower, tomato, sweet potato, taro, and potato. Not only did the ministries coordinate the collection of these types of materials, they also dictated a new sliding scale for their use.[32]

All this attention to substitution discloses an important shift that occurred during the Great Leap. Whereas cigarette production had been a source of tax revenue in China going back to the dawn of the twentieth century, and whereas the PRC nationalized cigarette manufacturers after 1949, the Great Leap set in motion a new set of government-cigarette relations. Government became no longer just a beneficiary and owner of cigarette factories during the Great Leap. It became increasingly a restless steward, striving to produce a stable supply of cigarettes, defining cigarette manufacture and supply as being a bedrock of the normal order of things even during periods of acute upheaval.

To grasp this point further, consider the cigarette butt. In the early twentieth century it became increasingly common for economizing smokers to repurpose tobacco shreds from discarded butts into hand-roll new cigarettes.

And collecting cigarette butts even became a known livelihood.[33] Carl Crow estimates, for instance, that more than a thousand people made a living at any one time in Shanghai during the 1930s gathering butts and reselling them.[34] During the Great Leap Forward, acquisition of butts shifted from free-market survival strategy to policy. Feeling pressure to provide the public a continuous flow of new cigarettes, in October 1959 the Ministry of Commerce issued the Notice for the Collection of Cigarette Butts to Process into Cut Tobacco. The document urges every work unit, service industry, and subdistrict government office to collect butts for repurposing into cut tobacco. The ministry even set a price range that cigarette factories would pay for harvested butts: 0.5–0.8 yuan per catty (abour 500 grams).[35]

Give Away Yet Leap Forward

Cardinal principles of modern cigarette manufacturing in and outside of China today are mechanization, automation, and efficiency. Mobilizing these very tenets became a primary concern of cigarette governance in the People's Republic during the Great Leap. As already noted, the iron, steel, and related industries (e.g., coal, power, and machinery) became a political priority during the late 1950s. So large was the expectation to provide these and other heavy industries new investments, so large was the pressure on all sectors of society to "stop and give way" to heavy industry, that a thorny question emerged for managers of other industries: how to "give way" but also perform a visible "leap forward" in one's own managerial domain?

The cigarette industry had several answers. Reducing labor costs through innovation was a favored one. And for that, the cigarette sector tapped into four objectives of the Great Leap's industrial agenda: mechanization, continuous process implementation, standardization, and automation. Championing these objectives for tobacco was once again the Ministry of Light Industry. In its 1960 "Report on the Technological Revolution in the Cigarette Industry since the Great Leap Forward," the ministry boasted about recent technological innovations, such as the fabrication of iron-wood packaging machines, implementation of wind-powered tobacco-feeders, installation of conveyor belts, and the introduction of stem-removal machines. These innovations, the ministry boasted, not only allowed a third of China's cigarette factories to achieve new forms of "continuous production," but also dramatically reduced labor costs. The stem-removal machines alone allowed the industry to cut 6,700 jobs.[36] Other technological advances included the creation of a pneumatic gun shooting tung extract to promote fermentation; a starch-scraping machine, reducing the amount of grain needed to produce starch paste; an oil-catcher on rolling machines, keeping cigarettes from getting stained; and a machine that automatically stopped conveyor belts when cigarette cartons were being improperly packed. In a 1958 document entitled "Pioneers of the Technological Revolution in the Tobacco Industry," these and other kinds of innovations are celebrated for raising various aspects of industrial productivity, including the ability to insert 20 cigarettes per pack rather than only 10.[37]

Another answer to the "give way yet leap forward" challenge was to foster industry efficiency and productivity by encouraging cooperation and competition among factories. Contemporary Chinese tobacco industry managers regularly try to prod workers to reach new heights of excellence through friendly competitions. During the Great Leap, cigarette factories deployed similar techniques under the Maoist principles of "study, compare, catch up, and overtake." Competitions were often tied to managerial conferences, such as the Northern Five Province Cigarette Manufacturers Conference and the Southern Fifteen Province Manufacturers Conference. In 1958, factory managers in Shandong joined with six northeastern factories to challenge cigarette manufacturers throughout the country in a competition to raise product quality, save resources, and boost profits.[38] Perhaps the largest of these competitions up to then took place in March 1959. Under the auspices of the National Tobacco Industry Manufacturing Conference in Zhengzhou, eighty-four cigarette factories, six cigar factories, seven cut-tobacco facilities, and three re-drying facilities vied for top honors in various categories of manufacturing excellence. This inter-factory competition encompassed some seventy thousand workers.[39]

Turning a blind eye to harm has become a hallmark of contemporary cigarette production.[40] Most often we associate such avoidance with the obfuscation of pathogenesis, that is, ignoring the causal links between tobacco and specific disease categories (e.g., cancer and heart disease). How do managers of cigarette factories learn to ignore such harm? One answer is that they have been long encouraged to acquire a more general skill set: turning a blind eye to all manner of harm (not just that caused by tobacco) and staying focused on the technocratic specificities of their jobs. The Great Leap Forward was certainly not the first time that managers of cigarette factories and their supervisory agencies in China had an opportunity to exercise this general skill set, but it was surely a profound one. By the summer of 1959, famine was already gripping much of the country. By then, one would imagine that, if any branch of government should have been devoting resources to attenuating this quickly accelerating humanitarian crisis, the Food Industry Administrative Bureau of the Ministry of Light Industry should have been in the vanguard. Of course that would have required a degree of political courage, a willingness to cast a critical pall over Mao's Great Leap campaign, that few government officials in that period possessed. Research for this chapter suggests that, during 1959, one of the ways that the Food Industry Administrative Bureau distracted itself, one of the ways it looked past famine and enveloped itself with technical busywork, was by prodding cigarette factories to innovate and compete.

In June, the Food Bureau released a report extolling just such managerial handiwork. The report outlines the "technological revolution" the bureau had been ushering in through its National Tobacco Industry Inter-Factory Competition Committee. Described is great progress the Competition Committee was making replacing manual labor with automated processing in cigarette factories nationwide by introducing packaging and threshing machines.[41] Managerial efforts like this continued through the autumn. In September, the Food Bureau sent out a communiqué to cigarette factories and Light Industry Ministry staff in every province and municipality. It directed everyone to learn from the Lianxin Cigarette Factory and redouble efforts. Located in Shandong's Jining Prefecture, the Lianxin factory had apparently introduced novel techniques to maximize the use of tobacco stems in fulfillment of its cigarette production quota.[42] Soon thereafter, the Food Bureau and its Competition Committee profiled another facility—Qingdao City's No. 1 Cigarette Factory—as a national model. What was the great success of this factory for "food governance" in a period of growing caloric insecurity? Effectively adding tobacco stems to the manufacture of cigarettes.[43]

This Is the Problem We Have to Solve

The Great Leap also helped enshrine two more principles of governance foundational to China's contemporary cigarette situation. First, the masses have a basic right to access cigarettes, and second, tobacco-related taxes should be maximized but not to the detriment of public access to cigarettes.

During the Republican era, the Guomindang regime neither regarded cigarette consumption as a basic right of citizenship nor as anything worthy of intervention, ensuring that most people could afford factory-rolled tobacco products. In fact, through propaganda, the Guomindang regime both chastised cigarette consumption as harmful to health and called it profligate.[44]

Compare that to the "party line" regarding cigarettes that emerged as the 1950s came to a close. This party line was disseminated in many ways over the decade, but was perhaps most succinctly delivered by the Ministry of Light Industry at a cigarette manufacturers' conference in 1958. There, Vice-Minister Wang Yuanxin explained to members of China's recently nationalized cigarette industry that they had an "especially important role" in fulfilling two tasks. In their order of priority, these were "satisfying the people's need, while raising capital for the government."[45] In Maoist China, the word "people" was of course highly coded. It designated an aspirational unified citizenry that transcended class. Within this cosmology, if cigarettes were a need of the people, than it was a need that was not to be impeded by income. No matter how modest one's livelihood, one should be able to buy and smoke cigarettes. And if government had a responsibility to "satisfy" that need, then it had a responsibility to ensure that satisfaction was enjoyed by all.

The second part of the party line is a little easier to grasp. Cigarettes had become a significant source of state revenue for successive regimes in China from the late nineteenth century onward. During the Nanjing decade of the Nationalist regime (1927–1937), consolidated taxation from cigarettes accounted for about 10 percent of the government's revenue. In 1934, this figure jumped as high as 20 percent, owing to an economic depression spreading across the country, driving down taxes from other sources.[46] After 1949, Beijing had high expectations for cigarette-related revenue. During the First Five-Year Plan (1953–1957), the cigarette industry generated more than 4.6 billion yuan in government income. Reflective of the political atmosphere of the late 1950s, government planners wanted to see a revenue leap. And so at the outset of the Second Five-Year Plan in 1958, they set an income quota of 10 billion yuan, double that of the preceding five years.[47]

But how to achieve such lofty levels of revenue? The easiest answer would have been to emphasize the production of higher-quality (A-grade and B-grade) cigarettes. Cigarette manufacturers in the People's Republic have typically preferred to produce A- and B-grade cigarettes. Reputedly better-quality cigarettes bestow more cachet on the enterprise and, because of their higher price and tax rate, they can generate far more state revenue. This taxing differential remains today: higher-grade cigarettes earn Beijing more per stick than lower-grade cigarettes. But back in the 1950s, there was not enough raw material of sufficient "quality" for cigarette factories to emphasize the production of A- and B-grade brands, and any emphasis on higher-quality brand production had another problem: running afoul of the principle of "satisfying the people's need."

Today, not only does China have more daily tobacco smokers than any other country in the world but also even the poorest of its citizens typically smoke cigarettes rather than loose-leaf tobacco. Back in the 1950s, the situation was different. Many people, notably farmers, preferred to smoke loose-leaf tobacco—sometimes rolling it up in pieces of discarded newspaper or more often smoking it by pipe—for the very reason it was cheaper than cigarettes. How did cigarette smoking become so commonplace among the public in the latter half of the twentieth century? One answer is that cheaper cigarettes became much more readily available.

This occurred not by happenstance. It was a program set up in the early years of the People's Republic and which became supercharged at the outset of the Great Leap by the very government agency then most responsible for the tobacco industry. At the same 1958 Ministry of Light Industry conference, Vice-Minister Wang lamented that loose-leaf tobacco belonged to a completely different price range than cigarettes, largely because of tax structures, with the price of loose-leaf tobacco being only half that of cigarettes. "This is the problem that we have to solve, and it's also the only way out," Wang declared.[48] "We need to do all we can," he said, "to cut prices."[49] Another vice-minister of Light Industry attending the conference, Di Jingxiang, clarified:

> It's true that low-grade cigarettes contribute less to national income than high-grade cigarettes, but if you can produce and sell more low-grade cigarettes then the picture changes. In fact, low-grade cigarettes represent real income, because you can actually sell them, and they realize a profit—high-grade cigarettes may be worth more, but if they're just sitting in a warehouse without realizing any profit, then they won't generate any income for the government.[50]

Government archives consulted for this chapter lend credence to the efficacy of Vice-Ministers Wang and Di's program. Consider Table 3.1, which shows important shifts occurring in the balance of cigarettes sold in one

TABLE 3.1.
Percentages of product sold annually by cigarette grade in Shanghai, 1957–1960

Grade	1957	1958	1959	1960 (expected)
A-grade	4	2	1.7	2
B-grade	63	53	47	45
C-grade	28	38	41	43
D-grade	5	7	10	9
E-grade			0.3	1

SOURCE: Shanghai Municipal Archives, B98-1-775-49.

important locale, Shanghai, between 1957 and 1961. These shifts correspond closely with the Ministry of Light Industry's agenda. During those four years, the percentage of cigarettes made and sold of A- and B-grade in Shanghai fell precipitously whereas C- and D-grade grew dramatically. What's more, lowly E-grade cigarettes started to appear in Shanghai in 1959 and thereafter rose in production and sales. That all these shifts occurred in Shanghai of all places must not be overlooked. More than anywhere else in China, Shanghai boasted cigarette makers who prided themselves for producing some of the country's most valued brands.

Table 3.1 also supports our point that, during the Great Leap, efforts were made to dissolve the stereotype of cigarette smoking as a trapping of bourgeois elitism, repositioning the practice as something suitable for all men irrespective of background. The Ministry of Light Industry was at the forefront of this project.

Conclusion

The Great Leap Forward had a profound and complex influence on China's cigarette industry. It eroded the manufacturing hegemony of places like Shanghai, prompting numerous new regional cigarette factories to take root. It helped to redefine the role of government vis-à-vis the cigarette industry as one of anxious steward, a hovering parent always ready to help resolve logistical problems, including scarcity, spoilage, and glitches in distribution and sales. It prodded into the modern era the design and formulation of cigarettes. It proletarianzed the cigarette, transforming it from an item largely enjoyed by the elite to something that "the people" had the right to access, acquire, and smoke. It furthered an institutionalization of cigarette fabrication as a domain wherein Communist officials could extol technical achievement while ignoring encompassing human misery. And it helped to cement cigarette manufacturing as a bedrock of the normal order of things across China, something to be expected during periods of both acute upheaval and relative calm.

Notes

1. "Zhongguo yancao gongzuo" bianjibu ["China Tobacco Work" Editorial Department], comp., *Zhongguo yancao shihua* [The history of tobacco in China] (Beijing: Zhongguo qinggongye chubanshe, 1993), 283–85.

2. Frank Dikötter, *Mao's Great Famine: The History of China's Most Devastating Catastrophe, 1958–1962* (New York: Walker & Co., 2010); Kimberley Manning and Felix Wemheuer, eds., *Eating Bitterness: New Perspectives on China's Great Leap Forward and Famine* (Vancouver: UBC Press, 2011); and Yang Jisheng, *Tombstone: The Great Chinese Famine, 1958–1962*, introduction by Edward Friedman and Roderick MacFarquhar, translated by Stacy Mosher and Jian Guo (New York: Farrar, Straus and Giroux, 2012).

3. Wang Guobin [Bin Wong], "18 shiji yilai Zhongguo caizheng bianqian ji xiangguan wenti" [Changes in Chinese finance since the eighteenth century], *Shilin* [Historical Review] 2 (2000): 2.

4. Dangdai Zhongguo yanjiusuo [Institute of Contemporary China Studies], *Zhonghua renmin gongheguo shigao* [History of the People's Republic of China], vol. 2 (Beijing: Dangdai Zhongguo chubanshe, 2012), 64.

5. Wang Haibo and Dong Zhikai, *Xin Zhongguo gongye jingjishi, 1958–1965* [New China's industrial economic history, 1958–1965] (Beijing: Jingji guanli chubanshe, 1995), 8–9.

6. Wang Wen-yu, "Ming Qing de yancao lun" [A discussion of tobacco in the Ming and Qing periods], PhD diss. (Taiwan Normal University, 2002).

7. Nongyebu [Ministry of Agriculture], "Guanyu kaoyan huibaohui de baogao" [Report on the debriefing meeting of tobacco conference], August 18, 1959, maintained by the Shanghai Tobacco Museum, Cigarette Industry 1959, 43–46.

8. Ibid.

9. Ibid.

10. Nongyebu dangzu [CCP Group in the Ministry of Agriculture], "Guanyu yaoqiu jiejue kaoyan jiagong wuzi wenti de baogao" [Report on requirements for resolving the problems of tobacco processing supplies], August 26, 1960, maintained by the Shanghai Tobacco Museum, Cigarette Industry 1960, 32–33.

11. Nongyebu dangzu [CCP Group in the Ministry of Agriculture], "1959 nian

shangbao kaoyan bozhong mianji de luoshi qingkuang" [The implementation of tobacco sowing in 1959], May 15, 1959, maintained by the Shanghai Tobacco Museum, Cigarette Industry 1959, 31.

12. Nongyebu dangzu [CCP Group in the Ministry of Agriculture], "Guanyu yaoqiu jiejue kaoyan jiagong wuzi wenti de baogao" [Report on requirements for resolving the problems of tobacco processing supplies], August 26, 1960, maintained by the Shanghai Tobacco Museum, Cigarette Industry 1960, 32–33.

13. Ibid.

14. "Di fubuzhang zai beifang wu sheng juanyan huiyi shang de zongjie baogao" [Final report of Vice-Minister Di at the Five Provinces Cigarette Conference], May 12, 1958, maintained by the Shanghai Tobacco Museum, Cigarette Industry 1958, 69–73.

15. Guojia jingji maoyi weiyuanhui [State Economic and Trade Commission], *Zhongguo gongye wushi nian: Xin Zhongguo gongye tongjian* [Fifty years of Chinese industry: A comprehensive study of the industry of New China], part 3 (Beijing: Zhongguo jingji chubanshe, 2000), 71.

16. Cheng Li, *The Political Mapping of China's Tobacco Industry and Anti-Smoking Campaign* (Washington, DC: Brookings Institution, 2012), 91, 119.

17. "Di fubuzhang zai beifang wu sheng juanyan huiyi shang de zongjie baogao," 60.

18. "Taiyuan yancaochang changzhang Chang Yingui zai Shanxisheng 1960 nian yanye shengchan huiyi shang de fayan" [The statement of Chang Yingui, manager of Taiyuan Tobacco Factory, at the Shanxi Province Conference of Tobacco Leaf Production in 1960], February 28, 1960, maintained by the Shanghai Tobacco Museum, Cigarette Industry 1960, 9.

19. Shangyebu, Qinggongyebu [Ministry of Commerce and Ministry of Light Industry], "Guanyu jiaji yan de shengchan baogao" [Report on the production of A-grade cigarettes], June 15, 1959, maintained by the Shanghai Tobacco Museum, Cigarette Industry 1959, 46–47.

20. Ibid.

21. Dong Haolin, ed., *Shanghai yancao zhi* [The historical record of tobacco in Shanghai] (Shanghai: Shehui kexue yuan chubanshe, 1998), 50.

22. Ibid., 7.

23. Guojia jingji maoyi weiyuanhui, *Zhongguo gongye wushi nian* part 3, 1112.

24. Shangyebu, Qinggongyebu, "Guanyu jiaji yan de shengchan baogao," 46–47.

25. Robert Proctor, *Golden Holocaust: Origins of the Cigarette Catastrophe and the Case for Abolition* (Berkeley: University of California Press, 2011).

26. Chen Hansheng, *Diguo zhuyi gongye ziben yu Zhongguo nongmin* [Industrial capitalism and Chinese peasants], translated by Chen Jiang (Shanghai: Fudan University Press, 1984), 89, 91.

27. Shipin gongyebu gongye guanli ju, hezuo zongshe yan lian ju [Industry Administration under the Ministry of Food Industry, the General Cooperative of Allied Tobacco Bureau], "Guanyu dingjiyan (zhi xinpai) chanyong yanjiepi de lianhehan" [The joint letter on incorporating tobacco stalk skin into D-grade cigarettes (referring to the new brand)], January 7, 1958, maintained by the Shanghai Tobacco Museum, Tobacco Leaf 1958, 24.

28. Qinggongyebu, Shangyebu [Ministry of Light Industry and Ministry of Commerce], "Guanyu dali shougou yan'ganpi, yan'gan nenshao de lianhe tong-zhi" [Joint notice on large-scale purchase of tobacco stalks and shoots], September 25, 1959, maintained by the Shanghai Tobacco Museum, Tobacco Market 1959, 7.

29. Qinggongyebu, Zhongguo qinggongye gonghui quanguo weiyuanhui [Ministry of Light Industry and National Committee of the Light Industry Trade Union], "Guanyu zhuanfa yanjie chuli jishu huiyi zongjie, qing jinyibu fadong qunzhong gengduo gengkuai chuli yanjie de han" [The letter on forwarding the summary of experience-sharing meeting on techniques for dealing with tobacco stalks, in order to further mobilize the masses to deal with tobacco stalks faster, greater, better], March 10, 1960, maintained by the Shanghai Municipal Archives, B189-2-387-27.

30. Guowuyuan shou dian yaoqiu hejian juanyan shengchan renwu [The incoming telegram to the State Council requiring reducing the production target], July 27, 1960, maintained by the Shanghai Tobacco Museum, Tobacco Industry 1960, 19.

31. Qinggongyebu, Shangyebu [Ministry of Light Industry and Ministry of Commerce], "Guanyu shengchan juanyan chanyong yanjie jinxing qingkuang de lianhe baogao" [Joint report on the process of incorporating tobacco stalks in producing cigarettes], April 14, 1960, maintained by the Shanghai Tobacco Museum, Tobacco Industry 1960, 6–8.

32. After the expansion into non-tobacco material, 5 percent of the B-1-grade cigarette had to consist of substitutes, 10 percent in the case of the B-2, 15 percent for the C-1, 20 percent for the C-2, and 25 percent for the D-grade—E-grade cigarettes were withdrawn from production altogether. Qinggongyebu, Shangyebu [Ministry of Light Industry and Ministry of Commerce], "Guanyu juanyan bu chanyong yanjie gaiyong qita tianchongliao de baogao" [Report on using alternative tobacco substitutes instead of tobacco stalks], September 1960, maintained by the Shanghai Tobacco Museum, Tobacco Industry 1960, 10–19.

33. Carl Crow, Siwanwan guke [Four Hundred Million Customers], translated by Xia Boming (Shanghai: Fudan daxue chubanshe, 2011) (originally, London: Hamish Hamilton, 1937), 43.

34. Anonymous, "Shi yanwei" [Collecting cigarette butts], Wenzhai [Readers Digest] 1(4) (April 1, 1937): 115.

35. Shangyebu [Ministry of Commerce], "Guanyu kaizhan huishou yantou, jia-gong yansi de tongzhi" [Notice on collecting cigarette butts to process into cut to-bacco], maintained by Shanghai Tobacco Museum, Tobacco Industry 1960, 37–39.

36. Qinggongyebu shipinju [Food Bureau of the Ministry of Light Industry], "Guanyu juanyan gongye dayuejin yilai jishu geming qingkuang de baogao" [Re-port on the "technological revolution" of the tobacco industry after the Great Leap Forward], March 28, 1960, maintained by the Shanghai Tobacco Museum, Tobacco Industry 1960, 13–16.

37. Dongbei san sheng he Huabei san sheng gongyeting [Industry Department of Three Provinces of Northeast China and Three Provinces of North China], Juan-yan gongye jishu geming de xianjin renwu [The pioneers of the "technological revo-lution" in the tobacco industry], April 1, 1958, maintained by the Shanghai Tobacco Museum, Tobacco Industry 1958, 53–54.

38. Dongbei qu juanyan gongye xiezuo zu [Cooperative Group of the Tobacco Industry in the Northeast district], Dongbei qu juanyan gongye xiezuo zu xiang Shandong sheng yingzhan xiang quanguo tiaozhan shu [Announcement of the Cooperative Group of the Tobacco Industry in the Northeast district to accept a challenge from Shandong, and throw down a challenge to the rest of the country], April 1, 1958, maintained by the Shanghai Tobacco Museum, Tobacco Industry 1958, 51.

39. Qinggongyebu shipin gongye guanli ju [Food Industry Administration of the Ministry of Light Industry], Quanguo yancao gongye kaizhan changji jingsai de qingkuang he jinyibu kaizhan changji jingsai yijian de baogao [Report on the inter-factory competition in the national tobacco industry and the suggestions on further promoting the inter-factory competition], October 1, 1959, maintained by the Shanghai Tobacco Museum, Tobacco Industry 1959, 14.

40. See Matthew Kohrman's chapter in this volume about the China Tobacco Museum.

41. Qinggongye shipin gongye ju, Quanguo yancao gongye changji jingsai wei-yuanhui [Food Industry Bureau under the Ministry of Light Industry, the National Tobacco Industry Inter-Factory Competition Committee], "Guanyu juanyanchang zili gengsheng shixian jixiehua shengchan zizhi baozhuangji he daye jichugengji qingkuang de tongbao" [Notification on self-dependently realizing mechanization of tobacco factories by creating packaging machines and threshing machines], June 22, 1959, maintained by the Shanghai Municipal Archives, B189-2-349-17.

42. Qinggongyebu shipin gongye ju, quanguo yancao gongye changji jingsai weiyuanhui [Food Industry Bureau under the Ministry of Light Industry, the Na-tional Tobacco Industry Inter-Factory Competition Committee], "Guanyu zhuanfa Jining Lianxin yanchang fanyouqing guzuganjin da'nao jishu gexin liyong yanjie juanyan baozheng le quanmian chao'e wancheng 1959 nian 8 yuefen shengchan

jihua zongjie de han" [Summary of how Jining's Lianxin Cigarette Factory's bold, anti-rightist, giving-it-their-all, technological innovation in tobacco stalk usage enabled the factory to exceed its production quota in August], September 16, 1959, maintained by the Shanghai Municipal Archives, B189–2–349–72.

43. Qinggongyebu shipin gongye ju [Food Industry Bureau under the Ministry of Light Industry], "Guanyu jieshao Qingdao diyi juanyanchang zengyong yanjie shengchan juanyan de han" [Notice on introducing the experiences of No. 1 Cigarette Factory in Qingdao, which had added tobacco stems to its manufacturing process], September 19, 1959, maintained by Shanghai Municipal Archives, B189-2-349-77.

44. Huangfu Qiushi, "Xinshenghuo yundong de 'bianzou': Zhejiangsheng jin xi juanyan yundong yanjiu (1934–1935)" [The variations of the New Life Movement: A study focusing on the anti-cigarette campaign in Zhejiang province, 1934–1935], *Jindaishi yanjiu* [Studies in Modern History], 6 (2010): 95–112.

45. Dongbei san sheng he Huabei er sheng gongyeting [The Industry Department of Three Provinces of Northeast China and Two Provinces of North China], "Wang Yuanxin fubuzhang zai beifang wu sheng juanyan shengchan huiyi shang de baogao (jilu)" [Report of Vice-Minister Wang Yuanxin at the Northern Five Province Cigarette Manufacturers Conference (record)], April 20, 1958, maintained by the Shanghai Tobacco Museum, Cigarette Industry 1958, 65–68.

46. Jiangsusheng Zhonghua renmin gongheguo gongshangshui shoushi bianxiezu, Zhongguo di'er lishi dang'anguan [The Writing Group of History of Industrial and Commercial Tax in Republican China, Second Historical Archive of China], *Zhonghua minguo gongshang shuishou shiliao xuanbian* [Compilation of historical documents of industrial and commercial tax in Republican China], series 3 (vol. 2) (Nanjing: Nanjing daxue chubanshe, 1996) 4667–68; Yang Yinpu, *Minguo caizheng shi* [Financial history of Republican China] (Beijing: Zhongguo caizheng jingji chubanshe, 1985), 47.

47. Dongbei san sheng he Huabei er sheng gongyeting, "Wang Yuanxin fubuzhang zai beifang wu sheng juanyan shengchan huiyi shang de baogao (jilu)," 65–68.

48. Ibid.

49. "Di fubuzhang zai beifang wu sheng juanyan huiyi shang de zongjie baogao," 60.

50. Ibid.

PART TWO

Cultural Legitimation through
Visual and Historical Manipulations

CHAPTER FOUR

Bourgeois Decadence or Proletarian Pleasure?
The Visual Culture of Male Smoking in China across the 1949 Divide

Carol Benedict

Cigarette smoking in China today is a highly gendered practice. With more than 300 million Chinese smokers, China has the highest rate of cigarette consumption in the world. However, most Chinese smokers are men. The 2010 Global Adult Tobacco Survey found that 53 percent of men over age fifteen smoke while only 2.4 percent of adult women do.[1] This stark difference in the pattern of men and women's smoking behavior in China today is often attributed to lingering cultural taboos against female smoking, assumed to have been in place for centuries. In fact, the gender exclusivity of male smoking in China is of fairly recent vintage, dating only from the mid-1900s. In the opening decades of the twentieth century, many Chinese women smoked tobacco in pipes and some even smoked cigarettes. Over time, however, fewer and fewer Chinese women initiated smoking and by 1949, prevalence rates among women had greatly diminished.[2] After 1949, these rates sharply declined: whereas the proportion of women who smoked before age twenty-five was 10 percent for all urban women born before 1940, it was only 1 percent for those born between 1950 and 1964.[3] In contrast, smoking prevalence among men remained consistently high, with roughly seven men out of ten using tobacco at peak ages of consumption across the entire century.[4]

Many social, economic, and cultural factors have contributed to the distinctively gendered pattern of smoking that emerged in China.[5] An essential aspect of this history was the transformation in social and political norms that made smoking less rather than more respectable for women over time. Whereas in 1900, pipe smoking was entirely respectable for Chinese women of all ages, in the twentieth century it was increasingly regarded as an old-fashioned habit retained only by older women. At the same time cigarettes, widely associated with Shanghai's fast-paced urban lifestyle, in the 1930s and 1940s came to be identified with a stigmatized type of "new woman" known as the "Modern Girl." Portrayed in popular culture and political rhetoric alike as extravagant and frivolous, the Modern Girl's pursuit of luxury came to symbolize bourgeois decadence and suspect national loyalty. These associations continued into the post-Liberation period and, as a consequence, most women born after 1949 elected not to smoke at all.

In contrast to fluctuating norms for female smokers, those for men remained relatively stable across the 1949 divide. Certain forms of tobacco—notably cigars and imported cigarettes—were associated with luxurious excess, but most men who smoked after Liberation faced no particular social or political censure. Indeed, the period between 1949 and 1978 arguably saw smoking become increasingly masculinized. With women by and large eschewing both pipes and cigarettes, tobacco use came to be identified as an exclusively male habit. Whereas female smoking was perceived as a bourgeois vice, smoking among men under socialism was transformed into a legitimate proletarian pleasure.

This chapter, a survey of Chinese visual representations of men smoking as presented in tobacco advertisements, cartoons, and propaganda posters from the 1920s to the 1970s, argues that the gendered pattern of tobacco use in twentieth-century China had an important *visual* dimension that both reflected and contributed to changing gender norms as pertains to smoking. Although many women traditionally smoked tobacco, they did so only privately at home. Only in the first two decades of the twentieth century did bold "new women" begin to take their smoking public, daring to smoke in venues where they could be seen doing so. Around the same time, pictures of cigarette-smoking women began to appear in the burgeoning print media, and by the 1930s such images were ubiquitous. This explosion in the visibility of female smokers encouraged even more women to smoke openly. Yet, after Liberation, female smokers disappeared almost entirely from both the public and the visual realms. The absence of such imagery reflected the new improprieties of female smoking that emerged from its association with "bourgeois" Modern Girls in the 1930s and 1940s, an association that carried over into and was strengthened after Liberation.

In contrast to the vanishing female smoker, the visibility of male smokers never diminished. Chinese men had been smoking publicly since at least the 1600s and they did not stop doing so in the twentieth century. After 1949, they continued to smoke prolifically while at work, in meetings, and on the street, a fact that was amply represented in the visual culture of the early PRC. The many images of male smokers that appeared in officially sanctioned publications and posters from 1949 to 1978 portrayed it as a legitimate form of proletarian consumption for adult men. Such illustrations reinscribed long-standing associations between smoking and Chinese ideals of masculinity even as they erased Republican-era connections between cigarettes and "bourgeois" luxury for men (China's "Republican era" dates from 1912 to 1949).

Men Smoking in Republican China: Haohan Sociability, Wenren Connoisseurship, and Bourgeois-Liberal Individuality

Tobacco smoking among men had been a very public activity since its introduction into China in the late Ming period (1368–1644). The proffering of cigarettes among men, common throughout the twentieth century, was a variation on the smoking rituals performed during the Qing dynasty (1644–1911) when men hosted friends or guests. Since such entertainments often occurred in teahouses, restaurants, or other semi-public venues, men's smoking behavior was always highly visible. Men of all social classes smoked freely when out and about, a historical reality reflected in many Qing scroll paintings and woodblock prints.[6] Elite male smoking culture was also amply on display through a learned tradition of tobacco connoisseurship.[7] Tobacco smoking was common among farmers and laborers as well as scholar-officials, so elite smokers set themselves apart by carefully adhering to certain rules of smoking etiquette as outlined in guidebooks for connoisseurs.[8] They also took to using snuff, a very expensive type of tobacco that was out of reach for ordinary consumers. Smoking and snuffing fine tobacco were thus part of the refined lifestyle that marked highly educated men as members of an exclusive group. At the same time, the literati elite shared with their social inferiors the imperative to be open-handed with guests and friends. Offering tobacco to guests became the quintessential expression of hospitality among elite and non-elite alike and consuming it together became an integral part of male conviviality from at least the early Qing on.[9] Smoking among men was above all a social act, meant to be shared and to be seen.

Late imperial male smoking culture thus embodied two powerful and long-standing gender ideals that historically shaped the construction of Chinese masculinity: the talented Confucian scholar (*caizi* 才子/*wenren* 文人) and the martial hero (*yingxiong* 英雄/*haohan* 好漢).[10] The *haohan* model calls up images of physically strong, fearless, and loyal "good fellows" who are dedicated to their comrades, generous with friends, and have large appetites for food and wine.[11] The primary loyalty of the *haohan* is to other men; friendship and fidelity are demonstrated above all through the exchange of material goods (such as pipe tobacco, snuff, or cigarettes). *Caizi* (talented scholars), by contrast, are refined and accomplished gentlemen whose careful cultivation of their innate talents have elevated them to the socially admired ideal of the educated *wenren* (cultured man) who is capable of taking on the public role of a scholar-official. Together the *haohan* and *caizi*/*wenren* ideals form the "dyad of *wen-wu* (cultural attainment—martial valor)" discussed by Kam Louie as a defining feature of Chinese masculinity both in the past and the present.[12] Although the *caizi*/*wenren* and *haohan* models are often contrasted as two opposing poles on the *wen-wu* (文武) axis of Chinese masculinity, Louie points out that historically there were complementarities between the two.[13]

In the opening decades of the twentieth century, as cigarette smoking began to displace other modes of tobacco consumption, the historical ideals of the *caizi*/*wenren* tobacco connoisseur and the magnanimous *haohan* continued to shape male smoking culture. In their advertising, tobacco companies targeted men using both tropes. Although cigarettes were mass produced and sold to consumers on all levels of the socioeconomic hierarchy, proprietary branding enabled marketers to appeal to the refined sensibilities of modern-day aficionados, such as the "patriotic gentlemen" (*aiguo junzi* 愛國君子) depicted in a 1923 Tower cigarette ad (Figure 4.1).[14] At the

FIGURE 4.1.
Tower cigarette advertisement. *Shenbao*, April 15, 1923, p. 8.

same time, even the most sophisticated smoker participated in the indispensable ritual of sharing cigarettes with other men, a gesture that demonstrated the manly virtue of *haohan* generosity (Figure 4.2).[15]

While the visual culture of smoking in Republican China reproduced "traditional" Chinese masculine ideals, it also reflected newer associations between smoking and masculinity appropriated from abroad. The manly "bourgeois-liberal culture of smoking" that emerged in England and North America in the second half of the nineteenth century permeated Republican-era representations of smoking both in visual images and

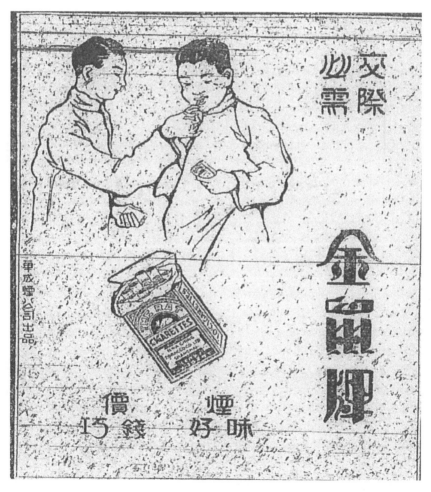

FIGURE 4.2.
Advertisement for "The Rat" brand cigarettes. *Shenbao*, July 4, 1928, p. 8.

in literature.[16] Front and center here was the bourgeois-liberal celebration of individuality: respectable male smokers were represented as discriminating connoisseurs whose smoking habit reflected well on their character. As Charles Laughlin points out, the many reminiscences about the pleasures of smoking that appeared in popular literary magazines from the 1930s, particularly those in the Analects group edited by Lin Yutang (林語堂, 1895–1976), associated smoking with freedom, individuality, idle contemplation, and creative genius.[17] In the pages of the journal *The Analects Fortnightly* (*Lunyu banyuekan* 論語半月刊) and other publications promoting the "literature of leisure," smoking emerges as a symbol of eccentricity in much the same way that Victorian literature portrayed idiosyncratic smokers such as Sherlock Holmes.[18] Lin Yutang's inaugural editorial for the first issue of *The Analects* even depicts his associates as modern eccentrics by describing their individual smoking habits: one is fond of Luzon cigars, one a pipe, one a cigarette, one is a nonsmoker who provides others with smokes, and so on.[19] The celebration of the tobacco "fiend" as an unconventional eccentric articulated the belief that each man smokes in his own individual way. His discerning choice of particular brands made him an enthusiast, not a market-driven consumer.

In the bourgeois-liberal aesthetic as well as that of the traditional Chinese literati, men smoking together set the tone for mental creativity and high-minded discussion. Lin Yutang and other intellectuals in the 1930s greatly admired what Xu Zhimo (徐志摩, 1897–1931) termed England's "smoking-ism" (*chouyanzhuyi* 抽煙主義), by which he meant engaged debate and discussion (carried on while chain-smoking cigarettes).[20] Many of the essays written in the style of the "literature of leisure" echoed Xu Zhimo's sentiments about the connections between smoking and the life of the mind.[21] Lin Yutang's journals, like British periodicals of the Victorian age, also included many histories of cigarette and tobacco use (both worldwide and in China), smoking-related anecdotes, and stories about famous European and historical smokers. Linking tobacco to scholarly knowledge and learning in this manner not only carried forward the *caizi/wenren* tradition of tobacco connoisseurship, it also allowed male intellectuals to legitimate a pleasurable act of consumption as weighty and important when done by men even as they denigrated the same act as frivolous and extravagant when done by women.

The influence of the refracted Western bourgeois-liberal culture of smoking on Republican-era visual imagery is readily apparent in the pages of popular pictorial magazines such as *Liangyou* (The Young Companion 良友).

Aimed at Shanghai's white-collar workers who constituted many of the city's "petty urbanites," *Liangyou* included numerous photographic collages and cartoons in which cigarettes figure prominently. The humorous "Character In Cigarets," for example, depicts the many ways an individual smoker might hold his cigarette and what each pose reveals about his unique personality (Figure 4.3).[22] Yet another photographic montage illustrates the importance of the cigarette break for the modern office worker.[23] Fourteen pictures of a young male clerk taken throughout the day are laid out sequentially, moving in a clockwise direction from morning until night. A mechanical clock is positioned in the center of the spread, further emphasizing the temporal discipline imposed on the man by his office job. The first of the office worker's smoking breaks comes when he returns home from the office for lunch, collapsing into his easy chair, bow-tie askew and utterly exhausted. In the afternoon, he returns to the office for the rest of the workday. In the evening, he again reclines at home, puts his feet up, and has a smoke, this time with the cigarette held in an elegant long holder. The collage illustrates how smoking allows the modern man to refine his individuality by taking him momentarily away from the pressures of a competitive world, then allowing him to reenter the public realm refreshed and renewed.[24]

The many tobacco advertisements that appeared in the pages of *Liangyou*, *Shenbao*, and other Republican-era newspapers and periodicals similarly proclaim the individuality of the "new" modern man even as they celebrate smoking as a form of elevated leisure enjoyed by those well-off enough to appreciate the "good life." Many advertisements show men in

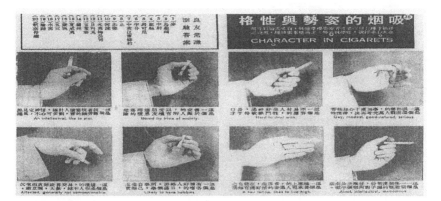

FIGURE 4.3.
"Character in Cigarets." *Liangyou*, no. 155 (June 1940), p. 36.

dressing gowns smoking at home (Figure 4.4).[25] On the surface, these illustrations are reminiscent of those that show women smoking while reclining in armchairs.[26] Solitary female smokers, however, are often portrayed in dreamy sexually evocative poses, with heads rolled back, eyes closed, and arms held loosely at their sides or open to expose their armpits (Figure 4.5).[27] Some even show women smoking in bed (Figure 4.6).[28] In contrast, men sit upright and straight in their chairs, smoking with deliberate purpose.[29] Moreover, many ads that feature men leisurely smoking at home include images of wives dotingly waiting upon their husbands.

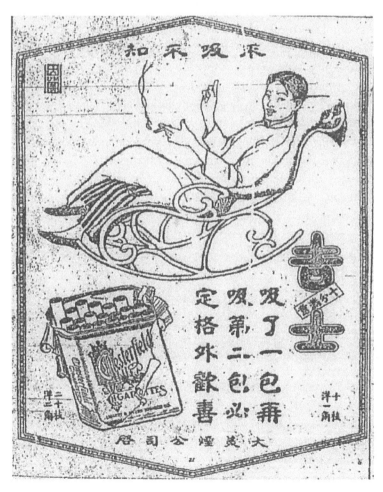

FIGURE 4.4.
Chesterfield cigarette advertisement. *Shenbao*, May 24, 1921, p. 3.

FIGURE 4.5.
My Dear cigarette advertisement. *Shenbao*, January 5, 1928, p. 6.

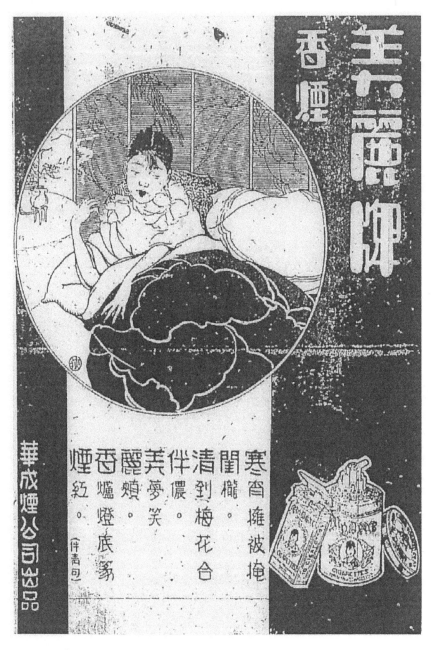

FIGURE 4.6.
My Dear cigarette advertisement. *Shenbao*, February 23, 1928, p. 7.

One ad for Three Stars cigarettes that appeared in *Shenbao* in May 1928, for example, shows a very substantial man sitting squarely in his oversized armchair smoking while his wife peeks out from an interior room (Figure 4.7).[30] Such images reinforced patriarchal gender hierarchies even as they underscored the autonomy and personal choice of the individual smoker.

Tobacco industry advertisements in the Republican period did not shy away from showing images of women smoking together with men in intimate or romantic settings (Figure 4.8).[31] Often the woman is depicted offering the man a light in highly suggestive ways.[32] Many advertisements also placed men and women smokers sociably together in semi-public settings such as restaurants, tennis courts, ballrooms, or hotel lobbies.[33] They also feature men and women smoking together at parties or weddings (Figure 4.9).[34] Occasionally, cigarette-smoking women will be placed alongside men on a public street (Figure 4.10).[35] They do not, however, generally show women and men sharing a cigarette at work. Such images are reserved for sociable smoking among men. The fraternal bond created by men sharing cigarettes is reinforced again and again in illustrated advertisements from the period.[36] Men smoke together in cafés, they smoke together on the way to work, and they smoke at the office (Figure 4.11).[37] Such images draw upon the masculine *haohan* ideal as well as the globally circulating bourgeois-liberal prescriptions of smoking that identified the homosocial male environment as the only place for respectable gentlemen to indulge their habit.

While many Republican-era images meld the sociable *haohan* smoker with that of the bourgeois-liberal ideal of important and substantive discussion carried on in segregated smoke-filled rooms, others link traditional literati associations between smoking and mental creativity to new ideas about the benefits of smoking for enhanced work performance. For example, a cartoon that appeared in *Liangyou* in June 1934 entitled "Smoking His Idea" depicts a writer at his desk clearly suffering from writer's block (Figure 4.12). Many cigarettes and much smoke later, the young man has filled the page, presumably with great thoughts.[38] Tobacco advertisements also made connections between productivity and smoking: in one for The Rat brand that appeared repeatedly in the pages of *Shenbao* in July 1928, one clerk complains to another that he is always sleepy at work. The second one offers a cigarette, saying "Have a smoke." The final panel shows the first man newly invigorated, working away with cigarette in hand (Figure 4.13).[39]

FIGURE 4.7.
Man leisurely smoking at home. Three Stars cigarette advertisement. *Shenbao*, May 8, 1928, p. 3.

FIGURE 4.8.
Romantic theme for female smokers. Good Chance cigarette advertisement. *Shenbao*,
January 17, 1928, p. 1.

FIGURE 4.9.
Men and women partying with smokes. Hwa Li cigarette advertisement. *Shenbao*, March 6, 1928, p. 1.

FIGURE 4.10.
Woman smoking with men in public. My Dear cigarette advertisement. *Shenbao*, June 2, 1928, p. 9.

FIGURE 4.11.
Male cigarette sociability while dining. Ruby Queen cigarette advertisement. *Shenbao*, November 1, 1931, p. 1.

FIGURE 4.12.
"Smoking his idea." *Liangyou*, no. 89 (June 15, 1934), p. 35.

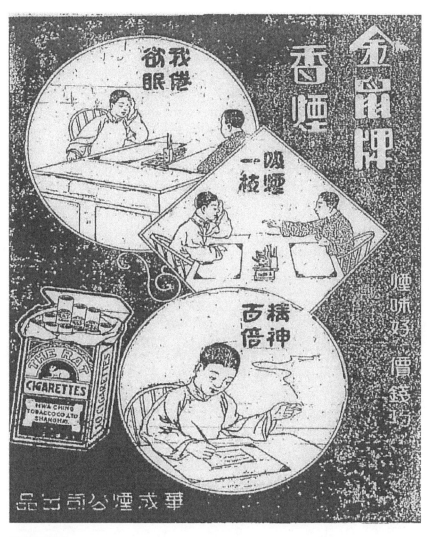

FIGURE 4.13.
Smoking to enhance work performance. The Rat cigarette advertisement. *Shenbao*, July 6, 1928, p. 7.

Still other advertisements focused on the physicality of the male body rather than the mental acuity to be gained from smoking. Images of powerful athletes, for example, graced advertisements for Huacheng Tobacco Company's My Dear cigarettes (Figure 4.14).[40] An ad for BAT's Three Castles brand featured a blacksmith stripped to the waist, revealing a muscular torso (Figure 4.15).[41] As noted by Matthew Kohrman, illustrations of this sort "trumpeted male smoking as an antidote to colonial discourses that had been framing the body politic of China as shamefully enfeebled and backward, epitomized by the label 'The Sick Man of Asia.'"[42] By utilizing images of brawny laborers more reminiscent of *haohan* masculinities rather than those of cultivated *caizi* gentlemen, such advertisements not only played upon anxieties about

FIGURE 4.14.
My Dear cigarette advertisement. *Shenbao*, May 4, 1934, p. 1.

FIGURE 4.15.
Advertisement for Three Castles cigarettes. *Shenbao*, May 8, 1925, p. 4.

China's national standing vis-à-vis the West and Japan, they also underscored the point that at least in some areas and among some occupational groups, cigarette smoking had already become a staple of working-class culture.

Men Smoking across the 1949 Divide: From Bourgeois Luxury to Proletarian Pleasure

After 1949, male smoking remained part and parcel of socialist masculinities and modernity even as earlier associations of cigarettes with bourgeois individuality were suppressed. In the People's Republic, male smokers remained highly visible both in public and in officially sanctioned publications. While tobacco advertisements in newspapers in the 1950s no longer contained images of smokers, many cartoons and other illustrations did. Propaganda posters and pictorials from the 1960s and 1970s often featured workers with cigarettes or peasants with short-stemmed pipes. To be sure, such representations were altered to fit the new socialist aesthetic. Whereas the visual culture of male smoking in the Republican era celebrated the "good life," that of the early PRC emphasized themes of male comradeship, male physicality, and manly authority. Earlier visuals alluded to the unique individuality of each eccentric smoker, but those produced after Liberation explicitly linked modes of smoking (cigarette or pipe) to newly institutionalized categories such as cadre, worker, or peasant. The paucity of images of young male smokers in post-1949 publications indicates new sensitivities about juvenile smoking not fully evident in preceding decades. And, significantly, female smokers are entirely absent from the visual discourse of the early PRC. Tobacco smoking by mature men, however, including by China's premier leaders, was amply on display throughout the entire 1949–1978 period.

During the first decade after 1949, the newly established PRC government nationalized all tobacco companies and combined advertising agencies into one state enterprise.[43] Tobacco advertising continued for a time in the 1950s before disappearing altogether in the 1960s. For the most part, tobacco ads from the 1950s were simple and featured only text or illustrations of the product itself.[44] When such illustrations did feature smokers, they were invariably men (never women). One tobacco advertisement from the 1950 *Shanghai City Directory*, for example, shows the new socialist man on his way to work at a factory, jauntily smoking an International brand cigarette as he walks along (Figure 4.16).[45]

FIGURE 4.16.
Advertisement for International cigarettes from the 1950 *Shanghai City Directory*. Andrew S.
Cahan, *Chinese Label Art* (Atglen, PA: Schiffer Publishing, 2006), p. 148.

The greatly diminished number of illustrated tobacco advertisements did not mean that images of men smoking cigarettes disappeared entirely. Quite the contrary: images of male smokers can readily be found in a wide array of visual media from the early PRC period, including newspaper cartoons, propaganda posters, and pictorial magazines. To be sure, male smokers were portrayed somewhat differently after 1949. For one thing, images of men smoking at home in moments of quiet repose almost entirely disappeared. When men were shown smoking alone, it was generally in a setting related to work or productive activity. For example, Liu Zhide's famous 1973 poster of the *Old Party Secretary* depicts a village party official taking a break from manual labor (breaking rocks) to smoke his briar pipe while studying.[46] Humorous cartoons from the 1950s also show men smoking alone at leisure but they generally do so in their work unit, not at home. A 1955 cartoon from *Gongren ribao*, for example, places a cadre in a communal reading room perusing the newspapers. When he finishes, he lights up a cigarette as he departs, leaving the room a shambles with papers scattered helter-skelter (Figure 4.17).[47] Cigarettes figure prominently in many other humorous cartoons about careless or irresponsible officials. One shows a rotund cadre putting up a fire hazard sign while puffing away on a cigarette (Figure 4.18).[48]

It goes without saying that after 1949 there are no images of men smoking with women, intimately or otherwise, since women were no longer portrayed as smokers in the new socialist visual culture. As in the Republican period, however, men were frequently shown smoking together in ways consonant with the *haohan* tradition. They do so not in cafés and restaurants but while at work. A *Gongren ribao* cartoon published in 1954 shows a worker at the door of a meeting room, asking the cadre for advice. The cadre chides

FIGURE 4.17.
Zhang Heming, "The unfortunate fate of books and newspapers." *Gongren ribao*, January 30, 1955, p. 4.

FIGURE 4.18.
Untitled cartoon mocking a careless official posting cautions about fire safety while smoking a cigarette. *Gongren ribao*, October 23, 1956, p. 3.

him, saying, "Can't you see we have meetings every day? When do we have time to manage [anything]?" Behind him in the smoke-filled room, chain-smoking cadres argue endlessly (Figure 4.19).[49] Newspaper cartoons, whether didactic or humorous, place cigarettes in the hands of officials working at their desks at virtually every turn, suggesting that smoking in the office was completely acceptable behavior.[50] *Renmin huabao* (China Pictorial), a large-format pictorial magazine established in 1950 and distributed both nationally and internationally, frequently included photographs of cadres and workers smoking on the job.[51] Since such publications were designed to put China's best foot forward, the inclusion of such images underscores that male smoking was entirely respectable at the time.

FIGURE 4.19.
Wang Hong, "Taking on everything except this one . . ." *Gongren ribao*, July 4, 1954, p. 3.

If smoking by men was perfectly appropriate during political study or when at work, it was also regarded, at least during the 1970s, as a much deserved leisure activity for hardworking peasants and proletarians. Propaganda posters such as Guo Zhiming's 1976 *Our Brigade Leader* showed peasants during off-hours, relaxing with cigarettes or pipes (Figure 4.20).[52] Another image that picks up the theme of smoking and leisure is that of *A Spring Breeze on a Snowy Night* (1976). Showing the interior of an urban shop filled with consumer goods, the poster includes several men smoking as they gather around tables to read and talk.[53]

While the occasional peasant was depicted with a cigarette, images of rural men with short-stemmed pipes were far more common. Indeed images of older peasants with pipes are ubiquitous in Cultural Revolution posters.[54] Peasants, however, are shown with cigarettes only very occasionally. More typically, cigarettes are reserved for urban factory workers, as in the 1964 poster *Early Morning on the Huangpu River in Shanghai* (Figure 4.21).[55] Soldiers in the People's Liberation Army are typically not portrayed as smokers in these posters but they are in some instances—the 1965 poster *Passing on Military Skills*, for example, which shows an older solider smoking a

FIGURE 4.20.
Guo Zhiming, *Ni duizhang* (Our Brigade Leader), 1976. Stefan R. Landsberger Collection, International Institute of Social History (Amsterdam), call number BG E15/93. http://hdl. handle.net/10622/B5BF7442-232C-4030-90FB-5F2FF14D61B6.

FIGURE 4.21.
Qu Fang, *Shanghai Huangpu jiang de zaochen* (Early Morning on the Huangpu River in Shanghai), 1964. Jean-Yves Bajon Collection, International Institute of Social History (Amsterdam), call number BG E39/810. http://hdl.handle.net/10622/2E05CE31-BA48-43FE-9726-3A7592F5F60B.

cigarette alongside an old peasant grasping a short-stemmed pipe (Figure 4.22).[56] Interestingly, the smokers portrayed in these images are always more mature than those around them, suggesting that in officially sanctioned publications there were generational as well as gender proscriptions against smoking. That the social disapprobation against female smoking also extended to young educated males is suggested by documents and memoirs from the Cultural Revolution period.[57]

Adult smokers, especially authority figures, were a different story. The link between manliness and male power was underscored above all by the many representations of Mao Zedong holding or smoking a cigarette (Figure 4.23).[58] Others, such as the one based on Liu Wenxi's 1972 painting entitled *New Spring in Yan'an*, humanize Mao by showing him smoking with representatives of "the people" (Figure 4.24).[59] Another example of this populist sensibility is Liu Wenxi's early 1970s *Heart-to-Heart Talk*, a poster in which Mao puffs on his cigarette while chatting amiably with pipe-smoking peasants (Figure 4.25).[60]

FIGURE 4.22.
Tang Guangtie, *Chuanshou wuyi* (Passing on Military Skills), 1965. Stefan R. Landsberger Collection, International Institute of Social History (Amsterdam), call number BG E15/558. http://hdl.handle.net/10622/93B829D0-C90F-45FC-836E-1CFC78473F36 (accessed August 28, 2016).

FIGURE 4.23.
Long Live Chairman Mao, the Reddest Sun in Our Hearts, 1967. Shanghai People's Fine Arts
Publishing House, 1967. Reproduced in Lincoln Cushing and Ann Tompkins, *Chinese
Posters: Art from the Great Proletarian Cultural Revolution* (San Francisco: Chronicle Books,
2007), p. 124.

延 安 新 春

FIGURE 4.24.
Liu Wenxi, *Yan'an xin chun* (New Spring in Yan'an), 1972. Stefan R. Landsberger Collection, International Institute of Social History (Amsterdam), call number BG E3/713. http://hdl .handle.net/10622/2220B9A5-0300-4DCC-AA52-9AA68700AA86.

知　心　话

FIGURE 4.25.
Liu Wenxi, *Zhixin hua* (Heart-to-Heart Talk), 1972. Stefan R. Landsberger Collection,
International Institute of Social History (Amsterdam), call number BG E13/125. http://hdl
.handle.net/10622/98C6BAF0-D613-4667-BD34-45EE0397C9E4.

While many images of Mao portray him smoking with peasants or workers in ways reminiscent of *haohan* sociability, still others revive the *caizi/
wenren* associations between smoking and scholarly accomplishment. In the
1972 poster *We Will Surely Bring the Hai River under Permanent Control,*
Mao stands at his desk with a freshly completed calligraphy scroll in front of
him (Figure 4.26).[61] On the desk are the accoutrements of scholarly work:
a brush and ink, teacup, and ashtray. Mao looks resolutely forward with
the cigarette held in his left hand. Photographs of Mao, such as one showing him relaxing in a long gown while smoking a cigarette and reading the
newspaper, also carry forward associations between a more refined masculinity and smoking in the person of the Great Helmsman. This photograph
is also the rare image from the early PRC period that shows a man, in this
instance Chairman Mao, in a casual pose reminiscent of the "bourgeois-
liberal" enjoying the good life relaxing at home and smoking a cigarette.[62]

一定要根治海河

FIGURE 4.26.
Zan Zheng, *Yiding yao genzhi haihe* (We Will Surely Bring the Hai River under Permanent Control), 1972. (Speech by Mao Zedong in November 1963.) Stefan R. Landsberger Collection, International Institute of Social History (Amsterdam), call number BG E12/740. http://hdl.handle.net/10622/7A1C3493-BFC1-4E7E-BDFC-7A5FEE3A635F.

Conclusion

Visual culture played an important role in shaping gendered patterns of smoking behavior in twentieth-century China. To be sure, pervasive images of people smoking pipes or cigarettes, whether before or after Liberation, did not compel Chinese to smoke—tobacco use was deeply entrenched in Chinese society long before advances in printing technologies allowed for the mass circulation of such images. But visual culture did help normalize smoking by increasing the perception that the behavior is commonplace, respectable, and integral to everyday life. It also successfully served to "de-normalize" smoking by utilizing censorious images of smokers, or by removing depictions of people smoking from the visual realm altogether. Understanding this helps us appreciate the logic behind the WHO Framework Convention on Tobacco Control (FCTC) requirement that signatory countries undertake a comprehensive ban on tobacco advertising, promotion, and sponsorship.

Transformations in how Chinese female smokers were represented in the early twentieth century arguably contributed both to an increase in cigarette smoking among women in the 1920s and 1930s and the dramatic decline in smoking rates among women that occurred between the 1940s and 1950s. Whereas in the teens and twenties such imagery made it respectable for women to smoke in public, the proliferation of images of the new Chinese woman in the guise of the all-consuming Modern Girl—the aesthetic that dominated tobacco advertisements in the 1930s and 1940s—actually in the long run served to undermine rather than enhance the respectability of female smoking. In the early PRC period, women who smoked were explicitly labeled "bourgeois" or "decadent" and, as a result, images of female smokers vanished almost completely except as negative role models. The paucity of such imagery was so profound that it must have been quite shocking when real women lit up in public.[63]

Although smoking by women became synonymous with bourgeois decadence after 1949, for men it remained perfectly acceptable. By representing smoking as entirely normative, the visual culture of the early PRC reinforced long-standing connections between smoking and masculinity even as its social and cultural meanings were altered by new revolutionary aesthetics. Associated in the first half of the twentieth century with refined tastes, idiosyncratic habits, and savvy connoisseurship, smoking among men emerged after Liberation as a marker of a new kind of Chinese manliness that was closer to the *haohan* ideal than it was to the scholarly *caizi/wenren* model. Whereas in the Republican period cigarette smoking was above all a form of refined consumption aimed at displaying one's individuality, in the post-1949 period the dominant gender ideal that appeared in images of men smoking was that of the *haohan* whose loyalty to his comrades (and by extension, the nation) was demonstrated by the simple proletarian pleasure of smoking cigarettes together. At the same time, however, the *caizi/wenren* ideal persisted in images of Chinese leaders, particularly those showing Chairman Mao smoking while engaged in the contemplative pursuits of reading, writing, or relaxing at home. On rare occasions, as in the photograph of Mao in his dressing gown, the refracted Republican-era bourgeois-liberal culture of smoking made an appearance in PRC imagery.

Whatever the particular trope, the associations between smoking and masculinity, long in the making and after 1949 sanctioned by official propaganda, remained deep and seemingly unshakeable. When commercial advertising returned to China in the late 1970s, tobacco companies had a rich unbroken tradition of cultural meanings and visual imagery to draw upon in promoting cigarettes to Chinese men. Themes that had remained consistent across the century, particularly the importance of smoking for male sociability, resurfaced quickly in cigarette ads from the 1980s.[64] Muscular *haohan* masculinity was also on display in the elaborately produced Marlboro ads Philip Morris ran on TV at Chinese New Years from 1990 to 1997 and then again in 2001 to congratulate China on winning its bid to host the 2008 Olympics. These spots featured phalanxes of powerful men beating on drums (to the theme of "The Magnificent Seven" used in Marlboro Man commercials!), running sure-footedly across mountainous landscapes, or rowing across open water, waving huge red flags or holding them upright in one hand with arm outstretched. Adhering to Chinese regulations in place since 1991 against directly mentioning cigarettes or showing people smoking, the ads end simply with the written words "Wan Bao Lu [Marlboro] wishes you a happy New Year."[65] The point is nonetheless clearly made: smoking Marlboro cigarettes is a particularly macho thing to do.

This chapter has emphasized continuities over time in the visual imagery that helped to maintain smoking as a normalized activity for Chinese men. The high prevalence of smoking among men recorded over the past thirty years can be largely explained by the continued identification of smoking with Chinese *haohan* masculinity and male sociability as well as the post-1978 return of associations between smoking and the "good life." It is important to recognize, however, that Chinese masculinities, like gender constructs everywhere, are not fixed and unchanging. Although the traditional *haohan* and *caizi/wenren* tropes continue to resonate in contemporary China there are, and always have been, multiple and diverse masculinities enacted by Chinese men in everyday life. As anthropologist Derek Hird says, to reduce the complexities of Chinese masculinities to an essentialized *wen-wu* dyad is to ignore the fact that "constructions of gender are necessarily composites, particularly in today's globalised world."[66] Moreover, gender ideals and norms are dynamic and, as illustrated by the dramatic transformation in female smoking rates that occurred in the twentieth century, smoking behavior can change. To be a Chinese man is not necessarily to smoke cigarettes. In ethnographic research conducted among Chinese white-collar men in Beijing in 2007, Hird found that among some men who fashioned themselves as particularly cosmopolitan and urbane, care and attention to health, including not smoking, is emerging as a new masculine ideal.[67]

Analyzing why some white-collar men now regard nonsmoking as a sophisticated cut above the rugged and aggressive type of masculinity associated with chain-smoking is beyond the scope of this essay. We can speculate however, that transformations in the visual field that occurred as a result of Chinese governmental restrictions on tobacco advertising put in place over the past two decades have played an important role in changing attitudes. Regulations banning images of people actually smoking cigarettes have increasingly been tightened since 1991.[68] A notable step was taken in December 2013 when the General Office of the Communist Party of China Central Committee and the General Office of the State Council asked government officials to set a positive example by refraining from smoking in public. The fact that China's leaders are no longer photographed smoking is also significant. In recent years, the government has moved to prohibit the display of cigarette brands or indirect advertising in films and television programs, although more can be done to ensure that smoking is no longer presented as normative for men.[69] Only when a majority of Chinese men begin to appreciate that smoking contravenes the norms of respectable behavior, as Chinese women did more than half a century ago, will the powerful associations between tobacco use and masculinity be broken. Attention to how Chinese visual culture has historically promoted smoking among men, whether directly through advertising or indirectly through propaganda, can help effect this transformation by illuminating just how pervasive and perfidious favorable images of male smokers have been over the past century.

Notes

1. Qiang Li, Jason Hsia, and Gonghuan Yuan, "Prevalence of Smoking in China in 2010," *New England Journal of Medicine* 364.25 (June 23, 2011): 2469–70.

2. A recent birth cohort analysis finds that over 25 percent of Chinese rural women born between 1908 and 1912 smoked tobacco (at ages 50–54) but that smoking declined among subsequent cohorts. Among urban women, those born between 1908 and 1912 again showed the highest prevalence (27 percent at ages 50–54) with the 1918–1922 cohort nearly matching the 1908–1912 cohort. The two youngest cohorts (1928–1932 and 1933–1937) displayed much lower smoking prevalence at each age and peaked at about 12 percent. Albert I. Hermalin and Deborah Lowry, *The Age Prevalence of Smoking among Chinese Women: A Case of Arrested Diffusion?* Population Studies Center Research Report 10-718 (Population Studies Center, University of Michigan, October 2010), p. 9.

3. Bo-Qi Liu et al., "Emerging Tobacco Hazards in China: 1. Retrospective Proportional Mortality Study of One Million Deaths," *British Medical Journal* 317 (November 21, 1998): 1411–22.

4. Hermalin and Lowry, *Age Prevalence of Smoking among Chinese Women*, p. 12.

5. Carol Benedict, *Golden-Silk Smoke: A History of Tobacco in China, 1550–2010* (Berkeley: University of California Press, 2011), pp. 199–239.

6. Lucie Olivova, "Tobacco Smoking in Qing China," *Asia Major*, 3rd series, 18.1 (2005): 225–50.

7. Benedict, *Golden-Silk Smoke*, pp. 65–73.

8. Timothy Brook, "Is Smoking Chinese?" *Ex/Change* (Newsletter of the Centre for Cross Cultural Studies, City University of Hong Kong) 3 (February 2002): 5–6.

9. Benedict, *Golden-Silk Smoke*, p. 68.

10. Kam Louie, *Theorising Chinese Masculinity: Society and Gender in China* (Cambridge: Cambridge University Press, 2002).

11. Song Geng, *The Fragile Scholar: Power and Masculinity in Chinese Culture* (Hong Kong: Hong Kong University Press, 2004), pp. 163–65.

12. Louie, *Theorising Chinese Masculinity*, p. 4.

13. Ibid., p. 11.

14. *Shenbao*, April 15, 1923, p. 8.

15. Ibid., July 4, 1928, p. 8.

16. Matthew Hilton, *Smoking in British Popular Culture, 1800–2000* (Manchester: Manchester University Press, 2000), pp. 17–40.

17. Charles Laughlin, *The Literature of Leisure and Chinese Modernity* (Honolulu: University of Hawaii Press, 2008), p. 124.

18. Hilton, *Smoking in British Popular Culture*, pp. 17–20.

19. Laughlin, *The Literature of Leisure*, p. 114.

20. Xu Zhimo, "Xiyan yu wenhua" (Smoking and culture), *Chenbao fukan* (Morning Post Literary Supplement), January 10, 1926, p. 21.

21. Laughlin, *The Literature of Leisure*, p. 127.

22. *Liangyou* (The Young Companion), no. 155 (June 1940): 36.

23. "The City Man's Life, Twenty Four Hours: A Complete Schedule," in *Liangyou*, no. 102 (February 1935): 40–41.

24. Hilton, *Smoking in British Popular Culture*, p. 21.

25. *Shenbao*, May 24, 1921, p. 3.

26. Weipin Tsai, *Reading Shenbao: Nationalism, Consumerism, and Individuality in China, 1919–37* (London: Palgrave Macmillan, 2010), pp. 35–42.

27. *Shenbao*, January 5, 1928, p. 6. On the sexual connotations of exposed armpits in Chinese iconography, see Francesca Dal Lago, "Crossed Legs in 1930s Shanghai: How 'Modern' the Modern Woman?" *East Asian History* 19 (June 2000): 103–44.

28. *Shenbao*, February 23, 1928, p. 7.

29. One example, among many, can be found in *Shenbao*, May 19, 1935, p. 1.

30. Ibid., May 8, 1928, p. 3.

31. Ibid., January 17, 1928, p. 1.

32. See, for example, advertisement for Saw cigarettes in *Shenbao*, May 25, 1934, p. 1.

33. See Shu-mei Shih's analysis of such images in "Shanghai Women of 1939: Visuality and the Limits of Feminine Modernity," in Jason C. Kuo (ed.), *Visual Culture in Shanghai, 1850s–1930s* (Washington, DC: New Academia Press, 2007), pp. 213–18.

34. *Shenbao*, March 6, 1928, p. 1.

35. Ibid., June 2, 1928, p. 9.

36. See, for example, ibid., May 3, 1935, p. 6; ibid., November 7, 1929, p. 8.

37. Ibid., November 1, 1931, p. 1.

38. *Liangyou*, no. 89 (June 15, 1934): 35.

39. *Shenbao*, July 6, 1928, p. 7.

40. Ibid., May 4, 1934, p. 1.

41. Ibid., May 8, 1925, p. 4. Another example is an advertisement for Chienmen brand cigarettes, which shows a bull wrestler similarly bared to the waist (ibid., June 9, 1925, p. 4).

42. Matthew Kohrman, "Depoliticizing Tobacco's Exceptionality: Male Sociality, Death, and Memory-Making among Chinese Cigarette Smokers," *China Journal* 58 (July 2007): 100.

43. James Chu, "Advertising in China: Its Policy, Practice, and Evolution," *Journalism Quarterly* 59.1 (Spring 1982): 40–45, 91; Hong Cheng, "Advertising in China: A Socialist Experiment," in Katherine Toland Frith (ed.), *Advertising in Asia: Communication, Culture, and Consumption* (Ames: Iowa State University Press, 1996), p. 77.

44. Examples include advertisements in *Gongren ribao* (Worker's Daily, Hebei), January 1, 1951, p. 7, and ibid., June 15, 1951, p. 2.

45. Andrew S. Cahan, *Chinese Label Art* (Atglen, PA: Schiffer Publishing, 2006), p. 148.

46. Liu Zhide, *Lao shuji* (Old Party Secretary) (1973), Stefan R. Landsberger Collection, International Institute of Social History (Amsterdam), call number: BG E27/321, http://hdl.handle.net/10622/6CBBFA94-C913-44F5-AA3A-187C3 F6ABBBF.

47. *Gongren ribao*, January 30, 1955, p. 4.

48. Ibid., October 23, 1956, p. 3.

49. Ibid., July 4, 1954, p. 3.

50. For examples, see ibid., January 3, 1952, p. 3; January 6, 1956, p. 2; July 29, 1956, p. 3; and August 21, 1956, p. 3.

51. *Renmin huabao* (China Pictorial), no. 1 (1975): 36; ibid., no. 10 (1975): 12.

52. Guo Zhiming, *Ni duizhang* (Our Brigade Leader) (1976), Stefan R. Landsberger Collection, International Institute of Social History (Amsterdam), call number BG E15/93, http://hdl.handle.net/10622/B5BF7442-232C-4030-90FB-5F2 FF14D61B6.

53. Lu Yifei, Zhang Guiming, and Xu Zhiwen, *Xue ye chun feng* (A Spring Breeze on a Snowy Night) (1976), International Institute of Social History (Amsterdam), call number BG E16/350, http://hdl.handle.net/10622/9B624BEE-73F7 -48DC-81F5-1DE4E8BEAD0D. See also Stefan Landsberger's collection, http://www.chineseposters.net/gallery/e15-98.php (accessed August 28, 2016).

54. The short-stemmed pipe emerged in the 1930s as a symbol of the virtues of "hard work and plain living" associated with farmers (Benedict, *Golden-Silk Smoke*, pp. 189–95).

55. Qu Fang, *Shanghai Huangpu jiang de zaochen* (Early Morning on the Huangpu River in Shanghai) (1964), Jean-Yves Bajon Collection, International Institute of Social History (Amsterdam), call number: BG E39/810, http://hdl .handle.net/10622/2E05CE31-BA48-43FE-9726-3A7592F5F60B.

56. Tang Guangtie, *Chuanshou wuyi* (Passing on Military Skills) (1965), Stefan R. Landsberger Collection, International Institute of Social History (Amsterdam), call number: BG E15/558, http://hdl.handle.net/10622/93B829D0-C90F-45FC-836 E-1CFC78473F36.

57. The Beijing No. 26 Middle School Red Guards, for example, listed smok-

ing as one of the bad habits that "absolutely must not be cultivated" and ordered "those under thirty-five to quit drinking and smoking immediately." Michael Schoenhals, ed., *China's Cultural Revolution, 1966–1969: Not a Dinner Party* (Armonk, NY: M.E. Sharpe, 1996), p. 220. Of course, many young men, especially those "sent down" to the countryside learned to smoke anyway.

58. Lincoln Cushing and Ann Tompkins, *Chinese Posters: Art from the Great Proletarian Cultural Revolution* (San Francisco: Chronicle Books, 2007), p. 124.

59. Liu Wenxi, *Yan'an xin chun* (New Spring in Yan'an) (1972), Stefan R. Landsberger Collection, International Institute of Social History (Amsterdam), call number: BG E3/713, http://hdl.handle.net/10622/2220B9A5-0300-4DCC-AA52-9AA68700AA86.

60. Liu Wenxi, *Zhixin hua* (Heart-to-Heart Talk) (1972), Stefan R. Landsberger Collection, International Institute of Social History (Amsterdam), call number: BG E13/125, http://hdl.handle.net/10622/98C6BAF0-D613-4667-BD34-45EE0397C9E4. See also Stefan R. Landsberger's collection at http://chineseposters.net/posters/e13-125.php (accessed August 28, 2016).

61. Zan Zheng, *Yiding yao genzhi haihe* (We Will Surely Bring the Hai River under Permanent Control) (1972), (Speech by Mao Zedong in November 1963), Stefan R. Landsberger Collection, International Institute of Social History (Amsterdam), call number: BG E12/740, http://hdl.handle.net/10622/7A1C3493-BFC1-4E7E-BDFC-7A5FEE3A635F.

62. See Getty image of Mao Zedong smoking that accompanies Martin Patience, "China to Ban Smoking in Public Places," BBC News, March 24, 2011, http://www.bbc.co.uk/news/world-asia-pacific-12844671 (accessed August 28, 2016).

63. Li Lanni, "Kan nüren xiyan" (Upon seeing a woman smoking), in Yang Guo'an, *Yanshi xianqu* (Leisurely delights of tobacco matters) (Beijing: Beijing Yanshan chubanshe, 1999), pp. 395–97.

64. Michael H. Anderson, *Madison Avenue in Asia: Politics and Transnational Advertising* (Rutherford, NJ: Fairleigh Dickinson University Press, 1984), p. 293.

65. Nan Zhou and Russell W. Belk, "Chinese Consumer Readings of Global and Local Advertising Appeals," *Journal of Advertising* 33.3 (Fall 2004): 71.

66. Derek Hird, "White-collar Men and Masculinity in Contemporary Urban China," Ph.D. diss. (University of Westminster, 2009), p. 36.

67. Ibid., p. 182. See also Geng Song and Derek Hird, *Men and Masculinities in Contemporary China* (Leiden: Brill, 2014), pp. 194–97.

68. Zhihong Gao and Sion Kim, "Advertising Law and Regulation in China," in Hong Cheng and Kara Chan (eds.), *Advertising and Chinese Society: Impacts and Issues* (Copenhagen: Copenhagen Business School Press, 2009), p. 151.

69. Lin Li and Hua-Hie Yong, "Tobacco Advertising on the Street in Kunming, China," *Tobacco Control* 18.1 (February 2009): 63; Tingzhong Yang et al.,

"Tobacco Advertising, Environmental Smoking Bans, and Smoking in Chinese Urban Areas," *Drug and Alcohol Dependence* 124.1–2 (July 2012), doi:10.1016/j. drugalcdep.2011.12.02; and Dan Xiao et al., "Implementation of the World Health Organization Framework Convention on Tobacco Control in China: An Arduous and Long-Term Task," *Cancer* 121, Suppl 17:3061-8 (September 1, 2015): 3061–68.

CHAPTER FIVE

Curating Employee Ethics
Self-Glory Amidst Slow Violence at the China Tobacco Museum

Matthew Kohrman

China's current building boom, often chided for effacing history, has been notably productive for at least one category of institutional memory making. During the past decade, hundreds of new museums have been built across the country.[1] One, on Changyang Road in the middle of Shanghai, appears decidedly out of place; its façade seems more at home in Mexico than China. Passing it initially, viewers may be lulled into believing they are seeing a replica of El Castillo, a famed site in the Yucatan. Replete with fortified gray windowless walls, a hefty external stone staircase, hieroglyphic-like carvings, and totem poles, the building is obviously a play on a Mayan temple.

Opened in 2004, it is called the China Tobacco Museum. It is the largest museum anywhere celebrating the cigarette, a commercial product that during the twentieth century became one of the most widely circulated, consumed, and criticized around the world.[2] The China Tobacco Museum is more than a tribute to the cigarette, however. It is, I argue, a carefully designed technology of self,[3] a building offering tobacco industry employees space for reflection and ethical nurturance.

My style of exposition here is likewise reflexive, with its object of inquiry, the museum, prompting how the pages below unfold, as something of a walking tour. Meandering from one exhibition space to another, I point out ways that the museum communicates an ethics tailored to its intended audience. As we journey through the museum, I detail how curators deploy themes aimed at fostering a sense of personal virtue and self-assurance among China's tobacco industry workforce.[4]

Before our tour gets underway, a few words regarding research methodology. Here too reflexivity has had a role. I draw on research that I have conducted during the last decade. Over that span, my fieldwork frequently has taken me to China's southwest province of Yunnan, but it has also involved periods of study elsewhere, including trips to Shanghai. I have spent more than twenty hours in the Tobacco Museum to date, touring its galleries, chatting with people, and extensively photographing exhibits. On my first visit, a colleague at Fudan University arranged for me to meet the museum's directors. They welcomed me with passionate handshakes, entry into their offices and library, overtures for long-term collaboration, and gifts of catalogues and other background information. Their flirtations ceased that same night, however, after a museum manager searched my academic record on the Internet and discovered that I had been funded previously by the U.S. National Institutes of Health and that I was open to making pointed assessments of the tobacco industry in my publications. These discoveries short-circuited initial passions, my Fudan colleague explained. My academic bona fides, dare I say my professional ethics, were simply too discordant with those that the museum exists to nurture. An upshot of this aborted relationship was that my subsequent visits to the building were less encumbered. I purposely let months go by between my unannounced museum trips, and the hours that I passed in galleries were pleasant and uneventful.

· · ·

Shanghai today has a long menu of museums from which to choose. For anyone wandering into the China Tobacco Museum for the first time, it can easily seem like little more than a blunt project of public relations, a mix of industrial triumphalism and product triage, a gambit by a rich state-run business sector to shore up the social standing of its leading and much maligned product, the cigarette. What is at stake for this business is a swelling pipeline of money resting on shifting sands. Cigarette manufacturing and sales have enjoyed meteoric growth over the past fifty years in China, generating in excess of US$170 billion in profits and taxes during 2015 alone, largely free of any foreign competition.[5] Buffeting this juggernaut are new and ongoing market uncertainties and ethical upheavals. The biggest ethical upheavals are evidence of tobacco smoke's toxicity and recent moves by Chinese health advocates to ally with global health programs to redefine cigarettes as highly pathogenic. Market uncertainties include everything from growing numbers of Chinese consumers increasingly attentive to health risks, to efforts by the party-state to restructure the competitive landscape of domestic cigarette manufacturing. Since the 1990s, Beijing has pushed for the state-run cigarette industry, partitioned by provincial protectionism, to consolidate production and to create only a few cigarette megabrands. Market shifts have also included swings in regulations, particularly regarding advertising.[6]

China's domestic tobacco industry has responded to all these uncertainties and upheavals through various means, including the mass media. Regional manufacturers have hired marketing experts to devise novel messaging platforms, skirting new restrictions on tobacco advertising, to bolster the cigarette's respectability in general and Chinese brand names in particular (Chunghwa, Yunyan, Panda, and many others). The audience for these public relations moves is far more than the 300 million Chinese who smoke daily. It has also been the country's nonsmoking majority.[7] The industry looks to that majority, particularly its younger members, to take up smoking as replacement customers for those lost to death and disease, and at least, in the years ahead, to remain tolerant of others smoking tobacco. Such tolerance is far from assured, however. Even mainstream media in China regularly report that cigarettes now kill over a million citizens annually and that the toll will triple by 2030, if current rates of smoking persist.[8]

So, when I first visited the China Tobacco Museum in Shanghai in 2011, I quickly assumed I was treading on just one more plank in the industry's crass public relations aimed at enhancing its cash cow, the cigarette. I also assumed, after a few visits, that the museum was a costly failure. Because, if the measure of the museum's success is encouraging members of the general public to continue seeing smoking as a laudable custom (rather than as a state-sponsored pathogenesis), doing so requires large numbers of people entering the building. But on almost all my visits, the place was a near ghost town. Even free admission and ample air conditioning on the hottest of Shanghai days fail to attract many people off the street and into the building, perhaps explaining why the museum is now only open to unscheduled visitors two days a week.

What I have come to understand, however, is that this institution was never built for any imagined general public. Rather, it was created for a narrow spectrum of Chinese citizens, a vocational demographic that includes those who oversaw its construction. It was built for people who most often wander its galleries, usually in groups, often at times when the museum is closed to the public. Its target audience is the tobacco industry's largely male, well educated, urban labor force: factory-line workers, managers, researchers, marketers, accountants, supply-chain personnel, and technicians. This focus is expressed patently in the institution's founding documents. For example, Jiang Chengkang, the director general of the museum's supervisory agency, the State Tobacco Monopoly Administration, when commemorating the institution's grand opening, emphasized: "The museum is to serve as a window and platform of communication, one that advances understanding of the industry . . . strengthening self-awareness among industry staff (加强行业职工对自身的认识)."[9]

Stated somewhat differently, this edifice in Shanghai was created as a grand project of self-enhancement for tobacco industry employees. It is a technology of self, in Foucauldian terms, a crucible of practices and logics by which a group of individuals represent to themselves their own ethical self-understanding. However, rather than the "manual of morals" that Foucault described when he coined the phrase "technology of self," what we have here is a museum of morals, a building designed by/and for an enigmatic group within the polity of the People's Republic.[10]

Self-referential industry museums can be found in many parts of the world, built on behalf of a variety of large business sectors.[11] Among its many characteristics, the tobacco industry in China is nothing else if not large. At current count, it produces well over two and a half trillion cigarettes annually, constituting more than 40 percent of the world's total production of rolled tobacco products. Despite automation, legions of laborers are required to feed this cigarette supply chain. Millions of farmers—growing and harvesting tobacco leaves at fixed government prices—are needed. Some 500,000 nonagricultural workers are also involved: procurement personnel, flue curers, factory-line staff, and experts specializing in everything from logistics to biochemistry, engineering, finance, law, management, medicine, insurance, transportation, marketing, and accounting.

These employees are comparatively well compensated, to be sure.[12] They have enjoyed salaries and bonuses the envy of other industrial sectors over the past fifty years. They have also started to receive something else at the turn of the millennium. As foreign business logics regarding human resource management have entered China and mixed with Mao-era pedagogies regarding labor and party rectitude, workers in the tobacco industry have received access to new forms of employee self-enhancement services. In the Southwest, for example, employees now have access to new psychological counseling services to help manage mental distress.[13] The China Tobacco Museum has positioned itself as a similar venture. It offers itself as a font of continuing education and as an adult resource center for industry personnel, providing them a perk, less material than spiritual. Of utmost concern is helping employee-subjects to perceive themselves as ethically directed and highly motivated individuals, impervious to temptations such as misconduct, corruption, and self-doubt.

Over the past decade, I have spoken to scores of people working in one capacity or another across China's State Tobacco Monopoly Administration, whether for local offices or manufacturing enterprises. These men and women have sometimes been forthright, sometimes dismissive regarding the dangers posed by cigarettes. But whatever their views on tobacco toxicity, the overarching message that they have communicated to me is that they self-identify as good, upstanding citizens who participate in making a product of great value to their country and community. And, when I have pushed any of them to defend their vocation, which many a media commentator chides as mercenary, malevolent, even murderous, they have consistently responded that, despite problems inherent to conventional tobacco combustion, they see themselves as contributing to an interwoven set of higher causes: providing consumers ever safer and more pleasurable choices through scientific innovation, building a stronger and more modern nation, and helping to finance strategic priorities of the party-state, both local and national.

How is the China Tobacco Museum designed to reinforce this ethical repertoire of self-understanding? What precisely are the curatorial strategies it deploys to prop up such a vocational subjectivity?

In this chapter, I offer a guided tour of the museum, describing ways that gallery designers advance an ethics of self for industry staff.[14] From exhibition space to exhibition space, I show how specific curatorial themes are deployed to represent an industrial history as moral epoch and a workforce as manufacturing more than just consumer products. I argue that, within these galleries, it is particularly notable that the museum repetitively depicts the source of history as actors who we see are not simply photographed but also are named. This representational strategy of calling out is not new to China, where Maoist propagandists long ago exalted model workers, naming and photographing them. Novel here is that this technique of person-alization is now being used in an effort to incite feelings of self-worth and allegiance for an industry facing a biopolitical struggle over the integrity of a consumer product.

Background to a Museum, Kickoff to a Tour

Formal planning for the museum began in the late 1980s, with China's State Council approving construction a decade later. Advocating for the museum were leaders of a then new branch of the party-state, China's State Tobacco Monopoly Administration (STMA), created in the early 1980s to supervise production and sale of cigarettes nationwide. The STMA's leaders not only advocated a national museum but arranged for all levels of their agency to pay for it. Because they won the right to host the museum, beating out a bid from the city of Kunming, the Shanghai branch of the STMA and the Shanghai Cigarette Factory financed over half the cost of construction. An additional hundred different branches of the STMA and a large percent-age of STMA-supervised cigarette factories also contributed. All told more than RMB 180 million (US$23 million) was raised by non-Shanghai enti-ties, with Yunnan province's factories and offices leading the way, giving a total of RMB 20 million. Provinces like Hainan, where tobacco production is less prominent, gave as little as RMB 100,000. Tibet did not contribute at all. The museum opened in the summer of 2004, across the street from the Shanghai Cigarette Factory, on a site where before 1949 a factory of the Brit-ish American Tobacco Company once sat.[15] The exhibition spaces of this new beacon of corporate self-acclamation occupy the first three floors and a portion of the basement; floors four and five are taken up by administrative offices and a library.

.   .   .

Entering a museum, anywhere, always means subjecting oneself to concep-tual and bodily management. The China Tobacco Museum is no exception. On each of my visits, I was required to show identification and to sign in at the front gate. Guards direct visitors to walk to the top of the external stairwell and to enter on the third floor, past socialist expressionist images, engraved on stone panels, depicting muscular proletarians, wrenches and revolutionary flags in hand. At the apex of the stairs, the panels conclude with two three-meter-tall workers operating cigarette rolling machines, doves hovering above. Once inside, visitors are expected to traverse each floor's gallery spaces, traveling downward from floor to floor, with overhead lights automatically switching on or off as you enter or exit a particular exhibit space. Guards sit in a central control room watching visitors on closed-circuit monitors, and reprimand any infractions over a speaker system (e.g., for touching a display case or using flash photography).

Within this managed environment, several rhetorical lines or themes are persistently communicated. These are the organizational touchstones of the tour that I offer here. One by one, I walk you through the themes' curatorial deployment.

Theme 1: Cigarettes were originally foreign products but they quickly underwent processes of bentuhua (本土化, "localization")

Before viewing anything inside the museum, the visitor must first walk through a large circular third-floor entry, seemingly providing a spatial primer on China's capacity to absorb and localize. The entry features a floor-to-ceiling mural in gold leaf. It portrays sights widely recognized as native to China, such as Tiananmen Gate, and others with more exogenous roots, everything from the Buddhist sculptures of Leshan to the contemporary Shanghai skyline and Tibet's famous Potala Palace in Lhasa.

Crossing the entryway, life-sized Native American manikins greet the visitor in a darkened room surrounded by displays depicting tobacco's American origins and its transoceanic dissemination. The viewer is enveloped by monochrome colors, cobblestone flooring, and raw-wood-framed exhibits. Maps explain the movement of tobacco out of the Americas, its arrival in Asia during the seventeenth century, and its spread across Old China. Graphics portray differing Chinese responses, including Ming court hostilities, Qing court praise, and public efforts to cultivate tobacco leaf.

A few meters along, the exhibits get to the heart of the matter—the making of the modern cigarette. Although tobacco was introduced into Asia more than 250 years before the advent of machine-rolling,[16] the designers of the museum are interested mostly in the era of *juanyan* (卷烟; literally, rolled tobacco). The first few exhibit walls to portray *juanyan* and its manufacture do so in the context of late imperial China, as initially foreign and thus at once suspect and fascinating. Here early cigarette production is mostly depicted through black-and-white photos: of Anglo-American businessmen; of factories designed, financed, and supervised by foreigners; and of poorly dressed Chinese toiling on the assembly lines at the British American Tobacco Company in Shanghai. The difficulty conveyed by the photographs, if any, is not of a harmful product being manufactured, in contrast to opium, for instance. Rather the difficulty is that of a deficient local citizenry, not yet poised to govern modern machinery, not yet able to operate cigarette factories free of foreign influence.

Theme 2: Localization of the cigarette has been the result of proud human actions carried out by Chinese patriots

Several rooms of the museum offer celebratory visualizations of how precisely a once-foreign product becomes a localized commodity. Prioritized are efforts and workspaces of people portrayed as decidedly "Chinese," proud and proactive. Men lead the way, with few exceptions.

In one room, we see a full-sized reproduction of the workspace in which the foreman of the Yee Tsoong Tobacco Factory (颐中烟厂) once held sway. Nearby a group of photos depicts two enterprises founded in 1926: the Fuxin Tobacco Company and Minfeng (China's first domestic cigarette paper maker). Some of the photos are of building exteriors; others feature well-dressed local workers overseeing the companies' massive machines. Portraits of Minfeng's cofounders, Messrs. Jin Runyang and Zhu Meixian, are displayed prominently.

The next wall is labeled "Tobacco Industry's Patriotic and Anti-Imperialist Activities." Of the many cigarettes a Chinese consumer could choose from in the early twentieth century, "Patriotic Brand (爱国牌) was warmly welcomed," a plaque explains. Nearby, a newspaper clipping describes how, in Shanghai in 1919, 600 tobacco workers took part in strikes of the May Fourth movement, the protonationalist campaign that gave birth to the Chinese patriot, pitting Chinese nationalism against feudal and foreign enemies. Also prominently shown are portraits of two early Communist luminaries, Xiang Jingyu and Li Lisan. A major figure in China's embryonic women's liberation movement and a CCP activist, Ms. Xiang organized the first Communist Party branch inside a tobacco company and helped orchestrate a strike in Shanghai during 1924. The equally renowned Mr. Li, someone who oversaw the CCP in the late 1920s and was assigned various third-tier posts until his demise in the late 1960s, we are told, emerged out of the very same party branch of a tobacco company.

That the industry was a spawning ground of nationalism, communism, and the rise of New China is bluntly communicated on the next wall with two displays. On the left, a display depicts Japanese military occupation during the Second World War. Here we see three images, each seemingly chosen to disturb the viewer more than the next and incite a sense of allegiance to workers who heroically embodied both Chineseness and tobacco production. The first image comes with a caption, "British and American tobacco factory capitalists humiliated Chinese employees. Workers were subjected to bodily searches." Guards are shown during the Japanese occupation, checking ID papers and searching workers at a factory gate. The second photo portrays Japanese imperial soldiers brandishing bayoneted rifles and loading domestic tobacco workers into a truck. The last photo shows a soldier beheading a man lying face up; an imperial officer stands above, hands in his pockets. The caption reads, "Japanese invaders mercilessly butchering Chinese tobacco workers."[17]

The display to the right offers a recuperative, psycho-political pivot, a nod to the reputed powers of manufacturing to heal and nurture the nation.[18] This display is devoted to cigarette manufacturing that occurred under the aegis of the Chinese Communist Party's wartime Revolutionary Base Areas. Photos show exteriors of three CCP factories in simple rural buildings. There are portraits of Messrs. Ji Bao and Song Changhe, director and vice-director of the Donghai Cigarette Factory, established in 1942 within the Third Division of the New Fourth Army. To one side of these portraits, a brightly lit plaque states that workers at another Revolutionary Base Area factory, Baojiafang, had to struggle constantly for resources to feed the factory's hand-cranked machines, but that at its height Baojiafang produced as many as 20,000 cigarettes daily for the Red Army.

Theme 3: Chinese cigarette makers have dutifully served the needs of the People's Republic's most important personages

If not the soldier, Mao is the embodiment of the revolutionary era cigarette consumer. The next display is devoted to the special care the CCP and the industry gave to Mao's tobacco habit during a period of pitched Communist fervor, the Cultural Revolution (1966–1976). Marshal He Long, a plaque explains, proposed in 1964 that Sichuan's Shifang Cigarette factory should set up a special enterprise to supply Mao and other top leaders with distinctive lines of rolled tobacco products. The factory sent samples to Beijing and, among these, leaders chose four. In 1971, at the height of the Cultural Revolution, the General Office of the central government assigned Shifang workers and equipment to set up a manufacturing facility at 80 Nanchang Road in Beijing, across the street from Zhongnanhai, the compound of China's highest leaders.[19] The actual physical entry to this address now stands in the museum, relocated in 2006. As if being given privileged access to an inner sanctum, we are invited to walk through the (repurposed) Nanchang Road entryway past the original set of stone lions. We are met by a large photo of Mao reclining in a rattan chair reading a newspaper and smoking a No. 2 cigarillo, his personal line. Also in this display is Fan Guorong, the Nanchang factory director; now retired, he is shown teaching young women from the Beijing Cigarette Factory how, during the Cultural Revolution, he would choose materials and roll special offerings like No. 2's for the CCP luminaries in Zhongnanhai.

This is not the only exhibit where one encounters government elites. Elsewhere, other members of the Communist Party's pantheon loom large through visible representation. Whether simply smoking or formally administering to the cigarette industry, icons like Liu Shaoqi, Zhou Enlai, Hu Jintao, Chen Yi, He Long, and Song Qingling (also known as Madame Sun Yat-sen) make appearances. Special attention is given to Deng Xiaoping along with his personal line of Panda brand cigarettes produced by Shanghai Tobacco. Packaged in blue, these cigarettes today remain highly prized and are rarely available for purchase in stores (Pandas wrapped in orange are more readily found). By emphasizing Deng's use of Pandas, the political domestication of the cigarette in China seems to be complete. This is especially evident in a section of the museum titled "Great Men, Celebrities and Tobacco," where a video clip runs on a continuous loop. In this 1986 clip, Deng Xiaoping is being interviewed in Beijing by CBS News' Mike Wallace, a US journalist. Deng pulls out a pack of his trademark Pandas and asks Wallace politely, "May I smoke?" Wallace warmly approves, certainly knowing he has no option, and he entreats Deng for a cigarette. Asking a superior for tobacco is impolite, according to current custom in China, but unfazed, Deng hands over a cigarette, smiles wryly, and says something that seems to communicate his affection for the Chinese tobacco industry, for providing him a special product and for using technical mastery to build him an ostensibly safer cigarette. Deng states, "To deal with me, they make these [cigarettes] especially on my behalf. The filter is long. Ha, the filter is even longer than the tobacco!"

Theme 4: Under the banner of tobacco culture, cigarette makers have contributed to the production of not simply an industry but all manner of Chinese society

In almost every gallery, the museum posits a theme of historical coproduction, that China's cigarette industry and its society have mutually enhanced each other. This is especially prominent in the second-floor gallery devoted to "tobacco culture" (烟草文化). There, a large plaque proclaims: "Tobacco has been around in China for over 400 years, since its introduction from abroad. It has merged with social life and joined Chinese tradition, leading to the birth of a rich and colorful tobacco culture." Along these lines, this gallery gives as much attention to chronicling the rise of the State Tobacco Monopoly Administration as it does to twentieth-century architecture. A string of photos displays the architectural pathway of the STMA and its predecessor. First comes a dilapidated redbrick barracks in Beijing's You'anmen area that once housed the China Tobacco Industry Corporation (established in 1964). Next are photos of the ever more modern buildings of the STMA (established in 1982), keeping pace with the architectural and economic efflorescence of urban China in the post-Mao era.

What does the museum portray as the engine of such "cultural" work? As with localization, it is more than an anonymous effort. It is the handiwork of specific actors, whom we meet by name and through visual portrayals. Gallery designers throw a wide, albeit gendered, net in giving a face to China's tobacco culture. In addition to photos of high party officials, in the Tobacco Culture Hall we are offered full-sized figurines embodying mid-century smoking personages of the revolution, from the People's Republic's most famous writer Lu Xun to the rugged soldier Yang Jingyu, someone whom we are told fiercely battled "Japanese invaders."

More direct personification of the STMA starts in the hall with an image from 1965, just before the Cultural Revolution. We see Wang Yizhi, director of the China Tobacco Industry Corporation, posing with a friendly group of cigarette factory workers, the women in the front row tenderly holding hands. Personification pulsates through the next display, which treats the viewer to a red wall of fame: a 10-meter-long glass case containing large portraits of the STMA's top executives (all male) from 1982 to the present. Directly across from this wall of named nomenklaturas is a plaque reading: "Party-state leaders have poured tremendous hope and concern into developing China's tobacco industry since the founding of the PRC. . . . They have encouraged generations of tobacco peasants to fight off poverty and march toward a good life."

Corporate social responsibility messaging appears not far away, presumably to reinforce the message that an ethic of generosity textures China's tobacco culture and to dampen any alienation a viewer might feel toward the STMA's handsomely remunerated executives. Former STMA director Jiang Ming and Shanghai Tobacco executive Dong Haolin are shown in separate photos, presenting poster-board checks to the China Charity Foundation and the China Children Development Foundation.

Theme 5: The State Tobacco Monopoly Administration is an august agency built by noble people

As should be obvious already, much of the museum is devoted not just to humanizing but also extolling the STMA/China Tobacco system. This comes across most strongly in one of the largest exhibit rooms, the Tobacco Administration Hall (烟草管理馆). Against a sienna-tinged background with elegant gray metal cases ringing the room, dozens of displays chronicle an origin story, wherein the STMA emerges from a seemingly logical progression of late dynastic and early twentieth-century political events. Throughout, the STMA is treated as a sacred telos, offering China's tobacco industry a long-needed "unified leadership, vertical administration . . . approaching perfection."

Portraiture here again is prominent. Late-Qing figures like Sheng Xuanhuai and Xiong Xiling appear as founding fathers of state tobacco monopoly "theory." Photos of financial administrators from the Soviet Base era also loom large. And in a display titled "Heroes of the Day, Guardians of the Golden Leaves," are contemporary photographs of named STMA employees receiving awards on stages festooned with flags of the People's Republic. In military-style navy-blue uniforms and accessorized with STMA insignias, these awardees are recognized for risking their lives to break up counterfeit cigarette factories. The last case in this hall depicts the monopoly system and China's arrival onto the global stage, showing male executives of the STMA, Philip Morris, Japan Tobacco, and British American Tobacco— with mutual respect and in harmony—signing a turn-of-the-millennium contract to fund an International Tobacco Anti-Counterfeiting Alliance.

Theme 6: Leading figures within the industry have been product modernizers, making cigarettes that have been progressively cleaner and more scientific

The museum's basement houses a sentimental machinist's fantasy. It offers perhaps the largest display of mothballed cigarette manufacturing equipment anywhere in the world, progressing from hand-crank devices used during the early twentieth century to sundry apparatuses of automation decommissioned in the past decade: cutters, rollers, packers, filter assemblers, and much else. Scrubbed since service, the machines exude no lubricants or odors, only tidy narratives of industrial advancement. The oldest ones often have neatly dressed, life-sized Chinese-featured manikins astride them, and labels acknowledging the country in which the device was originally fabricated.

Amidst this parade of hardware are photographic displays of Chinese-owned cigarette factories, helping to place the machines in grand narratives of localization and modernization. The first photos, in black-and-white, show factory exteriors of the 1920s, the Republican period, and before/after the founding of the PRC. The next, shifting to color photography, depict facilities built in the 1980s–1990s, some commissioned at the turn of the millennium and others renovated over the last decade. The final sequence, "Modern Cigarette Production," offers exemplary interiors of China's most recently outfitted factories, no workers in sight, only streamlined machinery. Nowhere does this sequence betray the machinery's origins, let alone the harm they generate. Much of the newest equipment in the photographs has actually been sourced from Europe. For instance, a large photo shows one of the speediest filter cigarette makers currently available for sale in the world, a stainless-steel encased Protos-M5, fabricated by the Hauni Corporation of Hamburg, Germany, capable of rolling 20 million cigarettes per day. Beneath its image, the caption only reads, "Ultra Rapid Production Equipment of the Shanghai Cigarette Factory."

While the museum's basement glorifies automation and a teleology of clean, modern production, the Tobacco Agriculture Hall trumpets human

achievement. It starts with dioramas communicating a cheerful vision of tobacco leaf production. "Leaf Tobacco Harvesting and Curing," for instance,
is set against a blue sky and verdant, rolling hills. Here we find cleanly dressed
four-inch prototypical peasants bundling green tobacco leaves, transporting
tidy wheelbarrows of coal, and removing golden leaves from crisply painted
white flue-curing compartments. A nearby display offers a more rustic scene,
with a life-sized Bai minority woman seated in ceremonial white costume,
preparing leaves to be hung over pristine clay ovens. Communicating a ra-
cialized dichotomy of Han Chinese sophistication and minority meekness,[20]
these two exhibits celebrate human labor while obfuscating the risks of harvesting and curing tobacco leaf, such as green tobacco sickness and respiratory diseases triggered by exposure to coal dust and smoke.[21]

The Tobacco Agriculture Hall, however, is devoted less to farmers than
to agronomists. The focus is on male scientists who helped improve the
"quality" of tobacco used in twentieth-century Chinese cigarettes. Extolled are tobacco innovators and inventors, from anonymous lab-coat-clad
Chinese-looking figurines working for BAT and the Nanyang Brothers Tobacco Company in the early twentieth century, to named scientific luminaries of the post-Liberation era who developed new varietals (e.g., Yunyan
98, 201, and 203) well suited to the climates of Yunnan and Guizhou. In-
terspersed are photos of Chinese government patriarchs—Mao Zedong in
1950 visiting Henan, Hu Jintao in 2002 touring Yunnan—inspecting tobacco fields and applauding the scientific success of agronomists. Research
visionaries like Zhu Zunquan (朱尊权) are pictured, celebrated for having
"contributed extensively to the Chinese tobacco industry." Born in Hubei
in 1919, we are told, Zhu took degrees in agronomy from Nanjing's Central
University and the University of Kentucky, returning to China after 1949
to make important discoveries for the industry while holding posts in the
Chinese Academy of Engineering and the China National Tobacco Corporation's main research institute in Zhengzhou.

*Theme 7: Chinese tobacco industry staff and allies have helped the
world discover the dangers of cigarette smoking and have confronted
those dangers innovatively and forthrightly*

Designers of the museum do not dodge public health's twentieth-century in-
dictment of the cigarette. Instead, following the example of foreign tobacco

companies,[22] this is addressed directly, with a part of the museum communicating a market-friendly version of the "problem." A large four-sided exhibit space, the Smoking and Tobacco Control Hall (吸烟与控烟馆), sits in the middle of the building. Here, the party-state is praised for recognizing dangerous features of tobacco; plaudits are directed at Chinese industry/academy contributions to harm reduction; and primacy is given to individual choice over industry culpability for risks that smoking may pose.

In the center of this hall sits a phalanx of machines, smaller than those found in the basement. These gifts, from enterprises like the Qinghai Provincial Tobacco Corporation, Changsha Cigarette Factory, and Zhengzhou Tobacco Research Institute, are mostly tools of measurement—such as a multichannel smoking machine, an automatic polarimeter, a gas chromatograph mass spectrometer, and instruments to test cigarette firmness and burning speed. Why such analytical devices are exhibited in the hall is to be inferred from the surrounding wall displays, which are filled with photos, texts, and small items.

The first of the four walls tells a story in two parts. It acknowledges tepidly the dangers inherent to tobacco smoke, with one plaque intoning that "Smoking Is Harmful" (吸烟有害). It then pivots to showcase some responsible public health adaptations, most notably Beijing's 2005 ratification of the World Health Organization's Framework Convention on Tobacco Control. The rest of the gallery, however, takes up a different subplot. It communicates a story of Chinese science and industry joining hands during the past few decades to safeguard consumers by producing a "safer cigarette." Pride of place in the Smoking and Tobacco Control Hall is given not to dangers, nor to public health experts and their techniques for limiting access to cigarettes. Instead, the emphasis is on providing consumers the choice to smoke "light" cigarettes, with filter tips and tobacco leaf processed in ways to retain taste but with "reduced tar and nicotine." The gallery's overarching storyline is one of progress by Chinese cigarette makers, fusing "quality" and "safety" signposted by displays featuring the 1959 trial release to government elites of China's first domestically produced filter-tipped cigarette, the introduction of brands blended with Chinese herbal medicines, industry researchers wearing white coats in laboratory settings, and a 2003 nationwide low-tar industry conference held in Kunming. The exhibit culminates with oversized images of five-mg-tar-per-pack domestic brands and exhibits of important constituent parts. Near the end of the third wall a pack of Zhongnanhai Super Lights, in airbrushed marketing copy, hangs triumphantly over glass cases of various innovations in filter designs and cut leaf formulations. There is no mention that "light" and "low-tar" cigarettes are canards,[23] despite empirical studies demonstrating repeatedly that such products can be even more dangerous than the regular cigarettes they replace.[24]

Several men, named and photographed, play prominent roles in the Smoking and Tobacco Control Hall. At its entryway is a portrait of Jiang Zeming, the preeminent figure in the third generation of the Communist Party's leaders, someone catapulted into power after the Tiananmen protests of 1989. Jiang's portrait was taken during his plenary speech at the 1997 World Conference on Tobacco or Health in Beijing, and is accompanied by platitudes from the plenary: Jiang praising citizens for adopting healthy lifestyles and discouraging smoking among youth. A few steps away, Chinese scientists, embodied by Professor Lü Fuhua (吕富华) of Tongji Medical University, are credited as pioneers in tobacco-control research. A foil here again is the United States. On a wall display, "Why People Smoke Cigarettes," it is explained that "in 1948, the Journal of the American Medical Association reported that . . . tobacco can relax mental tensions. Therefore there is no need to object to cigarette smoking." In the next panel, Professor Lü is credited for being one of the first scientists in the world to isolate tobacco's carcinogenic effects, publishing his earliest findings in a 1934 German medical journal and helping establish links between tobacco tar and cancer.[25]

The Ethical Animation of Slow Violence

China's tobacco industry has built a history museum to nurture an ethics of self among its employees, highlighting a truism of contemporary markets. The popularity of any commercial product—the automobile, single-serving can of beer, or mobile phone—does not emerge in a moral or temporal vacuum. This is likely to be even more the case with products manufactured on a vast scale and extensively criticized as harmful to health. To sustain long-term market presence, certain ethical and historical groundwork must be laid; otherwise the products may be ignored, rejected, or reviled. Declarations laced with deftly chosen virtues of local cultural import must be imposed upon consumers regularly, and so, it would seem, upon production personnel.

The deployment of history and technologies of self to texture social and political life in China is nothing new to scholars. Various branches of the party-state, in particular, have devoted much effort to shape what Chinese residents know and feel about significant events of the past.[26] These efforts have overlapped with governmental projects of subject making, cultivating citizens who conform to the diverse and changing needs of the party—initially revolutionary farmers, proletarian workers, and soldiers, and more recently government-friendly entrepreneurs, netizens, home buyers, car owners, and rural risk takers willing to provide cheap migrant labor.[27] Since 1949, China's state-run tobacco industry has tailored its products to help differentiate and sustain this array of selves, manufacturing a wide selection of cigarette brands, many symbolically segmented to suit specific categories of citizen subjects. It has also catered to needs of labor extraction, providing workers easy access to a highly addictive stimulant, nicotine, able to induce a wide range of behavioral effects.

Shanghai's tobacco museum also points to new tensions in China, notably rising anxieties regarding dangers posed to health by industry. Industrial sectors are increasingly being called to task, not for overworking people, but for imperiling health. To appreciate the scope of this social shift, consider Chai Jing's 2015 media sensation *Under the Dome*, an online air pollution documentary viewed over 150 million times within the first three days following its release.[28] As this shift of problematization grows, as new questions arise about toxins generated by industrial production, the challenge of labor management is no longer simply that of sustaining a workforce immune to sloth, corruption, party disloyalty, and discontentment. A new challenge exists: cultivating industrial employees' self-perception that they are noble individuals involved in unimpeachable work.

How successful the State Tobacco Monopoly Administration's Mayan-looking museum has been at boosting the morale of industry employees is beyond the scope of this chapter. Many galleries in the museum come across to me as blunt, even burlesque, attempts to shore up a workforce. But this is not a sentiment shared by any industry employees I have met who have toured the museum. Perhaps that is because the building is not a novel technology of self; it is one channel of a multivalent messaging program that tobacco companies and supervisory state agencies direct at employees. Other channels include intra-industry newsletters, websites, and magazines, as well as weekend entertainment offerings and holiday pageants. Taken together, all these media outlets help industry employees feel not just sated by their supersized salaries but also embedded within an ethics celebratory of cigarette manufacturing across China.

A final implication pertains to theorization regarding mass death, a topic of increasing discussion in the Euro-American academy during recent years. In assessing how to theorize what Rob Nixon has come to call "slow violence," Lauren Berlant has encouraged scholars along two lines.[29] She pushes us to recognize that the power to produce mass human annihilation is frequently diffused through market mechanisms over long periods. And she admonishes us to avoid overemphasizing the importance of intentionality and individual decision making by any single national sovereign. The China Tobacco Museum allows us to add to this; it suggests that we need to attend not just to diffusion when studying slow violence, but also diffusion into ethics of self. What we need is consideration of how the power to kill is inscribed upon and maintained by broad systems of actors, networks of what Judith Butler calls "petty sovereigns."[30] The cigarette business is a large-scale diffused machine of slow violence, one run by networks of petty sovereigns. How they, even in the midst of public health criticism, come to feel ethically animated, and remain so, is an important and little studied question. The China Tobacco Museum, I suggest, is an apparatus designed for such ethical animation. It is a technology of self, drawing heavily on tropes of exaltation and personification to vitalize the ethical outlook of petty sovereigns who work in perhaps the most important region of the global cigarette industry today. It is a museum of morals for a deadly business, a patent illustration that even the most harm-inducing branches of contemporary manufacturing contain forms of self-care.

Notes

1. Xinhua, "Reviving Cultural Power of China's Museums," *People's Daily Online*, November 29, 2012.

2. Within the Anglophone academy, Shanta Varma et al., "China: Tobacco Museum's 'Smoky' Health Information," *Tobacco Control* 14, no. 1 (2005): 4–5, and Fan Wang et al., "The Museum as a Platform for Tobacco Promotion in China," *Tobacco Control* (2014), http://dx.doi.org/10.1136/tobaccocontrol-2014-051633, have commented on the China Tobacco Museum. Passed over in these trailblazing yet relatively short treatments of the museum is the institution's mission to cultivate a sense of ethical purpose among tobacco industry employees. In North American

contexts, tobacco museums have been discussed by Peter Benson, *Tobacco Capitalism: Growers, Migrant Workers, and the Changing Face of a Global Industry* (Princeton, NJ: Princeton University Press, 2011), 6–7, 95–97; another form of tobacco industry memorialization has been considered by Evan P. Bennett, "Dubious Heritage: Tobacco, History, and the Perils of Remembering the Rural Past," *Agricultural History* 86, no. 2 (2012): 23–40. Museums devoted to tobacco manufacturing can be found today in numerous countries across Europe and elsewhere, including Cuba, Australia, Indonesia, and Japan.

3. Michael Foucault, *Technologies of the Self: A Seminar with Michel Foucault*, ed. Luther H. Martin, Huck Gutman, and Patrick H. Hutton (Amherst: University of Massachusetts Press, 1988).

4. My analysis here—regarding the relationship between the tobacco industry and how its employees understand themselves and their work—is different from two seemingly related investigations, both set in U.S. contexts. Drawing upon interview transcripts, Roger Rosenblatt, "How Do Tobacco Executives Live with Themselves?" *New York Times Magazine*, March 20, 1994, suggests that the most important mechanisms in play when it comes to tobacco executives' thinking are psychological ones of denial, sublimation, and rationalization and that these are facilitated by tobacco industry efforts including corporate responsibility spending. Scouring industry archives, Robert Proctor, *Golden Holocaust: Origins of the Cigarette Catastrophe and the Case for Abolition* (Berkeley: University of California Press, 2011), 292–99, documents the ways that tobacco companies in the late twentieth century developed discursive procedures to foster and police ignorance among their North American workforce, procedures he calls "internal agnotology." By contrast, extending Foucault's term "technology of self," my discussion documents ways that an institution, built by branches of the China National Tobacco Corporation, offers industry employees a set of ethical frameworks scripted within historical narratives, encouraging staff to imagine themselves as virtuous people doing important work for honorable causes.

5. "Tobacco Sector Contributes More to China's Revenue," Xinhua, January 15, 2016, http://news.xinhuanet.com/english/2016-01/15/c_135013454.htm.

6. Consider that between 1949 and the late 1970s it was rare to see advertisements for cigarettes (or any other product) in China. During the twenty years after Mao's death in 1976, however, China started looking much as it did in the first decades of the twentieth century, with advertisements for cigarette brands blanketing the country. See Sherman Cochran, *Big Business in China: Sino-Foreign Rivalry in the Cigarette Industry, 1890–1930* (Cambridge, MA: Harvard University Press, 1980), 30–34. Then again, since the 1990s new regulations have been promulgated, banning many forms of tobacco advertising and requiring (modest) warning labels on packaging.

7. Currently, over 97 percent of all Chinese women and about half of all men do not smoke on a daily basis, although many of these people are habitually exposed to secondhand smoke. Qiang Li, Jason Hsia, and Gonghuan Yang, "Prevalence of Smoking in China in 2010," *New England Journal of Medicine* 364, no. 25 (2011): 2469.

8. "Experts Raise Estimate of Death Caused by Tobacco-Related Illness in China," *People's Daily Online*, January 6, 2011, http://en.people.cn/90001/90782/90880/7252785.html.

9. Wang Chuanqing, *China Tobacco Museum Album* (*Zhongguo yancao bowuguan huace*) (Shanghai: Shanghai Tobacco Industry Press, 2004), i–ii.

10. Foucault, *Technologies of the Self*, 21.

11. Of the many self-referential industry museums to be found around the world a few examples include Argentina's National Petroleum Museum in Comodoro Rivadavia, the Malaysian Natural Rubber Museum, Michigan's Iron Industry Museum, the Chemical Industry Museum of China, and France's Aviation Museum (adjacent to an Airbus factory).

12. Here are some income data for southwest China provided by acquaintances of mine who reside in Kunming. By year two of employment, a formal production worker in a cigarette factory in Yunnan is likely to earn an annual pre-tax income of US$33,400 (about RMB 200,000). In contrast, by year four of employment, a formal production worker at Kunming Iron and Steel, also a state-owned firm, is likely to earn an annual pre-tax income of US$10,000. By year five of employment, a junior civil servant for the Kunming city government or the Yunnan provincial government is likely to earn an annual pre-tax income of US$13,400.

13. Li Zhang, "The Rise of Therapeutic Governing in Post-Socialist China," paper presented at the Annual Meeting of the American Anthropological Association, Chicago, April 12, 2013.

14. To be clear, as I understand them, terms like *technologies of self* and *ethics of self* are related but not interchangeable. Technologies of self are discursive and material projects designed to generate ethics among everyday actors involved in (sometimes highly specific, sometimes more general) fields of social life. What are ethics within my Foucauldian-informed stream of thought? As Bob Robinson, "Michel Foucault: Ethics," *Internet Encyclopedia of Philosophy*, 2015, ISSN 2161-0002, http://www.iep.utm.edu/fouc-eth/, explains, under Foucault's pen, ethics involves a "relation of self to itself in terms of its moral agency. More specifically, ethics denotes the intentional work of an individual on itself in order to subject itself to a set of moral recommendations for conduct and, as a result of this self-forming activity or 'subjectivation,' constitute its own moral being."

15. For discussion of British American Tobacco (BAT) in early twentieth-century China, see Cochran, *Big Business in China*.

16. Carol Benedict, *Golden-Silk Smoke: A History of Tobacco in China, 1550–2010* (Berkeley: University of California Press, 2011).

17. The English translation of the original Chinese-language caption is mine. The translation offered by the museum below the Chinese-language caption is inaccurate.

18. Joan Burbick, *Healing the Republic: The Language of Health and the Culture of Nationalism in Nineteenth-Century America* (Cambridge: Cambridge University Press, 1994); Frank Dikötter, *The Discourse of Race in Modern China* (London: Hurst, 1992); Wolfgang Schivelbusch, *The Culture of Defeat: On National Trauma, Mourning, and Recovery* (New York: Metropolitan Books, 2003); and Jian Wang, "The Politics of Goods: A Case Study of Consumer Nationalism and Media Discourse in Contemporary China," *Asian Journal of Communication* 16, no. 2 (2006): 187.

19. For further background on the 80 Nanchang Road factory, see an account, first published by the *China Elderly Post* on September 30, 2008, and since then widely circulated on Chinese-language websites such as "The Birth of the '132 Small Group': The Secret of the Special Tobacco Production in Zhongnanhai," March 12, 2015, http://history.people.com.cn/n/2015/0312/c372327-26683909.html.

20. Louisa Schein, *Minority Rules: The Miao and the Feminine in China's Cultural Politics* (Durham, NC: Duke University Press, 2000).

21. Thomas A. Arcury and Sara A. Quandt, "Health and Social Impacts of Tobacco Production," *Journal of Agromedicine* 11, nos. 3–4 (2006): 71–81; and Natalie M. Schmitt et al., "Health Risks in Tobacco Farm Workers—A Review of the Literature," *Journal of Public Health* 15, no. 4 (2007): 255–64.

22. Elizabeth Smith, "Corporate Image and Public Health: An Analysis of the Philip Morris, Kraft, and Nestlé Websites," *Journal of Health Communication* 17, no. 5 (2012): 582–600.

23. That scientific research has thoroughly proven "low-tar" or "light" cigarettes fraudulent is reflected in Article 11, page 9, of the Framework Convention on Tobacco Control, which refers to such products as "false, misleading, deceptive." See "WHO Framework Convention on Tobacco Control," 2005, http://whqlibdoc.who.int/publications /2003/9241591013.pdf?ua=1 (accessed August 5, 2015).

24. Proctor, *Golden Holocaust.*

25. Lü Fuhua's public biography states he was born in 1904 and studied in Germany during the mid-1930s, initially working under the renowned pathologist Karl Aschoff in a laboratory at the University of Freiburg, where Lü reputedly helped establish the link between tobacco tar and cancer on rabbit skin, and later working in labs at the University of Berlin. Extensive bibliographic searches of German-language medical publications have turned up no sign that Lü co-authored research findings during this period, as indicated by the China Tobacco

Museum. However, in the 1930s, German medical science was at the forefront of establishing the earliest laboratory evidence that tobacco is carcinogenic (Otto Schürch and Alfred Winterstein, "Experimentelle Untersuchungen zur Frage Tabak und Krebs," *Zeitschrift für Krebsforschung* [*Journal of Cancer Research*] 42, no. 1 [1935]: 76–92), a chapter in the history of science little known to most contemporary tobacco-control scholars (see Proctor, *Golden Holocaust*), so it is highly plausible that Lü participated in such laboratory inquiry during his first years as an overseas student.

26. Prasenjit Duara, "Historical Consciousness and National Identity," in *Cambridge Companion to Modern Chinese Culture*, ed. Kam Louie (Cambridge: Cambridge University Press, 2008); Joshua A. Fogel, *The Nanjing Massacre in History and Historiography* (Berkeley: University of California Press, 2000); Rana Mitter, "Behind the Scenes at the Museum: Nationalism, History and Memory in the Beijing War of Resistance Museum, 1987–1997," *China Quarterly* 161 (2000): 279–93; Jonathan Unger, *Using the Past to Serve the Present: Historiography and Politics in Contemporary China* (Armonk, NY: M.E. Sharpe, 1993); and Rubie S. Watson, *Memory, History, and Opposition under State Socialism* (Sante Fe, NM: School of American Research Press, 1994).

27. Ann Anagnost, *National Past-Times: Narrative, Representation, and Power in Modern China* (Durham, NC: Duke University Press, 1997); Lisa Rofel, *Other Modernities: Gendered Yearnings in China after Socialism* (Berkeley: University of California Press, 1999); Li Zhang, *Strangers in the City: Reconfigurations of Space, Power, and Social Networks within China's Floating Population* (Stanford, CA: Stanford University Press, 2001); Xin Liu, *The Otherness of Self: A Genealogy of the Self in Contemporary China* (Ann Arbor: University of Michigan Press, 2002); and Fengshu Liu, *Urban Youth in China: Modernity, the Internet and the Self* (New York: Routledge, 2011).

28. Daniel K. Gardner, "China's 'Silent Spring' Moment? Why 'Under the Dome' Found a Ready Audience in China," *New York Times*, March 18, 2015.

29. Rob Nixon, *Slow Violence and the Environmentalism of the Poor* (Cambridge, MA: Harvard University Press, 2011); Lauren Berlant, "Slow Death (Sovereignty, Obesity, Lateral Agency)," *Critical Inquiry* 33, no. 4 (2007): 754–80.

30. Judith Butler, *Precarious Life: The Powers of Mourning and Violence* (London: Verso, 2004).

PART THREE

Money and Malfeasance

CHAPTER SIX

Wrangling the Cash Cow
Reforming Tobacco Taxation since Mao

Matthew Kohrman, Gan Quan, and Teh-wei Hu

China's Contemporary Tobacco Industry in Outline

China's tobacco industry today is a unique hybrid. It is a self-labeled national monopoly headquartered in Beijing, yet it is heavily structured around regionalized revenue generation and jurisdiction. Created in 1982, the State Tobacco Monopoly Administration (aka, STMA; aka, the China National Tobacco Corporation) oversees a patchwork of localized industry/government cartels, divided into zones of influence, each delineated by state geography, historically along provincial lines.[1] Several characteristics have typified these cartels. The first is protectionism: encouraging the free flow of cigarette brands produced locally and impeding market availability of brands produced under the auspices of exogenous cartels. A second characteristic has been close coordination between regional government authorities (provincial, prefectural, and county branches of the party-state) and regionally based cigarette-manufacturing entities (state-owned enterprises that are today labeled as "companies" and "groups"). These manufacturing entities, although they report to the State Tobacco Monopoly Administration, are deeply enmeshed with regional governments, united under the promise of fostering "local" economic prosperity. A third characteristic has been aggressive manufacturing and sales of locally produced cigarettes. By 2000, a surfeit of cigarette factories had come to exist across the PRC. A map of China then, with its cigarette factories pinpointed, looks like an overfilled pincushion. Overcapacity of cigarette production in many parts of the country had become so significant by then that the State Tobacco Monopoly Administration began urging decommission of smaller factories and entreating bigger factories to suspend production toward year's end, as local markets became supersaturated with unsold cigarettes.

To thwart this monopoly-cartel system's ability to imperil people requires deep understanding of factors that have facilitated its formation and helped normalize its presence in the minds of both government bureaucrats and everyday citizens. One of these factors is outlined in this chapter, one which international tobacco control advocates today increasingly see as a promising tool for intervention. We describe the history of tobacco-related tax reforms, a history that, so far as we know, has never before been chronicled for an Anglophone audience. The authority to write tax codes in the People's Republic is controlled by the highest rungs of the Chinese Communist hierarchy. Party leaders have exercised that power numerous times in regard to tobacco, tweaking and rewriting codes on nearly a dozen occasions since the nation's founding. After outlining the shifting sands of Mao-era tobacco taxation, we give special focus to two waves of regulatory reform. The first started in the 1990s and the second began just as this book was going to press.

We ask: how have changes to tax policy textured the cartel side of the tobacco industry's monopoly-cartel hybrid? How have shifts in national tax regulations encouraged regional protectionism, local industry/government coordination, and overproduction? In what ways have anti-tobacco activists been trying to rewrite tax policies recently in order to delimit the ability of the cartels to foist trillions of cigarettes upon Chinese citizens every year? In the near future, how might tax reforms be designed to tame the cartels and satisfy modernist ideals of biogovernance ("growing" both tax revenue and healthier citizens)?

Tobacco Taxes before the 1994 Reform

Government authorities in China have been taxing tobacco in various ways since the reign of Chongzhen, the last emperor of the Ming dynasty (1627–1644). Communist leaders wasted no time in promulgating tax codes for tobacco in the twentieth century. Just months after the PRC's creation, the Government Administration Council of the Central People's Government (now known as the State Council) issued nationwide tax regulations. The PRC's Provisional Regulations on Goods Tax, released in January 1950, set a

40 percent rate on the sale of both "air-cured" tobacco leaf and "dark-fired" tobacco leaf (later called "flue-cured" tobacco leaf). Cigarettes were grouped by "quality" into four categories and subjected to goods tax rates ranging from 90 percent to 120 percent.[2]

Over the next decade, Beijing tweaked the young nation's tobacco tax code in several ways. A 1953 reform renamed the tax pertaining to flue-cured tobacco leaf a "commodity circulation tax," retaining 40 percent as its rate, and it increased the goods tax on air-cured tobacco leaf to 45 percent. The 1953 reform also switched cigarettes over to a new commodity circulation tax and lowered rates on the four categories of sticks, from 90–120 percent to a new range of 60–66 percent. In September 1958, the State Council issued draft regulations regarding a consolidated industrial and commercial tax, which became the sole tax applied to the sale of flue-cured and air-cured tobacco leaf (50 percent and 40 percent, respectively). The four categories of cigarettes were likewise placed under the new consolidated industrial and commercial tax system, and once more were assigned new and lower rates ranging from 40 percent to 69 percent.[3]

Beijing revised its codes again in the early 1970s and 1980s. In 1971, the Ministry of Finance set the industrial and commercial tax at a uniform rate of 40 percent for both flue-cured and air-cured tobacco leaf. In 1984, the State Council issued regulations on a new product tax, and the Ministry of Finance issued a set of implementation procedures. Under these new arrangements, tobacco products were divided into three types (cigarettes, cigars, and cut tobacco) with seven different tax rate categories. The number of categories for cigarettes remained the same, but the rates of taxation were adjusted downward once more. Air-cured tobacco and flue-cured tobacco became taxed at a uniform rate of 38 percent.[4]

What were the guiding logics of these various tax reforms pertaining to tobacco from the early 1950s to the late 1980s? Interviews we carried out in Beijing reveal at least three. The first was to ensure that tobacco taxes remained a steady source of revenue for the party-state but never a hindrance for the smooth functioning of the tobacco industry or for eager smokers. The second was that of furnishing provincial and sub-provincial authorities with clear guidelines on how to supervise the collection of taxes. The third logic was, as tobacco merchandise flowed from "field to shelf," that tax collection should occur primarily at points of production rather than at points of consumption.

All three of these logics have significantly textured key characteristics of China's cigarette cartels. The first logic is decidedly pro-industry, guaranteeing that policy makers in the young People's Republic went out of their way to ensure that tobacco taxation never impeded cigarette production and consumption. The second—by placing much of the responsibility of collecting, sorting, and releasing tobacco taxes in the hands of intra-provincial government agencies—gave those agencies the motivation to build self-contained industrial cartels. And, the third logic reaffirmed that provincial officials will not only promote local industries but also protect them.

To appreciate logic three, consider for a moment another major cigarette-producing country: the United States. During the United States' now century-long entanglement with the machine-rolled cigarette, if a pack of Lucky Strikes or any other brand has been produced in one state, say North Carolina, and sold to a smoker in another state, say Arizona, sales tax has been earned by the state where the smoker made his purchase. However, because commerce in the PRC was originally designed along Communist principles, the government has favored taxes tied to production and only recently has begun to include some retail-level taxation. Thus, a pack of cigarettes produced by Shanghai Tobacco in 1961, 1981, or 2001 and sold a year later to a smoker in the city of Guangzhou, generated almost no revenue for local authorities in Guangdong province, a financial reality still largely in place today.

Taken together, all three logics have meant that tax policy in China, at least until recently, has afforded intra-provincial government much incentive to erect manufacturing facilities, work closely with those facilities to promote the production and sale of local cigarette brands, and impede exogenous competition.

Turn-of-the-Millennium Tobacco Tax Reforms

China's leaders were disposed to make another round of changes to the nation's tax system when the 1990s began. This time, though, their intention was not to tweak, but rather to overhaul the system. A primary impetus for overhaul was local government defiance. Irrespective of industry, until the 1990s, Beijing required most taxes to be collected by local authorities and for a fixed percentage to be transferred from provinces to the central government treasury. After four decades of Communist rule, provincial governments were regularly underreporting taxes they collected, finding this an easy way to boost their finances. By the time Deng Xiaoping had retired from all his leadership posts in the early 1990's, such fraud was so prevalent and some of the provincial governments had become so rich that they began to offer loans to the central government for infrastructural investment and national security. This was a state of affairs that party leaders loathed, seeing it as a direct threat to their supremacy. In response, they authorized the State Council to rewrite tax codes, under a principle of having taxes flow as directly as possible from source to central government.

The 1994 "tax-sharing reform," which applied to all parts of China, was the most thorough change to tax regulations since the founding of the People's Republic. The reform introduced several modifications. One reform replaced older taxes with new ones. This eliminated the product tax, for instance, replacing it with two new major categories: VAT and excise tax. Another cardinal feature of the reform was infrastructural, building a network of central government tax offices around the country. A further change was definitional, regarding core and periphery. Taxes were redefined as (a) central government levies, to be collected directly by Beijing's new network of tax offices without involvement by regional governments, (b) local government levies, to be collected by intra-provincial government tax bureaus alone, and (c) shared levies, to be collected by the central government offices with a certain percentage to be later returned to the provinces. This brings us to one more important element of the reform: the introduction of rebate mechanisms, wherein each year the central government awards to provincial governments a certain percentage of taxes that Beijing has collected. A straightforward example here is VAT. All VAT goes directly to the central government, but in most cases 25 percent is annually handed back to the province from which it was sourced.[5]

The 1994 tax-sharing reform came to influence nearly all pillars of China's socialist market, no less so the country's tobacco industry. And when it came to tobacco, the reform certainly succeeded in fulfilling Beijing's goals of channeling most tobacco revenue directly to the central government, in large part because of the introduction of the VAT and excise tax apparatuses. These new apparatuses came to represent the bulk of tobacco taxation and, since their inception, the central government has controlled them with an iron fist. It is the local branches of the National Taxation Bureau that ensure the VAT and excise tax are collected at their assigned rates and that all the money is channeled directly into the central government treasury.

One might assume that, because it was a power grab by the central government and because of its timing, the 1994 reform package would have rolled back entrenched characteristics of China's tobacco cartels. In an age when Beijing was affirming commitments to global health and corporate efficiency, wouldn't such a power grab have dampened local industry/government alliances, market protectionism, and overproduction of cigarettes? After all, by 1994, Deng Xiaoping's program of "opening up" to the outside world was well rooted, and the Chinese Communist Party had become increasingly fervent about dissolving inefficient state-owned enterprises and playing by the principles of biopolitics, which upheld the expectation that a state authority is only as credible as its ability to protect the health of its citizens. The 1994 package and subsequent tweaks to it, in fact, did little to roll back key cartel characteristics. If anything, the reforms and local responses to them caused retrenchment.

For example, fine tuning of excise tax regulations during the run up to the millennium ensured that cigarettes, particularly cheap ones, remained commonplace. When first introduced in 1994, excise tax on cigarettes was set within a narrow band between 45 percent for Grade A cigarettes and 40 percent for all other cigarettes. Around the same period, Beijing loosened its control over retail pricing of cigarettes. These two moves incentivized manufacturers to increase their production and marketing of high-end cigarettes, at prices upwards of a hundred times more than the cheapest offerings. Appealing to consumers in a period of rapid social stratification and rising GDP, high-end cigarettes can generate much bigger profit margins for producers than cheaper brands. By the late 1990s, the comparatively thin margins of low-grade cigarettes had triggered a manufacturing shortfall of the brands to which most smokers were habituated. To rebalance the system, the State Council made an adjustment to excise tax rates in 1998. Cigarettes were regrouped into three different categories instead of two, as in the 1994 reform.[6] The groups ("A," "B," and "C") were based on cigarette pricing, and different excise tax rates were applied to each group. Under the new policy, Grade A cigarettes, with a factory price of 7,500 yuan or more (including VAT) per case, were subject to an excise tax rate of 50 percent; Grade B cigarettes, with a factory price between 2,500 and 7,500 yuan (including VAT) per case, were taxed at a rate of 40 percent; and Grade C cigarettes, with a factory price of less than 2,500 yuan (including VAT) per case, were taxed at a rate of 25 percent. (A case consists of 50,000 cigarettes.) As a result, many manufacturers began to open the spout again on the production of low-grade cigarettes, although we must emphasize that the industry continued to place most of its marketing energy into promoting its higher-end/more-profitable products.[7]

How else did the 1994 reform package shore up cartel characteristics? The package put new tax burdens on cigarette manufacturers by requiring them to shoulder a combined VAT and excise tax rate of around 50 percent. This prompted many manufacturers, under the aegis of their regional governmental allies, to seek out new profit mechanisms. More than a few realized that a loophole in the tobacco excise tax system provided an opportunity to lighten the weight of what manufacturers were supposed to pay out to the central government. The regulations of 1994 required that excise tax be levied only during the production phase, and that the base price used for estimating excise tax would be the factory price. Manufacturers, initially those in Yunnan Province and then others, realized that if they built their own allocation stations, which were permitted under the 1994 regulations, and allowed those stations to buy cigarettes from factories at a much lower factory price than that of the allocation stations owned by the China National Tobacco Corporation, the manufacturers could pay less excise tax.[8] Cigarette manufacturers and their local government allies were taking advantage of this loophole to such a large extent that by the turn of the millennium, in 2001, Beijing released a new round of tax tweaks. Beijing banned manufacturers' allocation stations and implemented a series of other minor changes to tax codes.[9]

Nowhere have end-of-the-millennium tax policies served to solidify the workings of China's tobacco industry more than in the countryside. The 1994 reform package tightened the terms under which tobacco leaf taxes were levied and collected. The reforms merged the agricultural and forestry specialties tax with the agriculture, forestry, livestock, and fisheries product tax, folding them under a new unified agricultural product tax. Seven categories of agricultural products (including tobacco) were taxable under this streamlined mechanism, with new rules stipulating that anyone producing agricultural products within the borders of the PRC would be legally obliged to pay tax to the state. Levies on air-cured and flue-cured tobacco leaf, previously set at different rates, were newly united in 1994 at 31 percent. Tobacco farmers were required to absorb these taxes when selling leaf, and local governments were urged to collect them and then use the money as needed.[10]

Providing local governments newly streamlined powers to collect taxes on tobacco leaf intensified an already extractive relationship between agriculturalists, cigarette manufacturers, and rural state authorities. Farmers in many parts of the country found themselves far more likely to have county and village cadres press them to grow easily taxable products like tobacco than was the case before 1994. Tobacco leaf had already become a comparatively easy farm product to tax as the post-Mao era (beginning in 1976) progressed because the outflow of tobacco leaf from the countryside was being increasingly regulated, unlike products such as fresh vegetables. Whereas farmers since the 1980s have found it increasingly easier to sell vegetables to anyone anywhere, regulations have tightened on tobacco leaf sales. Farmers today may only sell leaf at fixed prices to buyers working for agencies attached to local cigarette manufacturers and local offices of the State Tobacco Monopoly Administration.

The 1994 reform package further intensified local industry/government collusion to extract tobacco leaf from farmers because of the ways the package overhauled key terms for the financial responsibilities of governance. In short, the 1994 reform required that local authorities pick up far more of the tab for basic services in the provinces, such as health care and education, which had previously been financed by Beijing. Suddenly, local officials felt an urgent need to raise additional revenue.

So significant was the 1994 reform at supercharging leaf production that, within a couple of years, China's stock of flue-cured tobacco came to far exceed what manufacturers could unload in the form of cigarettes. This triggered the State Council to issue its 1998 "Urgent Notice Concerning the Adjustment of Prices and Tax Policies for Tobacco and Cigarettes." The Urgent Notice was a set of minor tweaks to the 1994 reform, designed to fine-tune the relationship between levies and farmer output. Its aim was to safeguard the industry's access to a well-balanced flow (not too large, not too small) of tobacco leaf.[11]

Using taxation to ensure a well-modulated and lucrative flow of tobacco leaf was affirmed anew not long after the fourth generation of the Communist Party's leadership took office. Because post-Mao market liberalization had been inequitably benefitting city dwellers, Beijing engineered a boon to the country's farmers in 2005. The National People's Congress abolished China's agricultural tax regulations, eliminating all Beijing-approved levies on farmers. This was a big win for most farmers nationwide. However, there was an exception. One agricultural pursuit, the People's Congress ruled, would remain firmly in the grip of China's tax system. Tobacco cultivation would continue to be taxed. The only change was a new name: "tobacco leaf tax." Otherwise, nearly all facets of the extant tax code covering tobacco leaf went untouched (from how the leaf levy gets collected, to methods for calculation, responsibility for payment, and level of taxation—20 percent—that had been set in 1998).

That tobacco leaf escaped the abolition of agricultural taxation is a testament to the cartel system, particularly the influence and vested interests of major tobacco growing provinces and their cigarette manufacturers. As Beijing prepared the 2005 abolition, we must assume that provincial governments in Yunnan, Sichuan, Guizhou, and elsewhere lobbied for an exception. Governments in these regions surely wanted to avoid being thrust into a position where they would have had to backstop county-level authorities hit hard by a loss of rural tax revenue. They surely wanted to avoid harming the extractive leaf system they had developed with local cigarette manufacturers, a system involving rural officialdom taking a pro-leaf position with farmers, leaf taxes paying for local government services, and farmers reaping relatively little from a highly lucrative resource. After all, without this extractive leaf system, farmers would be left free to choose whatever they wanted to grow and some would invariably switch to other, more profitable untaxable crops, a situation that would pinch local officials and put cigarette manufacturers at risk of losing stable inflows of their most important materiel.

Beyond leaf tax, a batch of other intricate rules introduced in the late 1990s has notably influenced the makeup of China's current tobacco economy. Consider the supplementary education tax and the urban construction and maintenance tax, both post-1994 inventions. They are earmarked to pay for vital aspects of governance in contemporary China, and both of these inventions are calculated for a province based on a fixed percentage of what that province generates in cigarette-friendly excise tax and VAT. In other words, the more cigarettes a province can manufacture and sell, the more money it will have on hand to pay for everything from schools and universities, to city parks, municipal hospitals, government office buildings, sanitation systems, and urban renewal projects.

Added to the mix were three other tax mechanisms, all rebate schemes, set up since 1994. The first has already been noted: 25 percent of the VAT collected each year automatically gets delivered from Beijing back to the province in which it was generated. The second rebate scheme is more complicated and involves both VAT and excise taxes. Since 1994, Beijing has returned money to provincial finance bureaus each year based on a set of excise tax/VAT calculations. The calculations are based on a fixed amount and a floating figure. The fixed amount is what Beijing determined each province earned in combined VAT/excise tax back in 1993. The floating figure is the difference in the combined excise tax and VAT that a province generates between 1993 and the current tax year. The rebate is based on a ratio (1:0.3) applied to the increase between the 1993 and current year figure. Thus, for instance, if during 1994, a province saw a 1 percent increase in the total excise tax and VAT generated within its borders, as compared to what it generated in 1993, its rebate component would be 0.3 percent of the increase. The third rebate scheme was created in 2002 and revolves around corporate income tax. Following the 1994 reforms, the central government collected and kept all corporate income tax tied to tobacco within a province. After 2002, 50 percent of this income tax was to be returned to the provincial government.[12]

However baroque in complexity, the message all these schemes have conveyed to many provinces has been the same. Whereas the 1994 reform introduced new macroeconomic challenges for provincial leaders, cigarettes offered a solution. In an age when keeping local GDP rates rising was the golden path to civil-service promotion, cigarettes offered a solution to a tax overhaul that, on the surface, allowed the central government to grab bigger slices of the nation's taxation pie and vacate its Maoist responsibilities of rule.

A net result was that, by the turn of the millennium, China's tobacco cartels were humming along with new vehemence. Regional authorities' zeal for building and protecting cigarette cartels surged to such a degree in this era that even the country's otherwise sober state-run media started to raise eyebrows. For example, in 2009, news outlets widely covered a Hubei case wherein the people's government of Gongan County was requiring that its cadres help peddle locally produced cigarettes and guarantee that "non-compliant" (exogenous) brands be shunned. Gongan cadres were issued sales quotas and instructed to criticize residents for smoking exogenous brands. Under the threat of the sanction, some cadres entered schools, inspected educators' ashtrays, and publicly shamed local teachers for smoking the wrong brands. Other cadres chose to appropriate government funds to buy out their individual quotas, and hid the costs as work-related expenditures.[13]

Tobacco Taxation Meets Tobacco Prevention

In 2009, Beijing once more announced rule changes to cigarette taxation. Beijing's purported goal for its 2009 reform was to offset downward fiscal pressure triggered by the then global financial crisis. Beijing feared that the crisis would undermine its inflow of taxes, so it announced that tobacco levies were going up. The existing ad valorem (Latin, meaning "according to value") rate for the excise tax on Grade A cigarettes would be raised from 45 percent to 56 percent and for Grade B cigarettes from 30 percent to 36 percent; and a new 5 percent ad valorem tax would be introduced at the wholesale distribution stage. In total, the 2009 reform would lead to a 16 percent increase in the excise tax for Grade A cigarettes and an 11 percent increase for Grade B cigarettes.[14] As to be expected, these changes piqued the attention of various interest groups. A relatively new group in the mix consisted of health experts united under the cause of tobacco prevention. These experts saw in the reform's announcement the glimmer of something they had been hoping for: tax hikes that might dampen cigarette consumption.

How did the 2009 reform package perform at offsetting the downward pressure the global financial crisis exerted on central government tobacco revenue? And how effective was the reform at fulfilling the hopes of tobacco prevention experts? The answer to the first question is that the package was a bonanza. It catapulted the central treasury's windfall from tobacco upwards by an estimated fifty billion yuan per year. This flood of new revenue, however, did little to decrease smoking rates as many tobacco-control advocates had hoped. Why? Because the 2009 rate increases were not passed on to consumers; retail prices of cigarettes were left unchanged. Tax reformers placed a pro-smoking wall around the consumer. All the increases in government revenue generated by the 2009 reforms were contributed from within the flush budgets of the tobacco industry.[15]

The disappointment that the 2009 reforms caused among health advocates speaks to an ongoing struggle over tobacco taxes underway in China. A group of international and Chinese economists have been ardently advocating changes to tax policy in China since the 1990s. With funding and support from international organizations, such as the WHO, the U.S. National Institutes of Health, Bloomberg Philanthropies, and the Gates Foundation, the economists have published a series of studies showing that raising cigarette taxes (resulting in an uptick in retail pricing) would be a double victory for the Chinese government. It would not only generate additional tax revenue, but also save lives and reduce medical costs by making smok-ing less financially viable for citizens.[16] The economists have presented their findings at numerous workshops in China, often inviting representatives from relevant government agencies—the Ministry of Health, Ministry of Finance, State Administration of Taxation, National Development and Reform Commission, State Council, People's Congress, and People's Po-litical Consultative Conference. They have also submitted policy briefs to top government leaders either through official channels or through private personal connections. All the while, they have been trying to leverage the World Health Organization's Framework Convention on Tobacco Control (FCTC), the global health treaty that Beijing joined in the early 2000s. A key plank of the FCTC is that member states should aggressively use tax increases, passed along to consumers, as tools for curbing cigarette smoking.

Some media observers thought that the economists had pulled off a public health victory in 2009 when Beijing announced changes to the to-bacco tax codes. However, it quickly became clear to the economists that such thinking was misguided. As noted above, because manufacturers ab-sorbed the 2009 rate increases, retail prices of cigarettes went unchanged, and smoking rates were consequently unaffected. Not missing a beat, the economists continued their advocacy. In 2010, they released a study that showed, all told, the effective tax rate for a pack of cigarettes in China was well below FCTC mandated rates. They calculated that the effective tax rate on a pack of cigarettes hovered somewhere between 40 percent and 43 per-cent, well below the WHO's 70 percent mandate.[17] The then best practices of the WHO indicated that when carrying out calculations in pursuit of the 70 percent level, tabulation of extant taxes should be restricted to those most effective at influencing consumption, or those holding the greatest sway over the retail prices of cigarettes relative to other goods and services, notably excise taxes.[18]

The question of how to measure the average tax rate on cigarettes in China came to a head in 2014. In late spring of that year, tobacco-preven-tion advocates organized a workshop in Beijing to celebrate the WHO World No Tobacco Day (May 31, 2014). Several economists at the workshop once again detailed that cigarettes in China have a relatively low effective tax rate, between 43 percent to 50 percent, citing an estimate based on excise tax and VAT data.[19] Within weeks, China National Tobacco Corporation (CNTC) economists counterpunched, releasing a competing assessment to the news media and to the State Council. The CNTC economists insisted that a technique for calculating the effective rate emphasizing only excise tax and VAT leaves out important types of taxation occurring in China as the cigarette flows along its supply chain from land to lip. Using their internal calculations, the CNTC economists claimed that the average total tax on a retail pack of cigarettes stood at 59.5 percent, considerably higher than tobacco-prevention scholars were estimating.[20]

Why did these CNTC economists suddenly deign to disagree with tobacco-prevention scholars, whom the CNTC had long ignored, and why in such a public way? The prevailing policy wind in Beijing had changed. By the summer of 2014, through internal communications, China's leadership had signaled to all involved that the key question to be settled was no longer *whether* the central government would raise taxes on cigarettes to better conform with the WHO and its Framework Convention. Rather, the puzzle to be resolved had become an issue of *how much* and *what kinds* of rate hikes would be promulgated. And to settle what had become the new problem of the hour, the debate between the competing camps of economists had crystallized around defining the baseline, defining what was then the relevant average tax rate on a pack of cigarettes in China. And these were the stakes: if government leaders agreed that the relevant current average tax rate was nearly 60 percent, as CNTC economists claimed, then the leaders would see China as already having nearly met the WHO-recommended target tax rate of 70 percent. Yet if leaders agreed that the relevant current rate was considerably lower, as claimed by the tobacco prevention economists, Beijing would likely insist on bigger rate increases.

At the heart of the matter was not only money, but also methodology: how to translate the muddle that is China's tax code into the WHO language of an "effective rate." To review, at the turn of the millennium, excise tax and VAT were not the only levies that the production and sale of cigarettes generated in China. An array of other fees were in the mix: the tobacco leaf tax, income tax, urban construction and maintenance tax, property tax, stamp tax, urban land-use tax, land value-added tax, and supplementary education tax, as well as post-tax profit contributions. Should these fees be included when setting a baseline and, if so, which ones?

A disagreement over translational methodology between the two camps of economists could have stretched on for years, but it was resolved relatively quickly. At an October 2014 workshop in Beijing, representatives from CNTC, the Ministry of Finance, and the State Administration of Taxation agreed to jettison their earlier methodology and adopt the WHO-endorsed method used by the tobacco prevention economists. What caused a sudden change in policy winds, such that two competing groups of economists were propelled together into workshops in 2014, and such that industry economists conceded important matters like definitional methodology? Certainly decades of anti-tobacco advocacy—domestic and international—lay the groundwork for the change. That said, two triggers seem to have been indispensable. The first pertains to the Third Plenary Session of the Eighteenth Central Committee of the Community Party held in November 2013. The committee recommended that China's tax codes for all commodities, including codes pertaining to consumption tax, should not only be tweaked again, but also significantly rewritten. To fulfill that recommendation, the Ministry of Finance and the State Administration of Taxation began carrying out discussions. Unlike in past waves of reform, however, China's leadership signaled that another group of stakeholders was to be given seats during preparatory discussions. On the grounds that China was to better fulfill its Framework Convention obligations, tobacco prevention researchers, including experts from the WHO, were allowed to attend the meetings and contribute models on how different kinds of reforms might influence government tobacco revenue and tobacco consumption. The second, and perhaps more important, trigger occurred not long after the Third Plenary Session. A renowned tobacco-prevention researcher based in Beijing intrepidly penned a letter to China's new paramount leader, Xi Jinping, asking him to support two FCTC-endorsed measures: an increase in tobacco taxes and the adoption of graphic warning labels. Equally dazzling was Xi's response. He did not let the letter disappear into the bureaucratic clutter. Instead, he reacted quickly and favorably, requesting that government agencies take steps to support the letter-writer's goals.

Tax code writers' initial responses to Xi's endorsement can be described as definitive and desultory. In May of 2015, Beijing opened a new chapter in its long liaison with tobacco tax reform. It announced that a further round of changes to tobacco levies would be forthcoming for an unprecedented purpose: disease prevention. It pronounced that tax changes would therefore involve increasing retail prices on cigarettes. Within weeks of the announcement, retail prices on packs of cigarettes in much of the country indeed rose for the first time in a decade. Brands priced above 20 yuan per pack increased about 2 yuan, whereas brands priced under 20 yuan rose between 0.5 and 1 yuan. This across-the-board uptick was accomplished through three rule changes: Beijing increased the ad valorem tax rate at the wholesale price level from 5 percent to 11 percent; it required wholesalers to pay an additional specific excise tax of RMB 0.10 per pack; and it barred the industry from defraying these increases, requiring instead that they be passed along to consumers.

We view the May 2015 reform as being, in equal measures, historic and insufficient. Following the 2015 reform, consumption of cigarettes in China recorded its first year of stagnant growth since 1995, with a minor drop of 2.4 percent. We concur with market analysts who have suggested that this modest drop was likely prompted in part by higher retail prices for an average pack of cigarettes brought on by the May 2015 reform.[21] But, no matter how historic, no matter how much it demonstrates the power of taxation to reduce human exposure to tobacco, the 2015 reform is patently inadequate. It only elevates the average effective tax on a pack of cigarettes in China to about 56 percent of the retail price, well below the 70 percent target recommended by the WHO. Furthermore, the reform does little to collapse the cavernous price differentials among brands or to address other systemic issues. Even the central government mouthpiece, the New China News Service, seems to agree with our assessment. Not long after the spring 2015 changes went into effect, Xinhua intoned, the reform will likely have "little impact."[22]

Our Policy Recommendations

We are hesitant to make policy recommendations in this chapter, lest they fall prey to the law of unintended consequences. We are nonetheless united in our opinion that the harm to health wrought by tobacco in China is unconscionable, that further taxation reforms must occur, and that future reforms ought to be unlike anything previously tried. Some of the reforms we recommend pertain to the issues discussed at length above: how tax policy in the People's Republic has come to incentivize provincial authorities to collude with local manufactures in the production and sale of cheap cigarettes, to protect local markets vigorously, and to pressure farmers to grow tobacco.

The first recommendation we make concerns tobacco leaf. Research over the last decade has shown that tobacco farmers in many regions of China are worse off financially because they grow tobacco instead of other crops.[23]

Also, because of the high labor demands of growing tobacco, farmers in China who cultivate these leaves are often left with little time to engage in other economic pursuits. Intensive tobacco agriculture, moreover, harms the soil, making it unsuitable for farming many types of crops for an extended time. For these reasons, cultivating tobacco should be unattractive to most farmers in China. A casual onlooker might have viewed Beijing's decision in 2006 to scrap all forms of agricultural tax, except for that levied on tobacco leaf, as an act of both progressive public policy and health enhancement. After all, what better way to hinder the supply of a crop like tobacco that is so harmful to public health than to make that crop more expensive for farmers to grow relative to other crops? However, as already noted, the 2006 reform encouraged tobacco leaf output and strengthened the alliance between the tobacco industry and county-level government authorities. Bereft of all other forms of agricultural tax, officials sitting in county seats colluded even more intensely with cigarette manufacturers to browbeat farmers into growing tobacco.

A timetable should thus be created to abolish the tobacco leaf tax. Opposition will likely come from tobacco companies and local governments, especially in intensive tobacco-growing regions. To attenuate such opposition, another central-government-managed rebate system could be created. This would be similar to the existing rebate system on the excise tax and VAT, but would instead be earmarked for county governments. The amount of rebate can be based on the average tobacco leaf tax of a county government during the three years prior to the reform. The introduction of this type of rebate, perhaps paid out of the existing excise tax system, would mean that government officials living in close proximity to farmers would come to have a less direct stake in tobacco farming, the hope being that such officials would therefore be less intrusive in agricultural activities, allowing farmers more latitude to choose what to grow than they currently enjoy. It would be vital for this rebate system to be time limited, perhaps running for no longer than five years after the tobacco leaf tax is phased out, and then gradually being shut down over a few years, so that local officials will eventually become entirely weaned off of tobacco taxation.

No less important, steps should be taken to increase what cigarettes cost consumers. However regressive (placing more of a burden on the poor than the wealthy), ratcheting up taxes that translate into retail price increases on cigarettes is a proven method for reducing smoker demand. Over the last decade, in the interest of public health, many countries have taken steps to raise tobacco taxes that push up retail prices of cigarettes. These countries have shown that, because of the low demand elasticity of cigarettes, raising what people must pay to smoke through tax hikes is a win-win for government. On the one hand, it saves lives by dampening tobacco consumption; on the other hand, it does not diminish the overall revenue that governments can expect to collect, at least not in the short to medium term.[24]

Adopting such measures in the People's Republic is complicated by the large price differential today between the country's most expensive and its cheapest cigarettes. It is imperative that any new tax increase, which gets passed along to what smokers actually pay out of pocket, does not end up widening the pricing differential of cigarettes, which would make it that much easier for smokers to respond to a tax increase by simply opting to switch to a brand varietal that is at the same price or lower than they were originally consuming.

Existing categories of taxation that are candidates for manipulation include two types of excise tax: specific tax and ad valorem tax. Of these, the best candidate for a rate increase is the specific tax. As this tax generates government revenue in proportion to how many cigarettes are actually consumed, raising its rate would not only elevate the cost to consumers of all cigarettes, but also narrow price gaps between cigarette brands.[25] Currently, the specific tax comprises only RMB 0.06 of the cost of a pack, too low to have any significant influence on tobacco control and fiscal revenue. We suggest that this tax be increased substantially to a range spanning from RMB 1 per pack for brands that are less popular among consumers to RMB 4 per pack for brands that are most popular.

Ad valorem forms of excise tax are a key contributor to the wide price gap between cheap and expensive cigarettes in China. To reduce the price-expanding effect of ad valorem excise taxation, we recommend the removal of a key division. At present, a higher ad valorem excise tax rate (56 percent) is applied to more expensive, Grade A cigarettes and at a lower rate (36 percent) to cheaper, Grade B cigarettes. This two-tier system amplifies the country's cheap-to-expensive-cigarette gap. It should be abolished and a unified rate, perhaps 56 percent, should be applied to all cigarettes.

We further suggest a change in the primary point of tax collection. Rather than the current system wherein tax collection occurs mostly at the level of the manufacturer, and to a lesser degree at the wholesale level, government agencies should collect taxes far more at the retail level. This will better ensure that, in the future, levies are more directly borne by the consumer (thus dampening user demand) and not simply absorbed into production/distribution costs. Having taxes collected more at the retail level would further serve to roll back protectionist impulses underlying the current cartel system.

Our final area of recommendation pertains to tobacco-prevention programming. Beijing needs to establish policies that require central government budgeters to dedicate a portion of tobacco taxes for funding the country's commitments to the World Health Organization's Framework Convention on Tobacco Control. After this treaty was created, a number of countries adopted practices for setting aside a portion of tobacco tax revenues to support FCTC implementation, but that has not been the case in China. Since 2006, Beijing has allocated funds for tobacco control as part of its central government subsidy system. The stated purpose of these funds has been to create a supportive national environment for tobacco prevention and to strengthen the capacity of local regions to implement the FCTC.[26] However, the amount of money Beijing has allocated has been woefully insufficient to address the country's yawning tobacco problem. More to the point, during the past decade tobacco-prevention advocates in China have been systematically starved by Beijing's budgeting practices, at the same time that overall government earnings from tobacco have ballooned to well over US$100 billion a year. Such bureaucratic starvation must end. Only then can China expect to turn the tide on what has become a diplomatically awkward and epidemiologically tragic development: the People's Republic ratified the FCTC in 2005, yet during the ensuing decade overall cigarette consumption nationwide jumped by nearly a third.

Notes

1. In the 1950s, cigarette factories in China were nationalized and many were merged. Shortly after it was founded in 1982, the State Tobacco Monopoly Administration (STMA) began encouraging mergers among cigarette factories, consolidating them into larger state-owned "companies" and even larger "tobacco groups." As in the 1950s, nearly all of these new waves of mergers have occurred within provinces. The resulting companies and groups are constitutive elements of what we are here calling cartels, cigarette-producing assemblages that are tied to spatial/administrative units, typically the province (省), but also sometimes the municipality (直轄市).

The operative political unit for the cartels is *shengji* (省级), which means "provincial status," a designation of political authority that the People's Republic affixes to provinces but also to major municipalities like Shanghai, Beijing, and Tianjin. The growth of the cartels has been contingent on the *shengji* authority enjoyed by provincial and municipal people's governments. In recent years, under the logics of economies of scale, STMA has been coordinating for some "tobacco groups" to expand across *shengji*-defined boundaries. Most important here have been tobacco groups historically based in Shanghai and Yunnan Province. STMA has helped these groups gain stakes in cigarette factories as far afield as Beijing, Xinjiang, and Hainan. These trans-provincial deals have involved carefully negotiated terms for how profits and taxes will be shared by the respective provincial and municipal authorities.

2. Chen Wendong, "History of Tobacco Taxation in China," in *Tobacco Taxation in China: History, Current Status, and Reform* (in Chinese), ed. Hu Dewei [Teh-wei Hu] (Beijing: Chinese Finance and Economics Press, 2009), 1–15.

3. Ibid.

4. Ibid.

5. Ibid.

6. For the purposes of simplicity, in the early 2000s the Ministry of Finance and the State Administration of Taxation returned to a two-tier system, again using the terms Grade A and Grade B. To some readers, there might be some confusion between this system and another one that appears in current literature about Chinese cigarettes. China's tobacco industry today uses its own internal categorization system for planning production and analyzing market share. Based on allocation price, the industry's system ranks the country's most expensive cigarette varietals as falling into the category Class 1A. From there the system runs down the price ladder as follows: Class 1B, 2, 3, 4, 5. Because our chapter is about taxation, we have opted to give primary emphasis in our discussion to the system favored by the Ministry of Finance and State Administration of Taxation.

7. Factory price is the price at which cigarette manufacturers sell cigarettes to allocation stations. In 1994, the rate of the newly created VAT for cigarettes was set at 17 percent, whereas excise taxes on tobacco products, drawing on an ad valorem calculation, were set at 45 percent for imported cigarettes and Grade A cigarettes, 40 percent for cigars and all other cigarette grades, and 20 percent for cut tobacco. See Chen, "History of Tobacco Taxation in China."

8. An allocation station purchases cigarettes from the manufacturer at the factory price and then distributes the cigarettes to wholesalers across the district under its management. (Ibid.)

9. In addition to banning manufacturers' allocation stations, the 2001 reform package required that a specific tax be introduced into the excise tax system, in-

volving manufacturers paying an additional 150 yuan per cigarette case. A new term, "allocation price," was also created—defined as the sum of the factory price plus the specific tax—and a procedure was added whereby the State Administration of Taxation must verify the validity of the allocation price, leaving little room for cigarette manufacturers to continue underreporting the excise tax. The 2001 tweaks further reduced the number of cigarette grades back to two. Grade A cigarettes were defined as those with an allocation price of greater than or equal to 12,500 yuan (not including VAT) per case and Grade B cigarettes were defined as those with an allocation price of less than 12,500 yuan (not including VAT) per case. The ad valorem calculation rate for excise tax was also adjusted to 45 percent for Grade A cigarettes and 30 percent for Grade B cigarettes. See Chen, "History of Tobacco Taxation in China."

10. Hu Dewei [Teh-wei Hu] et al., "The Reform of Tobacco Leaf Tax and Tobacco Control" (in Chinese), in *Tobacco Taxation in China: History, Current Status, and Reform*, ed. Hu Dewei [Teh-wei Hu] (Beijing: Chinese Finance and Economics Press, 2009).

11. Chen, "History of Tobacco Taxation in China."

12. Ibid.

13. Peter Foster, "Chinese Ordered to Smoke More to Boost Economy," *Telegraph*, May 4, 2009, http://www.telegraph.co.uk/news/newstopics/howaboutthat/5271376/Chinese-ordered-to-smoke-more-to-boost-economy.html *(accessed April 30, 2015)*; "Red Heading Document Selling Cigarettes" (in Chinese), *Xinhua News*, October 29, 2013, http://news.xinhuanet.com/politics/2013-10/29/c_117916582.htm (accessed December 14, 2013).

14. It should be noted that, because the cut-off point between Grade A and Grade B cigarettes was raised from 12,500 yuan to 17,500 yuan (not including VAT) per case, the ad valorem tax rate for cigarettes with an allocation price between 12,500 yuan and 17,500 yuan (not including VAT) per case actually dropped from 45 percent to 36 percent, which amounted to an overall decrease of 4 percent if the new 5 percent wholesale tax was also taken into account. The specific tax of 150 yuan per case was left intact. See Chen, "History of Tobacco Taxation in China."

15. Teh-wei Hu, Zhengzhong Mao, and Jian Shi, "Recent Tobacco Tax Rate Adjustment and Its Potential Impact on Tobacco Control in China," *Tobacco Control* 19, no. 1 (February 2010): 80–82.

16. Teh-wei Hu et al., *Tobacco Taxation and Its Potential Impact in China* (Paris: International Union Against Tuberculosis and Lung Disease, 2008); Hu et al., "Recent Tobacco Tax Rate Adjustment and Its Potential Impact on Tobacco Control in China"; Song Gao, Rong Zheng, and Teh-wei Hu, "Can Increases in the Cigarette Tax Rate Be Linked to Cigarette Retail Prices? Solving Mysteries Related to the Cigarette Pricing Mechanism in China," *Tobacco Control* (2011), doi:10.1136/

tobaccocontrol-2011-050027; Zheng Rong, Gao Song, and Hu Dewei [Teh-wei Hu], "Tobacco Tax and Tobacco Control—Global Experiences from the WHO Tobacco Tax Technical Management Handbook and Challenges for Tobacco Control in China" (in Chinese), *Policy Research on Raising the Tobacco Excise Tax*, ed. Shi Jian and Hu Dewei [Teh-wei Hu] (Beijing: China Taxation Press, 2013), 183–204; David Levy et al., "The Potential Effects of Tobacco Control in China: Projections from the China SimSmoke Model," *BMJ* 348 (February 18, 2014); and Lian Yang et al., "Economic Costs Attributable to Smoking in China: An Update and an 8-Year Comparison, 2000–2008," *Tobacco Control* 20 (2011): 266–72.

17. Hu et al., "Recent Tobacco Tax Rate Adjustment and Its Potential Impact on Tobacco Control."

18. See page 12 of *WHO Technical Manual on Tobacco Tax Administration* (Geneva: World Health Organization, 2011). Also see pages 10 and 16 of *IARC Handbooks of Cancer Prevention, Tobacco Control*, Vol. 14, *Effectiveness of Tax and Price Policies for Tobacco Control* (Geneva: World Health Organization, 2011).

19. Hu et al., "Recent Tobacco Tax Rate Adjustment and Its Potential Impact on Tobacco Control in China"; Zheng, Gao, and Hu, "Tobacco Tax and Tobacco Control"; and Bai Jingming, "Production Cost of Chinese Tobacco Industry and Analysis of Its Pricing and Mechanism" (presentation, Conference on Economics of Tobacco Control, May 29, 2014), a report prepared by Bai et al. from the Research Institute of Public Finance, Ministry of Finance, China (in Chinese).

20. Yan Dingfei, "A Debate between the Tobacco Industry and Tobacco Control Advocacy Groups on Using Tax as a Means for Tobacco Control: Full of Hope But Shivering in Reality" (in Chinese), *South China Weekend*, July 4, 2014.

21. Paul McClean and Lucy Hornby, "China Tobacco Sales Fall for First Time in Two Decades," *Financial Times*, June 20, 2016.

22. "China Hiked Its Cigarette Tax Early This Month, and the Extra Cost Has Pushed up Retail Prices," Xinhua, http://news.xinhuanet.com/english/2015-05/30/c_134284069.htm (accessed June 15, 2015).

23. Teh-wei Hu et al., "China at the Crossroads: The Economics of Tobacco and Health," *Tobacco Control* (June 2006) 15 Suppl 1: i37–41; Zhang Xiulan et al., "Cost-Benefit Analysis of Tobacco Leaf Production in China" (in Chinese), in *Tobacco Taxation in China: History, Current Status, and Reform*, ed. Hu Dewei [Teh-wei Hu] (Beijing: Chinese Finance and Economics Press, 2009); Virginia C. Li et al., "Tobacco Crop Substitution: Pilot Effort in China," *American Journal of Public Health* 102, no. 9 (September 2012): 1660–63; and Wang Chengyao, "Tobacco Leaf Tax Reforms, Controlling the Production and Consumption of Tobacco Leaves and Cigarettes" (in Chinese), *China Taxation Journal*, August 15, 2012: 5.

24. Prabhat Jha et al., *Tobacco Taxes: A Win-Win Measure for Fiscal Space and Health* (Mandaluyong City, Philippines: Asian Development Bank, 2012).

25. Teh-wei Hu et al., *Tobacco Taxation and Its Potential Impact in China* (Paris: International Union Against Tuberculosis and Lung Disease, 2008).

26. Ministry of Health Framework Convention on Tobacco Control Implementation Leading Group Office, *2007 China Smoking Control Report* (in Chinese), http://www.moh.gov.cn/open/web_edit_file/20070529161216.pdf (accessed December 14, 2013).

CHAPTER SEVEN

Tobacco Governance
Elite Politics, Subnational Stakeholders, and Historical Context

Cheng Li

Those interested in developing a more effective anti-tobacco campaign in China must first identify the stakeholders and obstacles to tobacco control, and then explore possible ways to persuade decision makers.[1] They must also better understand how political elites, local governments, and other interest groups interact when it comes to tobacco. Those are challenging tasks given that, in the PRC, tobacco production and use occurs within confounding shrouds of political power, commercial incentives, state-industry alliances, regional interests, government secrecy, and fabricated cultural norms. And, existing literature on China's tobacco industry and Chinese anti-smoking campaigns offers few insights into many key issues—including tensions between various levels of industry management and how tobacco governance can breed corruption.

China's top political leadership and the national tobacco bureaucracy are primary stakeholders when it comes to the governance of tobacco. One must not, however, downplay the role of subnational stakeholders in this multilayered "tobacco economy." Public health efforts to curtail tobacco in China irritate some of the most sensitive nerves of provincial governments, especially those that rely heavily on the industry's economic activity.

Public health advocates challenge Big Tobacco's authority by undermining some of its essential strategies for promoting cigarette use, including advertising, public relations, and political lobbying.

Today, the PRC is the world's biggest tobacco producer, the world's largest cigarette consumer, and the gravest victim of the many diseases caused by smoking. China is home to one-quarter of the world's smokers, who consume nearly half of the world's cigarettes. Over three hundred million Chinese citizens smoke every day. Cigarettes made in China account for nearly half of the world's total. Tobacco-related diseases cause 1.2 million deaths in the country every year, accounting for 12 percent of all fatalities. Those deaths are expected to increase to two million per year by 2020, with half of these people dying between the ages of thirty-five and sixty-four.[2]

Tobacco-control advocates want China's top political leadership and governmental agencies to become more concerned about this catastrophe. In particular, they wish to see China top leaders implement the Framework Convention on Tobacco Control (FCTC) with greater vigor, in recognition of the ongoing health crisis sparked by the cigarette epidemic and long-term harms to the Chinese economy caused by the manufacture and sale of this deadly and addictive product.

By contrast, local government officials in China seem to want something else. They are primarily interested in the economic growth of their localities. Those provinces and cities that have a sizable tobacco industry often aim to maximize the profits of the tobacco monopoly on their turf, with little concern for China's international commitments. Tobacco's long-term health and economic implications for the nation as a whole seemingly have no bearing on the thinking of these local governments.[3] In these provinces and cities, leaders (including party secretaries, governors, and mayors) have often personally participated in negotiations with national leadership bodies such as the National Development and Reform Commission (NDRC) and the State Tobacco Monopoly Administration (STMA), especially on matters of production, distribution, and revenue/tax divides. As for the tobacco companies themselves, they have been the most aggressive promoters of further tobacco development, using myriad strategic instruments—sometimes of an underhanded nature.

An incestuous relationship between government and industry in the cigarette sphere has complicated tobacco governance in China. The industry operates as an appendage of the government, but the opposite is also true. This shady and conflicted state-industry boundary is a defining feature of— and a major contributing factor to—China's tobacco enterprise. Tobacco-related corruption among government officials has been rampant, although the number of those caught and jailed is (thus far) very small. Some of the most widely publicized corruption scandals in China during the past decade or so have had roots in the tobacco industry, tainting political leadership at three different levels—national, provincial, and corporate. A reasonable conclusion is that more effective governance of the tobacco industry is urgently needed, especially in light of the public health catastrophe now in the making.

This chapter pursues two subnational levels of analysis. At the provincial level, attention is given to Yunnan Province, where tobacco is the biggest industry and tobacco taxes make up nearly half of local government revenue.[4] At the tobacco company or factory level of analysis, attention is given to the Hongta Group in Yuxi City, Yunnan Province. Examining these two prominent subnational entities in China's tobacco landscape, my goal is to reveal key tensions in tobacco governance. These include tensions over how different levels of government divide and allocate revenue. They also include tensions regarding how tobacco-related corruption penetrates politics and how provincial and factory leaders conduct political lobbying and form industry-based coalitions in Beijing.

Uneven Development and Local Protectionism

Uneven regional production of both tobacco leaves and finished cigarettes is a distinct feature of China's tobacco industry. Although most of China's provinces currently grow tobacco (twenty-seven of thirty-one, to be exact), the bulk of production has been concentrated in Yunnan, Guizhou, Henan, and Sichuan.[5] In 2001, these four provinces accounted for 61 percent of China's total land devoted to tobacco growing (see Table 7.1). According to one official account, in 2004 over 70 percent of tobacco leaves were produced in the central and western provinces, generally considered to be the less economically developed regions in China. Based on research by the American economist Teh-wei Hu and his Chinese colleagues, among the 510 counties that produce tobacco leaves, 185 have been designated national-level poverty alleviation counties. Others have been designated provincial-level poverty alleviation counties.[6]

Tobacco production is important for the economy in these regions. The contribution of the tobacco industry to local governmental revenue in some provinces and cities was 40–80 percent in 2004.[7] In the cities of Bengbu and Chuzhou in Anhui Province, for example, tobacco revenue and profits in 2009 accounted for 70 percent of total revenues and profits.[8] That same year, in a number of provinces (Yunnan, Hunan, Guizhou, and Henan,

TABLE 7.1.
Tobacco acreage in China in 2010 (by province)

Province	Tobacco acreage (1,000 hectares)	Flue-cured tobacco acreage (1,000 hectares)	Tobacco acreage as a percentage of the total sown area of crops	Tobacco acreage as a percentage of total cultivated area of tobacco in China
Yunnan	405.7	387.4	6.39	29.15
Guizhou	197.8	184.9	4.14	14.21
Henan	127	111.7	0.90	9.13
Sichuan	121.5	102.3	1.28	8.73
Hunan	96.3	93	1.20	6.92
Hubei	74.6	55.9	0.99	5.36
Fujian	69	68.5	3.05	4.96
Chongqing	52.6	43.9	1.59	3.78
Shandong	45.7	45.3	0.42	3.29
Heilongjiang	37.3	32.3	0.31	2.68
Shaanxi	36.8	36	0.89	2.65
Guangdong	24.7	22.6	0.55	1.78
Jilin	23.4	12.9	0.46	1.68
Guangxi	20.1	16.3	0.34	1.44
Jiangxi	18.1	17.5	0.34	1.30
Liaoning	12.5	11.4	0.32	0.90
Anhui	10.4	10.2	0.12	0.75
Gansu	4.4	3.5	0.11	0.32
Inner Mongolia	4.2	2.9	0.06	0.30
Shanxi	3.8	3.6	0.10	0.27
Hebei	3	2.4	0.03	0.22
Zhejiang	1.5	0	0.06	0.11
Xinjiang	0.6	0.6	0.01	0.04
Ningxia	0.4	0.4	0.04	0.03
Jiangsu	0.2	0	0.01	0.02
Qinghai	0.2	0	0.04	0.01
National total	1,391.9	1,265.4	0.88	100

NOTE: In Beijing, Shanghai, Tianjin, and Tibet tobacco acreage is zero.
SOURCES: National Development and Reform Commission (NDRC) Research Institute of Industrial Economics and Technology, *Woguo yancao chanye zhuanxing yanjiu* (A study of the transition of China's tobacco industry), February 10, 2011, pp. 3–4. Also *2010 nian Zhongguo tongji nianjian* (China statistics yearbook 2010) (Beijing: Zhongguo tongji nianjian chubanshe, 2011).

for example), tobacco revenue and profits accounted for double-digit percentages of governmental revenues and profits.[9] Even in Shanghai, with its impressively large, diverse, and well-developed economy, cigarettes still accounted for 10 percent of the city's total tax revenues in 2007.[10]

Table 7.1 also shows that several provinces grow a great deal more tobacco than is average for the nation as a whole, measured by the percentage of total acreage devoted to this crop: in Yunnan, 6.4 percent of all agricultural land is devoted to tobacco; this is followed by Guizhou at 4.1 percent, Fujian at 3.1 percent, Chongqing at 1.6 percent, Sichuan at 1.3 percent, and Hunan at 1.2 percent. In none of China's other provinces does that proportion exceed one percent. Nationwide, according to a recent NDRC report, there are over 500 counties and 4,400 towns and villages that still plant tobacco, with 570,000 households and 22 million farmers engaged in tobacco cultivation.[11] Many of these are located in Yunnan and Guizhou.

Tobacco Tax Divided between Central and Local Governments

Before 1980, provincial governments, rather than Beijing, managed most aspects of China's tobacco industry. Two major events—the establishment of the STMA and the China National Tobacco Corporation (CNTC) in the early 1980s and the central-local tax distribution system (*fenshuizhi*) adopted in 1994—have had profound impacts on the management and business incentives of this industry in terms of Beijing-provincial relations. In general, the tobacco industry contributes three types of revenue income: 1) tax revenue, 2) profits, and 3) other types of taxes and fees. Tax revenue is the main source, while the other two are small by comparison.[12]

Table 7.2 shows the distribution of tobacco-related tax revenue in China in 2009. Total tobacco tax revenue was 385 billion yuan, of which 208 billion (54 percent) was from the tobacco consumption tax. Value-added tax and corporate income tax accounted for 23 percent and 13 percent, respectively. Urban maintenance and construction tax, tobacco leaf tax, and tobacco business personal income tax were each around 1–5 percent of the total. Other taxes—such as tobacco production-related property taxes, stamp duties, urban land use tax, and land value-added tax—were trivial.

Table 7.3 illustrates the distribution of tobacco tax revenue between the central and local governments. The tobacco consumption tax, which accounts for the largest portion of the tobacco-related tax, goes entirely to the

TABLE 7.2.
Tobacco-related tax revenue in China, 2009

Tax type	Amount of tax collected (billion yuan)	Percentage of total
Tobacco consumption tax	208.4	54.2%
Value-added tax	87.3	22.7%
Corporate income tax	48.3	12.6%
Urban maintenance and construction tax	19.4	5.0%
Tobacco leaf tax	8.1	2.1%
Tobacco business personal income tax	4.0	1.0%
Other taxes*	9.1	2.4%
Total	384.6	100.0

* Other taxes include tobacco production-related property taxes, stamp duty, urban land use tax, and land value-added tax.

SOURCE: Wang Li et al., *Zhongguo shuiwu nianjian 2010* (Tax yearbook of China, 2010) (Beijing: Zhongguo shuiwu chubanshe, 2010), 552–95. Calculated and tabulated by Cheng Li.

TABLE 7.3.
Distribution of tobacco tax revenue between China's central and local governments

Tax revenue for the central government	Tax revenue shared by the central & local governments	Tax revenue for local governments
Tobacco consumption tax	Value-added tax (75% for central and 25% for local)	Tobacco leaf tax
Corporate income tax (for firms founded after 2002)		Urban maintenance and construction tax
	Corporate income tax (for firms founded before 2002, 60% for central and 40% for local)	Cigarette sales tax
		Tax surcharge for education
	Tobacco business personal income tax (60% for central and 40% for local)	

SOURCE: Hu Dewei [Teh-wei Hu], ed., *Zhongguo yancao shuishou: lishi yan'ge, xianzhuang ji gaige* (Tobacco tax in China: Past development, current status, and prospects for reform) (Beijing: Zhongguo shuiwu chubanshe, 2009), 63. Tabulated by Cheng Li.

central government. The central government also receives 75 percent of the value-added tax, the second largest portion of tobacco-related taxes. As for the third largest portion, the corporate income tax, the central government collects 100 percent from firms established after 2002 and 60 percent from those founded before that year. The central government and local governments also share the tobacco business personal income tax: 60 percent for the central and 40 percent for the local.

Local governments receive 25 percent of the value-added tax on tobacco, explaining why they pay so much attention to it. Some other relatively minor tobacco-related taxes—such as the tobacco leaf tax, urban mainte-nance and construction tax, cigarette sales tax, and tax surcharge for educa-tion—go entirely to local governments.[13] According to a study conducted by PRC scholars, between the years 1994 and 2000, on average, the central government received 81 percent of China's total revenue from tobacco taxes, with the remainder going to local governments.[14] Even though the central government collects a large percentage of all tobacco-related taxes, the small sum that goes to local governments can, in fact, still be a major source of revenue for certain provinces. As an NDRC report released in 2011 indi-cated, the revenue from tobacco taxes in China is higher than from any other product, and tax revenues from tobacco can be like "printing money" for some provinces.[15] This is especially true in the case of Yunnan Province, which has come to be known as the "Tobacco Kingdom."

Provincial Level Analysis: The Case of Yunnan

Yunnan is the epicenter of Chinese tobacco production. For the past two de-cades, Yunnan's tobacco industry has played the most prominent role in both the local provincial economy and the national tobacco industry. Yunnan has led all provinces in the "number of famous brands, total output, sales volume, portion of market, foreign exchange earnings, tariffs, and facilities and tech-nology."[16] As mentioned above, in recent years, Yunnan's tobacco acreage has accounted for 29 percent of the total cultivated land devoted to tobacco in China, the province's trading volume of cigarettes constituted 28 percent of the national total, and tobacco-related taxes contributed to 49 percent of local government revenue. In 2007, the province supplied one-third of China's flue-cured tobacco and one-fifth of the country's manufactured cigarettes.[17]

Yunnan has not always been the PRC's leading province in terms of to-bacco production, however. As recently as 1978, Yunnan was only the nation's third largest flue-cured leaf-producing province, after Henan and Shandong. Irene Eng, a scholar at the Hong Kong University of Science and Technol-ogy, has observed that Yunnan's cigarette production that year accounted for only 5 percent of national output, ranking sixth after Henan (14 percent), Shandong (11 percent), Anhui (7 percent), Shanghai (7 percent), and Hebei (7 percent).[18]

It was not until the 1980s that Yunnan's tobacco flower came into full bloom. In 1979, Yunnan's tobacco production contributed only 7 percent of the province's GDP. By 1995, however, that figure had increased to a remarkable 30 percent. Similarly, whereas in 1978 tobacco revenue (taxes and profits combined) made up only 25 percent of the province's total governmental revenue, by 1988 that had increased to 63 percent—and would reach nearly 80 percent by 1997.[19] In the late 1990s, approximately ten million of Yunnan's forty million people were involved in growing, processing, or selling tobacco in one form or another.[20] There is no greater concentration of tobacco enterprise anywhere in the world.

What contributed to the rapid development of tobacco in Yunnan in the late 1970s and early 1980s? The decline of sugar cane farming as a result of large imports of sugar from Cuba was certainly one factor, along with the growing availability of sugar substitutes, both of which led provincial leaders to look to alternative sources of agro-industrial development. A substantial rise in tobacco prices and tax revenues in the mid-1980s also created new incentives for local leaders to promote tobacco. The most important reason for the triumph of tobacco in Yunnan, however, can be traced to certain personal and political connections of top provincial leaders, who managed to rise in political power through tobacco linked economic initiatives.

Table 7.4 provides an overview of top leaders (party secretaries and governors) of Yunnan Province from 1977 to the present. Most seem to have advanced their political careers with the help of a powerful patron in either Beijing or Yunnan. Several, especially those born in Yunnan, played a critical role in the rapid development of regional tobacco. Pu Chaozhu and He Zhiqiang, for example, natives of the province, had the longest tenures as top leaders in the province in recent history. Pu served as governor of Yunnan from 1983 to 1985 and then as provincial party secretary from 1985 to 1995; He Zhiqiang served as governor for fourteen years (from 1985 to 1998), during which Yunnan saw its tobacco industry grow remarkably fast. Other top provincial leaders, in contrast, served for only a few years. For example, Gao Yan, a protégé of former premier Li Peng, served as provincial party secretary of Yunnan from 1995 to 1997. Gao, who later came under investigation for corruption charges, reportedly defected to Australia in 2002. He is one of the highest-ranking officials to have defected to the West in the PRC's history.

Pu Chaozhu's personal background and his decisive role in the development of Yunnan's tobacco industry are revealing. He was born in Yuxi City in Lixian County (now Huaning), Yunnan, in 1929. He spent almost his entire career in the province, including his involvement in pre-1949 Communist student movement activities and time served in the People's Liberation Army (PLA). In the 1950s, he served as head of the Tax Bureau of Yuxi, from where he moved on to become deputy head and then head of the Department of Finance and Commerce of Yuxi. From 1979 to 1983, Pu served as party secretary of Yuxi Prefecture, home to the Hongta Cigarette Factory (the heart of today's powerful Hongta Group). Pu was instrumental in expanding Hongta's factory, helping to generate financial investments and the purchase of state-of-the-art cigarette making machines (including machines from British manufacturers).[21] With the help of his mentor, Yunnan party secretary An Pingsheng, Pu made a great leap forward when he was promoted from a prefectural leader to deputy provincial party secretary and then governor of Yunnan in 1983.

As governor, Pu made the development of Yunnan's tobacco industry a top priority. In the following three years, the province purchased advanced tobacco production equipment from the United Kingdom and Japan. In 1984 alone, Yunnan purchased foreign equipment worth US$50 million, a large expenditure at that time, especially for a poor province.[22]

Pu also adopted two new policy initiatives for Yunnan's tobacco industry. The first was that the province would take advantage of its high-quality tobacco leaves to produce more high-grade (i.e., expensive) cigarettes. As a result, the proportion of high-grade cigarettes in Yunnan's total production increased from 3 percent in 1983 to 30 percent in 1995.[23] During that period, three high-grade brands of cigarettes—Hongtashan, Yuxi, and Yunyan—became the best-known brands of cigarettes in all of China. Second, Pu allocated more resources and instituted favorable policies to help the rapid growth of the Hongta Group, located in the city where he had been born and had served as a local leader. With strong support from Pu and the provincial government, Hongta adopted a "triple play" system to unify tobacco farming, production, and sales. Consequently, Hongta became more competitive in both national and international markets. In 1991, Hongta became the first tobacco factory in the country to earn the title "National Level Enterprise."[24]

During his tenure as party secretary, Pu and his colleague, Governor He Zhiqiang, frequently lobbied national leaders (such as Premier Li Peng) in person or by letter to adopt favorable policies for Yunnan's tobacco industry, including tax reductions for poverty and natural disaster relief.[25] In his

TABLE 7.4.
Provincial party secretaries and governors of Yunnan, 1977–2011

Name	Tenure	Year of birth	Birthplace	Main career experience	Political background
Party Secretary					
An Pingsheng	1977–85	1917	Shaanxi	Secretary of Guangxi (1975–77), Deputy Secretary of Guangxi(1968–75)	Protégé of Tao Zhu (former Politburo Standing Committee member)
Pu Chaozhu	1985–95	1929	Yunnan	Governor of Yunnan(1983–85), Secretary of Yuxi Prefecture (1979–83)	Protégé of An Pingsheng
Gao Yan	1995–97	1942	Jilin	Governor of Jilin (1992–95), Vice-Governor of Jilin (1988–92)	Protégé of Li Peng (former premier), defected to Australia in 2002
Linghu An	1997–2001	1946	Shanxi	Deputy Secretary of Yunnan (1993–97), Vice-Minister of Labor (1989–93)	Princeling* (son of Li Dongye [Linghu Junwen], Minister of Metallurgical Industry), and Tuanpai
Bai Enpei	2001–11	1946	Shaanxi	Secretary of Qinghai (1999–2001), Governor of Qinghai (1997–99), Deputy Secretary of Inner Mongolia (1993–97)	Unknown
Qin Guangrong	2011–	1950	Hunan	Governor of Yunnan (2006–11), Vice-Governor of Yunnan (2003–6), Secretary of Changsha (1993–98)	Tuanpai**
Governor					

Name	Years	Birth year	Province	Position	Notes
An Pingsheng	1977–79	See above			
Liu Minghui	1979–83	1914	Jiangxi	Vice-Governor and Deputy Secretary of Yunnan (1968–79)	Protégé of Chen Xilian (former Politburo member and Vice Premier)
Pu Chaozhu	1983–85	See above			
He Zhiqiang	1985–98	1934	Yunnan	Vice-Governor of Yunnan (1983–85)	
Li Jiating	1998–01	1944	Yunnan	Vice-Governor of Yunnan (1993–98), Assistant Governor of Heilongjiang (1992–93), Mayor of Harbin (1991–92)	Protégé of Wei Jianxing (former Politburo Standing Committee member), purged in 2001 and received a death sentence (on corruption charges), suspended for two years and then commuted to life imprisonment
Xu Rongkai	2001–6	1942	Chongqing	Deputy Chief-of-staff of the State Council (1998–01), Deputy Director of Research, State Council (1993–98)	Protégé of Li Lanqing (former Politburo Standing Committee member)
Qin Guangrong	2006–11	See above			
Li Jiheng	2011–	1957	Guangxi	Deputy Secretary of Yunnan (2006–11), Deputy Secretary of Guangxi (2003–6)	Unknown

* Princelings are children of high-ranking officials.
** Tuanpai (or "League faction") refers to an informal faction within the Chinese Communist Party consisting of leaders who moved up through the Chinese Communist Youth League.
SOURCE: Xinhua News Agency. Tabulated by Cheng Li.

memoir published in 2003, Pu stated proudly that the expansion of Yunnan's tobacco industry and the Hongta Group in particular were his greatest legacies.[26] One may argue that this sort of mythmaking exaggerates the role of provincial chiefs like Pu and He. Nonetheless, the input and decisions made by key individuals in a particular region's industry can be of enormous import in a political system lacking more formal policy-making processes.

Tobacco: The Largest Source of Official Corruption in Yunnan?

Pu Chaozhu and He Zhiqiang were both suspected of tobacco-related corruption throughout the 1990s, but neither was ever charged.[27] Some analysts observed that government officials in Yunnan were particularly famous for "writing little notes" (*pi xiaotiaozi*) to tobacco companies and factories in the province in order to obtain, free of charge, large quantities of high-grade cigarettes. Such seemingly trivial acts could actually turn corrupt officials into instant millionaires.[28]

And yet, over the past decade, relatively few officials in the tobacco industry, including those at various levels of the STMA, have ever been charged with corruption. According to official data from 2009, 7,730 people nationwide were arrested for tobacco-related illegal activities that year, and 3,905 were sentenced to prison.[29] In contrast, in that same year, only twenty-two officials in the tobacco industry were arrested on corruption charges.[30] A year earlier, in 2008, only two industry officials were sent to prison for corruption.[31] This is disturbing, because in the eyes of many in the Chinese public, officials in the various levels of the STMA, including those in the poorest areas, have long been notorious for their profligacy and corruption. In 2011, the official *China Youth Daily* revealed that in a poor county-level STMA bureau in Guangdong Province, officials spent 130,000 yuan for a banquet in the STMA's own cafeteria. Their monthly expenditure for business meals was an astonishing 2 million yuan.[32]

Yunnan's two largest corruption scandals in the past decade or so were tobacco-related. The first resulted in the purge and death sentence of Li Jiating, Yunnan's former governor. The second involved Li Wei, a woman who began her career in tobacco smuggling and later became the "shared mistress" (*gonggong qingfu*) of several Chinese ministerial and provincial leaders. Over the past decade, she has been involved in a number of large-scale corruption cases. These two scandals are examined in more detail below.

THE CASE OF LI JIATING, FORMER GOVERNOR OF YUNNAN

Li Jiating, of Yi ethnicity, was born into a poor farming family in Honghe Prefecture's Shiping County (near Yuxi City) in Yunnan in 1944. As a young man, he attended Tsinghua University in Beijing from 1963 to 1968. After graduation, he worked in Harbin City, Heilongjiang Province, for twenty-four years, during which time he became a protégé of Wei Jian-xing, a heavy-weight politician who later served on the Politburo Standing Committee with responsibilities in the area of party discipline. Both Wei and Li worked in the same machine industry in Harbin through most of the 1970s; Wei served as mayor of Harbin from 1981 to 1983. When Wei became head of the powerful CCP Organization Department in Beijing in 1985, Li was appointed executive vice-mayor of Harbin. Li was later promoted to mayor of Harbin and assistant governor of Heilongjiang before being transferred back to his native province in 1992. In Yunnan, Li served as executive vice-governor; and in 1998, one year after Wei became a member of the Politburo Standing Committee, Li was appointed governor of Yunnan.

As a native son of Yunnan, and with such a powerful patron in Zhong-nanhai, Li had an auspicious beginning as provincial governor. He also impressed some of the top leaders in Beijing, including General Secretary Jiang Zemin, for his work in organizing the 1999 Kunming International Horticultural Expo.[33] Li was reported to have formed strong ties with Deng Xiaoping's widow, Zhuo Lin, who herself was born in Yunnan's Xuanwei County. (Zhuo's father had served as head of the county Tobacco and Wine Monopoly Bureau for the Nationalist government.) Li was also a close friend of Deng Xiaoping's son Deng Pufang. During his tenure as a leader in Yunnan from 1993 to 2001, Li frequently went to Beijing to lobby the central government (sometimes through his friends in high places) for tax reductions and financial subsidies for the province, especially for its biggest moneymaker—tobacco.[34]

Li also developed a very close relationship with major tobacco factories in the province. The Xinhua News Agency reported (after he was arrested) that Li's five-bedroom residence looked like a cigarette shop (*yanpu*), filled with all sorts of expensive cigarettes sent to him as gifts by cigarette makers.[35] The two major corruption charges against him were both tobacco related. The first occurred in 1994, when Li Jiating planned to send his son, Li Bo, a graduate of the Harbin Institute of Technology, to study abroad. Sending children to study overseas is a common practice among provincial leaders in Yunnan, as elsewhere in China. One example is Pu Xiang, the son of Li's boss, then provincial party secretary Pu Chaozhu. The province sent Pu Xiang, then a medical doctor in Kunming, to study in the United States as a visiting scholar in 1992. Pu Xiang later abandoned his medical career and emigrated to Canada, where he became a businessman heavily engaged in trade with his native province back in China.[36]

To obtain the funding for his son's study abroad, Li Jiating asked Hong Kong businessman Yang Rong, chairman of the Huande Hong Kong Co., Ltd., for help in 1994. Yang first bribed a police bureau in Guangdong with 500,000 yuan to grant Li Bo a regular permit to visit Hong Kong and later wired a total of 6.4 million HK dollars to Li Bo's bank account in Hong Kong. To return the favor, Li Jiating called the head of the Yunnan Province's STMA to "take care of" Yang Rong's request to export 13,000 boxes of cigarettes, from which Yang immediately profited to the tune of over 10 million yuan.[37] Li Bo, however, never studied abroad. Instead he too became an entrepreneur, engaging in real estate, land leasing, automotive sales, road construction, and other businesses in Kunming, Harbin, and Hong Kong. He was, for instance, the principal representative for the Audi auto company in Yunnan.

Li Jiating was arrested in the fall of 2001. He was accused of numerous illegal activities, including taking bribes totaling 21 million yuan, for which he received a death sentence in 2003 (his sentence was suspended for two years and then commuted to life imprisonment). His son, Li Bo, was sentenced to fifteen years in prison. Soon after Li Jiating was arrested, his wife, Wang Xiao, who had been his schoolmate at Tsinghua University, committed suicide.

The tragedy of the Li family was apparently linked to the power of the tobacco industry and reflected the greed of government officials in this enormously lucrative business. This perhaps helps explain Li Bo's famous words, widely circulated on the Chinese Internet: "Which princeling does not do business nowadays? A princeling who does not possess several millions should not hang around with other princelings who will naturally look down on you."[38] Not surprisingly, many Yunnan officials and their family members seem to be interested in getting a piece of the province's over 70 billion yuan in revenue from the tobacco industry and its 40 billion yuan worth of brand name cigarettes.

No corruption scandal in the PRC's history has involved so many senior-level leaders in so many different sectors as the case of Li Wei, which involved about a dozen ministerial/provincial leaders, several of whom are now in prison serving life sentences. These include the former governor of Yunnan Li Jiating, a former deputy party secretary of Shandong by the name Du Shicheng, former Sinopec CEO Chen Tonghai, former vice president of the Supreme Court Huang Songyou, former vice-mayor of Beijing Liu Zhihua, former vice president of the Development Bank Wang Yi, and former assistant minister of public security Zheng Shaodong.[39]

It is also believed that other senior leaders had affairs with Li Wei. This includes former minister of finance Jin Renqing and former minister of foreign affairs Li Zhaoxin.[40] A Chinese-language book, published overseas, used the term "shared mistress" with reference to Ms. Li.[41] These alleged sex scandals have not been independently verified. But in February 2011, a leading news magazine in China, *Caijing*, ran a long cover story about her case, listing her high-powered patrons and presenting details about certain "exchanges of favors."[42]

Li Wei was under investigation when Li Jiating was arrested on corruption charges in 2001. She was, however, able to avoid being tried along with some of Li Jiating's other mistresses. An investigative report by Luo Chang-ping quoted a comment Li Wei had made to her friends about the lessons she learned from her early career: "One should never give all one's resources to one person, nor rely solely on one channel, but should instead form a huge network of relationships—an umbrella-like network."[43] Apparently, she has established such a network in the wake of the Li Jiating case. After 2001, she expanded her business from south and southwestern China to the central and northeast regions of the country, establishing some twenty companies in Beijing, Qingdao, Shenzhen, Hong Kong, and overseas. These companies include tobacco, real estate, advertising, oil, and securities, with combined total assets on the order of 10 billion yuan. Li Wei seems to have been well protected by her patrons in high places. She also seems to have mastered what some Chinese journalists call "a network of sex, power, and money."[44]

In 2003, during her affair with then party secretary of Qingdao Du Shicheng, Li Wei asked him to lease to her company a piece of land covering sixty-one thousand square meters in the Taipingjiao area, one of the most scenic spots in the seaport city of Qingdao. Li then resold the land to the Capital Group and the Qingdao Urban Construction Co., and almost immediately garnered a profit of 84 million yuan.[45] In return, Li gave Du Shicheng a total of 1.7 million yuan as a bribe, for which Du was later sentenced to life in prison. Similarly, in 2006, another lover of Li Wei's, former Sinopec CEO Chen Tonghai, helped her earn 200 million yuan within a month and a half through an equity transfer of Taishan Petroleum, a Sinopec holding company. Chen was arrested in 2007 for allegedly taking bribes in the amount of 195 million yuan. In 2009, he was convicted and sentenced to death, a judgment subsequently suspended for two years and then commuted to life in prison.[46] Interestingly enough, while Du Shicheng, Chen Tonghai, and other of Li Wei's lovers were sentenced to either death or life imprisonment, Li herself was only temporarily taken into custody, on alleged tax evasion, in 2006. Presently Li Wei is free, and her assets overseas have apparently continued to grow.

Company-Level Analysis: The Case of the Hongta Group

The headquarters of the Hongta Group (and its main factory, the Yuxi Cigarette Factory) are located in Yuxi City, in central Yunnan about 90 kilometers from Kunming. Yuxi is known as Tobacco City, honoring the fact that 80 percent of the city's revenue comes from tobacco taxes.[47] The Yuxi Cigarette Factory was established in 1956 as a small tobacco re-curing plant. It merged with several other tobacco factories to become a group company in 1995.[48] Over the past few decades, it has grown into a multinational modern enterprise. With an annual production of ninety-three billion cigarettes, the Hongta Group is the biggest cigarette manufacturer in China and one of the world's largest tobacco companies.[49]

In 2007, it was reported that sales of the Hongta Group's Hongmei cigarette brand exceeded that of Philip Morris International's core brand L & M. More recently, an official of the Hongta Group told foreign media that the Yuxi Cigarette Factory floor was "capable of handling 2.5 billion sticks per day."[50] In 2002, among the country's top ten cigarette brands, the Hongta Group produced four (Hongtashan, Yuxi, Gonghexinxi, and Hongmei).[51] The company's major brand, Hongtashan, was awarded first prize for being the "most valuable Chinese brand" for seven years in a row (1995–2001); in 2000 the value of the Hongta brand itself was figured at 43.9 billion yuan.[52] In 2011, Hongtashan contributed to the Chinese state

68.5 billion yuan in taxes and profits, compared with only 26 billion in 2003.[53] In the Chinese tobacco industry, the Hongta Group has often been praised as "a banner of China's national industry."[54]

It should be noted that the Yuxi Cigarette Factory had only 10 million yuan in assets as of 1975; by 1995, however, it had become a corporate giant with 7 billion yuan in assets. The Yuxi Factory's revenue had increased from 110 million yuan in 1980 to 20 billion yuan in 1996.[55] It is widely believed in Yunnan and elsewhere that one individual, Chu Shijian, general manager of the factory from 1979 to 1995, played an crucial role in the rapid rise of the Hongta Group and its predecessor, the Yuxi Cigarette Factory. His strategic approach to modernizing this factory, in conjunction with his legendary personal life, has earned him the nickname the "godfather" of the "Hongta Empire."[56]

CHU SHIJIAN: GODFATHER OF THE FLAGSHIP COMPANY
OF CHINA'S TOBACCO INDUSTRY

Chu Shijian was born to a farming family in Huaning County, Yunnan, in 1928. After graduating from high school, Chu went to work in a number of different sugar mills, wineries, agricultural and livestock farms, and paper mills.[57] He joined the Chinese Communist Party in 1952 and served as director of the Personnel Office of the Yuxi Prefecture government before being appointed general manager of the Yuxi Cigarette Factory in 1979. His appointment as head of the factory occurred at the same time that his patron and fellow Huaning native Pu Chaozhu was appointed deputy director of the Financial Department of Yuxi Prefecture. In 1979, Pu began to serve as head and deputy party secretary of Yuxi Prefecture before becoming governor of Yunnan in 1983.

It is unclear whether it was Pu Chaozhu or Chu Shijian who first initiated the idea of a "triple play" system integrating tobacco farming, production, and sales, though the system was first implemented at the Yuxi Cigarette Factory under the leadership of Chu. Chu called tobacco farming the "first workshop" (*diyi chejian*) of the Yuxi Cigarette Factory, which under Chu's guidance extended its operations also into tobacco leaf production. In terms of management, the Yuxi Cigarette Factory, the Yuxi Tobacco Company, and the Yuxi STMA became fused into one entity. Chu himself served as general manager of the factory, president of the company, and director of the entire STMA in the mid-1980s.

Drawing on his strong support from the top leaders of the prefecture and province, Chu made two important moves in the following years. The first came when, as part of the enterprise reforms in the early 1980s, the funding of enterprises began to change from "allocated funds" (*bokuan*) to "loans" (*daikuan*). Chu seized this opportunity and obtained almost all of the province's foreign exchange (US$23 million), which he then used to buy updated tobacco equipment from the United Kingdom. By 1985, the Yuxi Cigarette Factory had accomplished its technological transformation into a modern tobacco plant.

In 1988, Yunnan experienced a major earthquake. In the wake of this disaster, Chu urged the provincial government to ask for a policy of "enlarging production to offset the losses from the earthquake." The central government was under financial pressure, and thus adopted Chu's proposal. Consequently, the province was granted a two-fold increase in tobacco production quotas and US$30 million in loans. The Yuxi Cigarette Factory was the greatest beneficiary of this policy, as it was permitted to build the most technically sophisticated cigarette assembly line in the country. By the 1990s, the Yuxi Cigarette Factory boasted some of the most advanced tobacco technology in the world, from which it reaped huge rewards. In 1994 the Yuxi Company enjoyed profits of 6.1 billion yuan, much higher than the second largest firm in the country, the Shanghai Tobacco Company, which had profits of only 940 million yuan.[58]

The second important initiative by Chu Shijian began in 1994, when the Hongta Group established some twelve thousand specialized Hongta tobacco stores throughout the country. This new method of specialized distribution allowed the company to raise its annual production to nine hundred thousand cases in 1996, resulting in 4.1 billion yuan in profits.[59] Later, the Hongta Group also established stores that sold Hongta brand cigarettes exclusively in the airports of six major Chinese cities (Kunming, Chengdu, Shenzhen, Shanghai, Zhengzhou, and Xi'an). To promote its Hongta brand cigarettes, the Hongta Group also established two Hongta smoking rooms at the Shenzhen airport.[60] Chu also launched an aggressive public relations campaign. In 1988, for example, the Yuxi Cigarette Factory was a main sponsor of the Spring Festival TV Gala, a broadcast watched by an overwhelming majority of the Chinese population.[61]

During Chu's eighteen-year tenure as head of the Yuxi Cigarette Factory, tobacco production increased from 275,000 to 2,183,000 cases; the factory enjoyed total revenues and profits of 99.1 billion yuan; and the company's average annual increase in sales was a remarkable 44 percent.[62] From 1988 to 1996, the Hongta Group's revenue and profits were so impressive that the firm was always ranked among the top ten "model companies" in the country. In 1996, the Yuxi Cigarette Factory's revenues and profits constituted 56 percent of the total revenue and profits from all business activities in Yunnan Province.[63] Not surprisingly, Chu received many awards from both the provincial and national governments, including "the Model Worker of Yunnan Province," "the Model Worker of the Nation," "the May 1st Labor Medalist," "National Outstanding Entrepreneur," and one of the "Top Ten Reformers of the Year." Quite impressively, a number of national leaders— including Hu Jintao, Zhu Rongji, and Wu Bangguo—visited the Yuxi Cigarette Factory when Chu was in charge (see Table 7.5). Politburo members Tian Jiyun, Wu Bangguo, Jiang Chunyun, and Wu Yi also visited the Hongta Group, as did provincial leaders such as Pu Chaozhu, He Zhiqiang,

TABLE 7.5.
Visits by top leaders to the Yuxi Hongta Group

Leader	Position at time of visit	Date of visit
Hu Qili	PSC member*	January 1989
Tian Jiyun	Politburo member, Vice-Premier	April 1991
Zhu Rongji	PSC member, Vice-Premier	December 1992
Hu Jintao	PSC member	December 1993
Wu Bangguo	Politburo member, Vice-Premier	November 1995
Liu Huaqing	PSC member	April 1996
Jiang Chunyun	Politburo member, Vice-Premier	November 1996
Li Ruihuan	PSC member	March 1999
Tian Jiyun	Politburo member	April 2001
Wu Guanzheng	PSC member	June 2003
Zeng Peiyan	Politburo member, Vice-Premier	August 2003
Wang Zhaoguo	Politburo member	January 2004
Luo Gan	PSC member	July 2004
Huang Ju	PSC member, Vice-Premier	September 2005
Zeng Peiyan	Politburo member, Vice-Premier	August 2006

* PSC = Politburo Standing Committee
SOURCES: Hongta yancao jituan youxian gongsi (Hongta Tobacco Group Ltd.), *Hongta jituanzhi 1956–2005* (Annals of the Hongta Group, 1956–2005) (Kunming: Yunnan renmin chubanshe, 2006). Also, http://www .tobaccochina.com/zt/hongta100w/index.html; and http://www.tobaccochina.com/zt/2006 _ 50years/eneve .html. Tabulated by Cheng Li.

Linghu An, and Li Jiating.[64] These visits were often—and rightly—seen as a strong endorsement from the CCP leadership.

Ironically, this role model of Chinese state entrepreneurialism fell from grace in a very sudden and dramatic way. In the spring of 1996, Chu came under investigation for corruption. In December of that year, the police detained Chu at a border check point in southern Yunnan, where he was allegedly attempting to cross into Vietnam. A widespread rumor held that Chu brought with him a small suitcase in which he had many "little notes" (*xiaotiaozi*) penned by various levels of leaders in the country, asking for a large amount of free expensive cigarettes. This suitcase was never mentioned in Chu's subsequent trial, which lasted for roughly two years. In early 1999, Chu was sentenced to life imprisonment for receiving bribes equivalent to US$1.74 million. His daughter, Chu Yinghong, was also accused of taking at least three bribes worth 36.3 million yuan, HK$1 million, and US$300,000, respectively. Chu Yinghong never appeared in court, because she committed suicide after her father came under investigation. Three other senior leaders of the Yuxi Cigarette Factory were also sentenced to multiyear prison terms for economic crimes.[65] No provincial or national-level leaders, however, were ever implicated in this case. Zi Guorui, an official who later purchased a building in the swanky Jiahua Plaza in Kunming to help Li Jiating and his mistress, was appointed the new general manager of the Hongta Group in 1996 (for a list of general managers of the Hongta Group from 1979 to 2012, see Table 7.6).

TABLE 7.6.
General managers of the Hongta Group, 1979–2012

Name	Tenure as General Manager	Year of birth	Birthplace	Post prior to this position
Chu Shijian	1979–1996	1928	Yunnan (Huaning)	Head, Personnel Office of Yuxi County
Zi Guorui	1996–2002	1946	Yunnan (Fengqing)	Party Secretary of the Hongta Group
Yao Qingyan	2002–2005	1957	Shandong	President, Yunnan Tobacco Research Institute
Liu Wandong	2005–2006	1950	Yunnan (Yimen)	Party Secretary of the Hongta Group
Li Suiming	2006–	1957	Shanxi	Deputy General Manager of Hongta Group

SOURCE: Hongta yancao jituan youxian gongsi (Hongta Tobacco Group Ltd.), *Hongta jituanzhi 1956–2005* (Annals of the Hongta Group, 1956–2005) (Kunming: Yunnan renmin chubanshe, 2006), 541–54. Tabulated by Cheng Li.

A few years later, Chu Shijiang's sentence was reduced from life imprisonment to seventeen years. In the spring of 2002, he was released on medical parole. This legendary figure in China's tobacco industry now lives on Mount Ailao in central Yunnan, running a large orange orchard employing about two hundred workers. Since 2007, a new type of orange—the "Chu-Shijian-planted orange"—can be found at almost every fruit stand in Kunming and Yuxi.

The post–Chu Shijian Yuxi Cigarette Factory experienced a drastic decline between 1996 and 2004.[66] The STMA banned the direct sale of Hongtashan brand cigarettes in other regions—ending the initiative developed by Chu Shijian. In 2000, Hongtashan sold 560,000 cases (yielding 1.3 billion yuan in profits), representing a 40 percent decline in sales and a 70 percent drop in profits compared with those of 1996.[67]

Conclusion: Individual Leaders, Industrial Interests, and Institutional Development

A major obstacle to China's tobacco control lies in the inherent contradictions within the state apparatus. The STMA has a dual role as regulator and operator of the country's tobacco industry, but central government organs with vast interests in tobacco are also responsible for fulfilling China's obligations under the Framework Convention on Tobacco Control. The primary force responsible for promoting and managing China's tobacco market is, in fact, the principal player tasked with tobacco control coordination.

The close ties between government leaders and corporate entities are certainly not a new phenomenon in China. These ties are, however, increasingly becoming a public concern. Official corruption is rampant, and the amount of money involved has become enormous, as these companies have gained in financial and political power. "Black collar" is a term recently created in China to refer to state-owned corporate and industrial elites—including those who work in monopolized industries such as banking, oil, electricity, coal, telecommunications, aviation, railway, shipping, and tobacco. These rich and powerful elites dress in black, drive black cars, have hidden incomes, live secret lives with concubines, may even have ties to the criminal underground (*heishehui*, black society) and, most importantly, operate their businesses and wield their economic power in an opaque manner. It has been widely reported in the Chinese media that these business interest groups have routinely bribed local officials and formed an "evil coalition" with local governments.[68]

These corporate interest groups could well be just as powerful in Western countries. In the United States, for example, hundreds of lobbying groups have flooded into Washington, DC, and now constitute an essential feature of American politics. From time to time, these business lobbies have been caught attempting to manipulate the democratic system for the commercial gain of some individual company or class of products. Crucial for limiting the power of such groups, however, as one might expect in a democratic political system, are institutional and legal mechanisms to prevent the convergence of money and power. For present-day China, where the boundary between government and state-owned firms is often blurred, laws to prevent political nepotism and to promote greater transparency are urgently needed. From a broader perspective, public health in China depends on the healthy development of the Chinese political system and the growing role of Chinese civil society.

Both conceptually and practically, the Chinese public and anti-smoking NGOs should be mobilized with the goal of enhancing public understanding of the interests and motivations of stakeholders in all aspects of tobacco-related enterprises. This chapter has sought to contribute to this effort by reviewing the historical context of the industry as well as the personal backgrounds, political networks, economic interests, and business associations of key figures at the provincial and enterprise levels of tobacco leadership. By highlighting the many political barriers to effective tobacco control, this chapter has further illustrated the need for public health advocates to develop a strategic map with which to better navigate this complicated, largely opaque, and highly politicized terrain.

Notes

1. An earlier version of this chapter was presented at an innovative history conference on the Chinese cigarette industry from the mid-twentieth century to the present organized by the Asia Health Policy Program at Stanford University's Shorenstein Asia-Pacific Research Center and held at the Stanford Center at Peking University in March 26–27, 2012. A still earlier version appeared as a chapter in the monograph, Cheng Li, *The Political Mapping of China's Tobacco Industry and Anti-Smoking Campaign* (Washington DC: Brookings Institution's John L. Thornton China Center Monograph Series, 2012). The author thanks Eve Cary,

John Langdon, Jordan Lee, and Yinsheng Li for their research assistance and editorial help, and thanks Lincoln C. Chen, Sarah England, Gan Quan, Matthew Kohrman, Susan V. Lawrence, Kenneth Lieberthal, Liu Wennan, Andrew Marble, Andrew C. Mertha, and Robert Proctor for their invaluable and comprehensive suggestions for revision.

2. Zhongguo kongzhi xiyan xiehui he Zhongguo yiyuan xiehui (Chinese Association on Tobacco Control and Chinese Association of Hospitals), eds., *Yiyuan kongzhi xiyan zhidao shouce* (Hospital guidebook on smoking control) (Beijing: Beijing daxue yixue chubanshe, 2009), p. 27.

3. Liu Wei, *Jingji zhuangui guocheng zhongde chanye chongzu: yi yancaoye weili* (Industrial reconstruction in the change of the mode of economic development: The case of the tobacco industry) (Beijing: Shehui kexue chubanshe, 2005), p. 78.

4. Alexi A. Wright and Ingrid T. Katz, "Tobacco Tightrope—Balancing Disease Prevention and Economic Development in China," *New England Journal of Medicine*, vol. 356, no. 15 (April 12, 2007): 1493–96.

5. Four jurisdictions with provincial status that do not have any tobacco acreage are Beijing, Shanghai, Tianjin, and Tibet.

6. Hu Dewei [Teh-wei Hu], ed., *Zhongguo yancao shuishou: lishi yan'ge, xianzhuang ji gaige* (Tobacco tax in China: Past development, current status, and prospects for reform) (Beijing: Zhongguo shuiwu chubanshe, 2009), p. 41.

7. Liu Tienan and Xiong Bilin, eds., *Yancao jingji yu yancao kongzhi* (Tobacco economy and tobacco control) (Beijing: Jingji kexue chubanshe, 2004), cited in Hong Wang, *Tobacco Control in China: The Dilemma between Economic Development and Health Improvement* (New Haven, CT: Yale School of Public Health, 2006), p. S142.

8. "The Other Side" (in Chinese), Easy Net, February 28, 2012, http://news.163 .com/special/00012Q9L/tobaccoindustry.html.

9. *Zhongguo jingji zhoukan* (China Economic Weekly), January 11, 2011.

10. Gordon Fairclough, "Taxing Addiction: China Confronts Price of Its Cigarette Habit," *Wall Street Journal*, January 3, 2007, p. A.1, http://search.proquest.com /docview/399036755?accountid=26493.

11. National Development and Reform Commission (NDRC) Research Institute of Industrial Economics and Technology, *Woguo yancao chanye zhuanxing yanjiu* (A study of the transition of China's tobacco industry), February 10, 2011, p. 2.

12. Liu and Xiong, eds., *Yancao jingji yu yancao kongzhi*, p. 168.

13. For a detailed discussion of tax divides between central and local governments, see Hu, *Zhongguo yancao shuishou*, p. 62.

14. Tao Ming, *Zhuanmai tizhixia de Zhongguo yancaoye: lilun, wenti, yu zhidu biange* (China's tobacco industry under state monopoly: Theories, issues, and institutional reforms) (Shanghai: Xuelin chubanshe, 2005), p. 249.

15. National Development and Reform Commission (NDRC) Research Institute of Industrial Economics and Technology, *Woguo yancao chanye zhuanxing yanjiu*, pp. 10–11.

16. "The Biggest Tobacco Planting Area—Yunnan Province," Busiunion.com, January 20, 2010, http://www.busiunion.com/10-1//3830.jsp.

17. "Yunnan Province of China," *China Provincial Update*, published by the Confederation of Indian Industry, vol. 1, no. 3 (June 1, 2007): 2.

18. Irene Eng, "Agglomeration and the Local State: The Tobacco Economy of Yunnan, China," *Transactions of the Institute of British Georgraphers*, New Series, vol. 24, no. 3 (1999): 318–19.

19. Ibid., p. 320; and Zheng Tianyi and Xu Zugen, eds., *Yanmu: yancao shichang dasaomiao* (Smokescreen: An overview of the tobacco market) (Beijing: Xinhua chubanshe, 2009), p. 40.

20. Zi Guorui and Gao Fayuan, eds., *Hongta jituan kuashiji fazhan zhanlüe sikao* (Thoughts on the cross-century development strategy of the Hongta Group) (Kunming: Yunnan daxue chubanshe, 1999), p. 11.

21. For more detailed discussion, see Pu's memoir, Pu Chaozhu, *Wode chengzhang yu Yunnan de biange* (My growth and Yunnan's reform) (Kunming: Yunnan renmin chubanshe, 2003).

22. Zheng and Xu, *Yanmu*, p. 40.

23. *Shenghuo xinbao* (New Life Daily), April 24, 2008, http://www.shxb.net/html/20080424/20080424_89071_2.shtml.

24. Pu, *Wode chengzhang yu Yunnan de biange.*

25. For a more detailed discussion of their lobbying, see He Zhiqiang's memoir, He Zhiqiang, *Ershi shiji bajiushi niandai Yunnan jingji fazhan hongguan juece huigu* (A macroeconomic policy-making review of the economic development of Yunnan in the 1980s and 1990s) (Kunming: Yunnan renmin chubanshe, 2006).

26. Pu, *Wode chengzhang yu Yunnan de biange.*

27. For example, see Supesite Net, November 13, 2001, http://bbs.lasg.ac.cn/?action-viewthread-tid-28544.

28. Ibid.

29. Guojia yancao zhuanmaiju (State Tobacco Monopoly Administration), *Zhongguo yancao nianjian* (China tobacco yearbook, 2009) (Beijing: Zhongguo kexue jishu chubanshe, 2010), p. 216.

30. Ibid., p. 223.

31. Ibid., p. 103.

32. *Zhongguo qingnian bao* (China Youth Daily), January 26, 2011, also available online on January 26, 2011, http://zqb.cyol.com/html/2011-01/26/nw.D110000zgqnb_20110126_4-05.htm.

33. According to a source that was not verified, Jiang once commented that Li Jiating should be considered as a candidate for the vice-premiership in the future.

34. The above discussion is based on the author's interviews in Kunming and Zhaotong in March 2010, and interviews in Kunming, Lijiang, and Dali in March–April 2011.

35. Xinhua News Agency, May 20, 2003, http://www.yn.xinhuanet.com/yn news/zt/2003/szdl/xlym/_001.htm.

36. Shenghuo Xinbao Net (New Life Daily), September 7, 2008, http://www .shxb.net/html/20080907/20080907_108651_2.shtml.

37. Li Qingchuan, "Duomianren Li Jiating—cong shengzhang dao renmin gongdi" (Multifaceted Li Jiating: From governor to the enemy of the people), *Xinmin zhoukan* (Xinmin Weekly), July 25, 2003, http://news.sina.com.cn/c/2003 -07-25/22061414275.shtml.

38. Xia Handong and Cheng Gongyi, "Shibada changwei mingdan, paixi he bianshu" (The members of 18th Politburo Standing Committee: Factions and variables), *Neimu* (Insider), no. 1 (September/October 2011): 46. Princelings are descendants of prominent Communist Party officials.

39. Xia Handong and Cheng Gongyi, "Shibada changwei jingzheng renwu" (Competitors for the 18th Politburo Standing Committee), *Neimu* (Insider), no. 1 (September/October 2011): 119

40. Ibid.

41. Yang Yun and Fang Yanhong, *Gonggong qingfu* (Shared mistress) (New York: Mirror Books, 2008).

42. Luo Changping, "Gonggong qundai" (Public nepotism), *Caijing*, no. 4 (February 14, 2011).

43. Quoted from ibid.

44. Ibid.

45. For a more detailed discussion of this land transfer, see ibid.

46. Ibid.

47. As Louisa Lim observed, "Yuxi has a Hongta avenue, a Hongta hotel, a Hongta sports stadium—and even a tobacco culture museum devoted to extolling the pleasures of smoking." See Louisa Lim, "China Dependent on Tobacco in More Ways Than One," National Public Radio, February 18, 2011, http://www .scpr.org/news/2011/02/18/china-dependent-on-tobacco-in-more-ways-than-one.

48. For more discussion of the history of the Hongta Group, see Zi and Gao, *Hongta jituan kuashiji fazhan zhanlüe sikao*, p. 10.

49. "Hongta Group Aims to Become World's Leading Cigarette Maker," ChinaRealNews Net, December 18, 2008, http://chinarealnews.typepad.com/ chinarealnews/2008/12/hongta-group-aims-to-become-worlds-leading-cigarette -maker.html.

50. Mark Godfrey, "China's Largest Selling Cigarette Brand Shapes up for Exports with Low Tar and Better Packaging," March 9, 2011, http://www.thefree library.com/China's+largest+selling+cigarette+brand+shapes+up+for+exports+with ...-a0226476958.

51. Hu Dewei [Teh-wei Hu] and Mao Zhengzhong, eds., *Zhongguo yancao kongzhi de jingji yanjiu* (Economic research on China's tobacco control) (Beijing: Jingji kexue chubanshe, 2008), p. 117.

52. Liu and Xiong, *Yancao jingji yu yancao kongzhi*, p. 126.

53. *Hongta shibao* (Hongta Times), no. 826, February 15, 2011, p. 20.

54. Tobacco Market Net, March 5, 2012, http://www.etmoc.com/firm/FirmShow .asp?id=92.

55. Tao, *Zhuanmai tizhixia de Zhongguo yancaoye*, pp. 224–25.

56. "Chu Shijian—Ba yanchang guanli cheng yinchao gongchang" (Chu Shi-jian: Making a cigarette factory into a "money printing factory"), *Nanfang renwu zhoukan* (Southern People Weekly), September 23, 2008, http://news.hexun.com/2008-09-23/109127819.html.

57. Ibid.

58. This discussion is based on Tao, *Zhuanmai tizhixia de Zhongguo yancaoye*, p. 225.

59. Liu, *Jingji zhuangui guocheng zhongde chanye chongzu*, p. 131.

60. Hongta yancao jituan youxian gongsi (Hongta Tobacco Group Limited), *Hongta jituanzhi 1956–2005* (Annals of the Hongta Group, 1956–2005) (Kunming: Yunnan renmin chubanshe, 2006), p. 223.

61. Ibid., p. 471.

62. Zhang Fuyu, "Hongtashan—Yige pinpai zai zhuanmai zhidu xia de chenfu" (Hongtashan: The ups and downs of a brand name in a monopolized system), *Ershiyi shiji jingji daobao* (Twenty-first Century Economic Herald), June 30, 2003, http://finance.sina.com.cn/b/20030630/1455358374.shtml.

63. Zi and Gao, *Hongta jituan kuashiji fazhan zhanlüe sikao*, p. 11.

64. Zi Guorui, ed., *Hongta jituan kuashiji fazhan zhanlüe shijian* (The Hongta Group's cross-century development strategy) (Kunming: Yunnan renmin chubanshe, 2000), p. 193.

65. Hongta yancao jituan youxian gongsi, *Hongta jituanzhi 1956–2005*, p. 413.

66. See the website of the Hongta Group, March 5, 2012, http://www.tobacco china.com/zt/hongta100w/index.html.

67. Tao, *Zhuanmai tizhixia de Zhongguo yancaoye*, p. 255.

68. *Zhongguo xinwen zhoukan*, January 13, 2006; *Liaowang*, December 5, 2005; see also http://www.chinesenewsnet.com, December 12, 2005.

PART FOUR

Obstructing Tobacco Control

CHAPTER EIGHT

Filtered Cigarettes and the Low-Tar Lie in China

Matthew Kohrman, Ronald Sun, Robert N. Proctor,
and Yang Gonghuan

> She doesn't smoke at all. That's why she isn't very healthy.
>
> To deal with me, they make these especially on my behalf. The filter is long. Ha, the filter is even longer than the tobacco [portion].
>
> > *Paramount leader Deng Xiaoping—bantering about his wife, Zhuo Lin,*
> > *with George H. Bush in 1980; and chatting in 1986 with a journalist*
> > *regarding a version of Panda brand cigarettes that Deng's doctors and family,*
> > *worried about his health, had arranged to be manufactured for him.*

Of all the myths surrounding tobacco—and there are many—none is more pernicious than the notion that, if a person is going to consume combustible cigarettes, it is safer to smoke "low-tar" brands that come with clean white filters affixed to the end. The idea is pernicious, because it builds on a commonsense idea: isn't it better to filter out the bad bits, like tar, from cigarette smoke?

For decades, manufacturers have added "filters" to cigarettes and labeled some sticks as "low tar." Until surprisingly recently, many in the public health community actually believed that such cigarettes were safer. This myth was not discredited until around the year 2000, when scholars finally gained access to (some of) the industry's European and American archives which revealed that smokers who consume filtered cigarettes, or ones advertised as low tar, were inhaling just as much poison into their lungs. It turns out that filters don't really screen anything out of the smoke, and low-tar smokers don't inhale any less tar. Low-tar products are actually more dangerous because smokers tend to inhale particles deeper into their lungs, where they cause more serious types of cancer, and filters change the chemistry of smoke, introducing new poisons.[1]

How, though, did filter-tipped and low-tar cigarettes come to be produced and marketed in China? The story is interestingly different from what we find elsewhere. Cigarette makers in China originally attached filters onto cigarettes at the end of the 1950s in an effort to fête and cater to party elites. Years later they turned to profiteering off of expensive filtered brands, selling the cachet of modern science to smokers. The next phase involved more rampant fraud, when the industry started hyping—in the late 1990s— "low-tar" cigarettes as safer. Cigarette makers successfully capitalized on this deceit, at a time when savvy citizens were becoming more aware of tobacco's toxicity. Deception often has an interesting demography, and, like elsewhere in the world, in China, it has been some of the best-educated who have been most entangled by the low-tar/filter myth. This, as we shall see, helps explain how a tobacco industry scientist, someone Mandarin speakers have called the "father of low-tar cigarettes," could be elected to the prestigious Chinese Academy of Engineering in 2011.

Filter Frenzy Outside of China

Cigarettes tipped with so-called filters date from the nineteenth century, when European tobacco manufacturers first experimented with stuffing cotton or paper wadding into the ends of cigarettes to make them less harsh when inhaled. In 1925, Boris Aivaz carried out experiments while working in the Ortmann factory of the UK's Bunzl Paper Mills, and applied for a patent to use crepe paper and cellulose to produce cigarette filter tips. Fears of cigarettes causing harm were not yet an important part of American or European popular culture, however, and the few brands that did emerge with such appendages—Viceroy was the most notable in the United States—fared poorly in the marketplace.

That began to change in the 1950s, following publication of studies linking cigarettes to lung cancer. From 1952 to 1954 in the United States, cigarette sales suffered a significant decline, as millions of smokers began to quit or cut down, fearing for their lives. The "health scare" and conspiracy that followed are well known to historians, as are the industry's efforts to steer smokers toward cigarettes labelled filtered and low-tar as an alternative to quitting.[2] Marlboro, Winston and Kent emerged as popular filter brands at this time, thanks to aggressive mass marketing and nascent consumer fears that their cigarettes might be killing them. Filter-tipped cigarettes were advertised as a safer kind of smoke, and increased their market share from only about 1 percent in 1950 to more than 80 percent in the mid-1970s. The era of the "safer" cigarette had arrived (see Figure 8.1).

In China, the manufacture, promotion, and popularization of filter-tipped cigarettes commenced somewhat differently. Backstory for the roll-out of this entirely new category of cigarette was October 1, 1959, the tenth anniversary of the PRC. And the setting of the story was the historical hub of China's cigarette industry, Shanghai. Directors at the Shanghai Cigarette Factory (SCF) shrewdly used the country's looming anniversary. Specifically, they used a presumption of etiquette—that government agencies during the anniversary must demonstrate filial appreciation for party elites—in order to sway mid-level officialdom in Beijing to grant exceptional import authority allowing SCF to acquire novel items from abroad with the aim of creating a special homemade gift. From a Japanese supplier, SCF purchased filter-tips, and with help from a Hong Kong company, SCF bought a small selection of machinery built by the Hauni Corporation of West Germany. All this happened, notably, as one of the world's worst human disasters, the Great Leap Forward (1958–1962), was starting to unfold. Despite the growing turmoil, staff at the Shanghai Cigarette Factory fought off customs office resistance and technical confusion to manufacture a number of test batches.

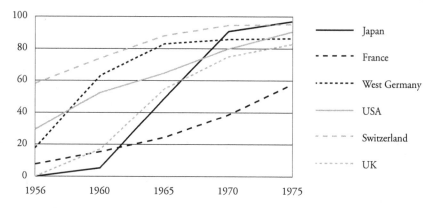

FIGURE 8.1.

Changing percentage of cigarettes with filter tips, 1956–1975, in six countries which were major cigarette producers during the twentieth century. "Recent Changes in Tobacco Products and Their Acceptance by the Consumer," *Proceedings of the Sixth International Tobacco Scientific Congress* (Tokyo, 1976), and *Tobacco Science and Technology*, issue 3 (1977).

Then, as October 1959 quickly approached, they officially launched China's first filter-tipped cigarettes under the factory's flagship brand, Chunghwa (China). Once wrapped and boxed, the first consignment was swiftly sent to Beijing for distribution to Mao and other party luminaries.

For decades thereafter, manufacture of filter-tipped cigarettes remained negligible, with most such product continuing to flow into the hands of high government officials. By the start of the 1980s, only a few factories were making filtered offerings, comprising at most 6 percent of cigarettes produced nationwide. And remember, cigarettes manufactured by foreign companies still remained largely inaccessible to Chinese consumers during this period, impeded by strict trade barriers erected after the founding of the People's Republic. Fast forward to the end of the millennium, though, and we find a very different situation. Foreign cigarettes still remained inaccessible, but by 2000 almost all cigarettes produced in China were filter tipped. How did this change occur, and so quickly? Interestingly, most of it transpired over a decade. From 1985 to 1995 filter-tipped offerings went from comprising 13 percent of all cigarettes made in China to 87 percent (see Table 8.1).[3]

Financial Rehabilitation through "Quality" Filtration

What prompted the dramatic shift? One explanation has to do with new expectations that party leaders had set for the Chinese tobacco industry. During the years when Mao guided the People's Republic (1949–1976), the industry was certainly expected to generate a steady stream of revenue to underwrite government finances. By the 1980s, however, much higher expectations had been set for this branch of China's planned economy. With the aim of rebuilding government institutions devastated by Maoist excess,

TABLE 8.1.
Proportion of cigarettes produced in China having filter tips

	1982	1983	1984	1985	1986	1987	1988	1989	1990	1995
Percentage of filter-tipped cigarettes among total cigarettes produced	6	10	11	13	18	28	36	42	48	87

SOURCES: State Tobacco Monopoly Bureau, *China Tobacco Yearbook 1981–1990* (Beijing: Economic Daily Press, 1991), p. 50; State Tobacco Monopoly Bureau, *China Tobacco Yearbook 1991–1995* (Beijing: Economic Daily Press, 1996), p. 25.

national financial authorities in Beijing issued clear instructions to cigarette makers to significantly increase earnings. This was not an easy expectation to meet, especially given extant limits on raw materials, technology, and labor training. One solution seized upon was to boost production of higher-grade tobacco products, which had larger profit margins and were more heavily taxed than cheaper brands. Higher-grade tobacco products, however, require leaf meeting relatively exacting standards set by industry purchasers. How to make the country's supply of "high quality" leaf go further? Adding filter tips held out the promise of reducing the amount of tobacco used in any given cigarette, while clearly differentiating the look and feel of more expensive brands.

To that end, the China National Tobacco Corporation established policies to ensure that filters were prioritized for higher grade cigarettes. Policies were also enacted prohibiting the use of A-grade leaf in non-filtered cigarettes. These measures were taken with the aim of minimizing wastage of higher-grade leaf, thereby increasing the profits of the industry and the financial reserves of the national treasury.[4] And it worked.

During China's Sixth Five-Year Plan (1981–1985), the country saw annual growth of industrial and agricultural output reach 11 percent, and cigarette production grew nearly as fast, at 9 percent per annum. But tobacco tax revenue grew far faster, at the rate of 17 percent per year! Similarly, during the Seventh Five-Year Plan (1986–1990), GDP growth came in at about 8 percent per year and cigarette production grew by 6 percent per year. But cigarette tax revenues grew by an astonishing 21 percent per year.

How was this momentum to be kept up? The most obvious answer was to produce more filter-tipped cigarettes, along with increasingly differentiated brand offerings, priced sufficiently high enough to maintain large margins. That plan was at the heart of the industry's efforts to increase national financial reserves during the Eighth Five-Year Plan (1991–1995). And even though cigarette *production* grew by only 1.3 percent per year during those years, *tax revenues* from cigarettes surged a whopping 18 percent per annum, well ahead of GDP annual growth. Indeed, tobacco tax revenues grew faster than all other sources of state revenue during those fifteen years. So much so that by the mid-1990s, revenues from the tobacco trade were funding more than ten percent of the entire Chinese government.[5]

But it was not just policies set in Beijing that kept throwing ever more filter-tipped cigarettes onto the Chinese market. Local governments also played a part by drafting their own policies, including tax relief for local factories. Prominent among these tax breaks were special earmarks for factories that used cigarette filter materials. The goal was to boost local productivity and profits by encouraging sales of "higher quality" cigarettes, meaning higher-priced brands outfitted with "filter tips."[6]

Where to Find Enough Filters?

One thread of this story is that competition emerged over which factories would have access to the best filter feedstocks and finished filter fibers. Ever since Shanghai Tobacco began making filter-tipped cigarettes in the late 1950s, China's cigarette industry had been largely dependent on imported cellulose acetate "tows," the fibrous materials from which filters are made. Only government-approved agents were allowed to import these tows. Once inside the country, the tows were permitted to be resold, and resale prices were allowed to float starting in the 1980s. The price of tow rose dramatically once that float was authorized, as official resellers hoarded goods and manipulated prices, with demand usually outpacing supplies. By 1988, when national production of filter-tipped cigarettes broke through the 500 billion stick mark, the price of acetate tow had reached 75,000 yuan per ton inside China—much higher than the import price of 18,000 yuan.[7]

Eventually, industry leaders proposed several remedies. For instance, China Tobacco spent considerable time and effort to rationalize filter imports, issuing a "Notice on the Strengthening of Management for Imports of Cigarette Filter Materials" and "Regulations on the Strengthening of Management for Cigarette Filter Costs and Prices." And it started laying the groundwork for tow to be made domestically, assisted by foreigner experts specializing in filter technology. Experimental polypropylene filter plants were launched toward the end of 1988, with the goal of imitating the filter-making methods then in use in the United States and in Czechoslovakia. Leaders also made plans to build what would be called the Nantong China-US Acetate Fiber Joint Venture.

If everything had gone according to schedule, acetate fiber from the Nantong factory would have become the first Chinese cigarette tow to be produced on an industrial scale, with polypropylene destined to catch up in a few years. The political disruptions of spring and summer 1989, however, shocked the domestic and international scene. And repercussions spread to every aspect of the Chinese polity. For the tobacco industry, one consequence was the collapse of the Nantong joint venture and an expedited launch and promotion of what were called "patriotic cigarette tows" made out of polypropylene, a fibrous alternative to acetate. In the words of Jiang Ming, then head of China Tobacco:

> The development of polypropylene cigarette tows embodies the full realization of the principle of self sufficiency; it symbolizes our resistance to the West's anti-revolutionary attempts to isolate and punish China. From this perspective, polypropylene cigarette tows are patriotic. . . . Provincial-level companies and all factories need to take this on board. Everyone needs to strengthen their resolve, we need to develop and use Chinese cigarette tows: "patriotic cigarette tows."[8]

As this passage implies, the tension that emerged between China and the rest of the world following the events of June 4, 1989, made the PRC's reliance on imported filter materials a politically sensitive situation. It also created an opportunity for China Tobacco to press party leaders for a special allocation. China Tobacco used the specter of international sanctions as a way to convince the central government to increase funding for the industry, so that a new and as-yet untested polypropylene filter material could be directed into domestic cigarette production.

Domestic manufacture of polypropylene filters was far from smooth, however. Most early production lines ended up being little more than modified versions of petrochemical facilities used to make textile fibers. Their polypropylene tows were strong and tough, which meant that they could not easily be formed into rods, were hard to work with, and did not cut evenly. They were also adhesive-resistant, which meant that their density could not be increased via traditional glues. As a result, the new filters were either acceptably airtight but insufficiently hard, or acceptably hard but too tight when compared with acetate filters of similar specifications. Since polypropylene filters could not meet the technical standards established for acetate, they could only be used for C-grade cigarettes or lower, and needed further modification if they were to be promoted on a larger scale.

By the early 1990s, market forces and government intervention had alleviated much of the shortage, with imports of acetate rising so fast that there was actually a surplus of it in China. Between 1992 and 1997, the market value of acetate fibers stabilized at 20,000 to 30,000 yuan per ton, domestic prices that had existed before 1987.[9] Also, because of all the trouble encountered trying to manufacture propylene tows, China Tobacco had by then convinced the central government to invest in more expensive overseas technology so that acetate tows could be made domestically, first in Kunming and subsequently in Zhuhai and Xi'an. Domestic acetate filter manufacturing reached 60,000 tons by 1997, fulfilling the 1989 goal of producing a significant portion of "patriotic cigarette tows."[10]

Factory Managers and Foreign Mercenaries

One thing that this tale of tows helps illuminate is that, despite all being subsidiaries of the China National Tobacco Corporation since 1982, cigarette factories in the PRC have regularly competed against one another for resources. Something else it reveals is that, for the industry, the decision to retrofit factories to produce filter-tipped cigarettes had little to do with any consensus in matters of "smoking and health." After the Cultural Revolution, neither tensions over tows nor fervor to produce filter-tipped cigarettes came to prominence in China because industry personnel or average smokers had become adamant that tobacco consumption was dangerous.

That is not to say that industry leaders had no reason to believe that cigarettes were harmful. For hundreds of years, Chinese medical experts had been raising red flags, however tepidly, warning that tobacco use had its dangers. When Shanghai Tobacco first made filter-tipped cigarettes in the late 1950s, ample evidence was already circulating outside of China regarding the deadly harms of cigarette smoking. By 1958, Chinese academics were beginning to hear about some of the epidemiology and animal experiments from the Anglo-American world linking cigarette smoke to cancer.[11] By the end of the 1970s Chinese journals had already published dozens of articles citing and treating as settled fact the 1964 report of the U.S. Surgeon General, which robustly declared causal links between cigarette smoking and acute disease.[12] To be sure, Chinese medical journals were not unanimous in their views of tobacco in the 1960s and 1970s, something which provided industry leaders ethical cover. A paper translated from English and published in the *Tianjin Medical Journal* in 1963, for instance, offered experimental evidence against any kind of link between smoking and pulmonary maladies.[13]

We do not find, though, the kind of massive denialist campaign notorious in the United States—and we cannot assume that this Tianjin translation was funded by anyone connected with the tobacco industry. What we can say is that this article was one of a number published from the 1960s onward that helped muddy the waters. As a consequence, within Chinese academic circles and among the general public concrete consensus regarding the dangers posed by cigarettes remained elusive to the end of the millennium. That was a godsend for industry leaders. The absence of a clear expert consensus, and prolonged public ignorance, meant that, even though they had ample reason to question the safety of their products by the late 1970s, industry leaders had a free hand to ignore pretty much everything pertaining to health, apart from ensuring factory hygiene.[14]

Let's not yet depart from the intellectual history of experts or their knowledge about smoking and health, because it helps reveal something interesting about the rise of filter-tipped cigarettes at the end of the twentieth century. If, in the early years of the People's Republic, academic journals in China were publishing contradictory articles about smoking and health, that all came to a screeching halt during the Cultural Revolution (1966–1976), when academic practices of all kinds were suspended. Health-related research resumed in fits and starts in the 1970s, as the nation's new pragmatic leaders started to steer China onto a path of market liberalization and "seeking truth from facts." Researchers began to explore again some of the diseases caused by cigarettes, and foreign literature and technology began finding their way into China with greater force and frequency.

This truth-seeking line likely influenced at least some of the researchers with positions inside the Chinese tobacco industry to become more cognizant of tobacco's toxicity and to begin discussing internally possible remedies. As early as 1972, we can find an article released by the industry's Zhengzhou-based journal, *Tobacco Science and Technology*, ceding ground regarding the question of harm.[15] The unauthored article was released in the first year of the journal's existence. It concedes that conventional smoking practices can indeed hurt human health, citing statistics of the U.S. Department of Health from the 1960s, and then goes on to suggest that any such harm, however, could be mitigated through various means, first and foremost being the adoption of filter tips.

But does an article like this one published in an obscure journal help explain why, in the 1970s, the industry began to request and receive large sums of government funding to retrofit factories to make filter-tipped cigarettes? We have found no documents to support that position. Indeed, as much as some within industry research institutes had quietly admitted by the end of the Cultural Revolution that cigarettes could cause harm, those concessions themselves were not driving decision-making processes among factory managers who sought to increase filter-tipped cigarette production at the end of the Mao era. This is interestingly different from the situation in Europe and especially in the United States, where filtered cigarettes were brought to market so the industry could alleviate credible fears among the public that cigarettes are deadly.

This reminds us of how important it is for historians to distinguish between a few words found in a technical journal like that published in Zhengzhou from what an industry pronounces more broadly. If tobacco companies in China were not yet regularly telling their employees or the broader Chinese public about cigarettes being dangerous and needing filtration, then what kind of message were they actually sending? What kind of language was used to rationalize filter-tipped cigarette production in the late 1970s and, beginning in 1983, the reduction of "tar and nicotine" deliveries of cigarettes?

As already emphasized, reducing production costs and raising revenue were clearly stated goals. Filter materials are usually much cheaper than quality tobacco leaf, and China's pricier Grade-A filter-tipped cigarettes generate more profits than lower grade non-filtered sticks. But was this the only rationale factory managers had for the sudden shift? After all, being able to make and save money manufacturing filter-tipped cigarettes presumes that all the machinery needed to produce such cigarettes was already in place. In the late 1970s, however, that was not yet the case in China. Very few cigarette factories were outfitted with the machinery required to make such products—which required substantial investments. The only possible source of investment funding at that time was the central government, which was preoccupied with strategizing new economic policies following decades of Maoist mayhem.[16] So, how did local factories convince Beijing to supply them with funds for a filter revolution? What was the vocabulary of persuasion?

Archives in and outside of China suggest that a crucial linguistic well-spring was renewed contact with foreign corporations. Searches of tobacco industry documents from the 1970s illuminate a notable uptick in international interactions on numerous levels.[17] More to the point, we see that the Chinese Communist Party green-lighted its domestic tobacco industry, for the first time in years, to send factory groups abroad on fact-finding missions and to invite experts from Canada, Japan, and elsewhere to engage in technical exchange.[18]

Given the new pressure they were under to turn bigger profits, managers of local cigarette factors in China were hungry for interactions with companies from more industrialized parts of the world in order to learn new ways to make money. Thanks to frequent exchanges with foreign companies and their affiliates, including Philip Morris, Germany's Hauni, and the Agricultural Research Service of the USDA (notably its top tobacco researcher, T. C. Tso), Chinese manufacturers were able to develop a more detailed understanding of how global manufacturers were making and marketing their cigarettes. Exchanges were not limited to the sharing of technical information or scientific reports; such exchanges blossomed into research visits, joint conferences, and direct supervision and guidance accompanied by technology transfer. Foreign Big Tobacco firms had long recognized the People's Republic as a potentially lucrative market for all things related to cigarettes, and, during the first phases of post-Cultural Revolution reform, they competed with one another to visit Chinese manufacturers. Moreover, suppliers of seed and machinery from the United States, the United Kingdom, Italy, and West Germany vied fiercely for contracts to upgrade China's technology. All told, these foreign companies were happy to hype, sell and otherwise transfer into China the same kinds of techniques and rhetorics of "advanced manufacturing" common to their own factories and boardrooms.[19]

Chinese cigarette factories, long starved for funds, tended to be quite receptive to ideas and equipment from foreign manufactures, once the dust began to settle on the Cultural Revolution. Indeed, the first local factory leaders to successfully wrest scarce foreign capital from party leaders for infrastructural upgrades were those who lobbied the earliest and loudest that any domestic manufacturing facility capable of making cigarettes closely approximating the look, feel and quality of the "modern" smokes sold abroad would prove to be a boon, symbolic and financial, for the party-state. Initially, some of these factory managers, with modest purchases of equipment from overseas, modified existing 81mm wrapping machines to accommodate filters. But managers typically wanted much more. They wanted to procure from abroad a wide variety of new machines and to receive approval for building new factory campuses in which to house those machines. In documents from local cigarette enterprises, newly funded foreign machines and factories are sometimes celebrated as a means of economizing on tobacco leaf usage but more often they are extolled for their scientific luster, for promoting technological progress.[20]

What this all suggests is that the shift in the post-Mao era to producing low-tar, filter-tipped cigarettes cannot be explained simply as a top-down decision by a few party leaders ensconced in Beijing. Nor can it be explained as simply an industry satisfying a public hunger for safer cigarettes. Far more, the shift to so-called low-tar, filter-tipped cigarettes in the 1970s and 1980s began as a result of problem solving among subnational administrators, supercharged by long-desired contacts between foreign and domestic tobacco enterprises. These contacts sensitized a local industry and its factory managers in particular to the marketability of filtration and low-tars, not so much as founts of health promotion, but rather as flashy scientific novelties eye-catching to a population hungry for novelty, innovation, and a taste of worldliness. Filter-tipped cigarettes in China took off in the 1970s and 1980s so that the industry could retrofit, the public could be sold something more modern, and the government could make more money.

Transforming "Tar" into the Enemy of the People: Mobilizing Harm to Sell More Cigarettes

By the turn of the millennium, a new round of hoodwinkery regarding cigarettes was well underway across the PRC, centered around an STMA-led campaign heralding the virtues of "harm reduction." The so-called "fragrant, low-tar, low-harm" (高香气，低焦油，低危害) "Chinese-style cigarette" had been born, accompanied by a disingenuous message that filters could contribute to safer smoking.[21]

As already noted, "tar reduction" had begun quietly in the early 1980s. Copying techniques developed abroad, manufacturers in China set out initially to lower machine-measured tar deliveries, calculating such deliveries down to two decimal points (see Figure 8.2). They achieved tar reductions as they had learned from foreign experts: by the use of tiny holes punched into the sides of filter tips ("ventilation"), the incorporation of expanded or "puffed" tobacco (which is rather like puffed rice), and the inclusion of less tobacco in the cigarette rod, all of which made it seem like tar yields were falling. From 1983 to 1992, tar deliveries per cigarette on average dropped from 27.27 mg to 18.72 mg, according to the industry's overly exact (and deeply deceptive) measurements. One might imagine that domestic manu-

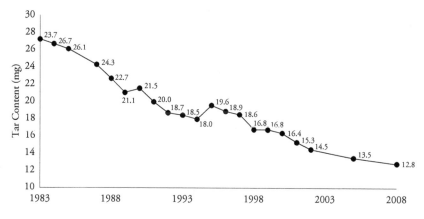

FIGURE 8.2.

Deceptive measures: Declining tar content of Chinese cigarettes over a 25-year period--according to standardized smoking robots that do not consider "compensation." Reproduced from Quan Gan et al., "Chinese 'Low-Tar' Cigarettes Do Not Deliver Lower Levels of Nicotine and Carcinogens," *Tobacco Control*, volume 19, issue 5, ©2010, with permission from BMJ Publishing Group Ltd.

facturers would have made such reductions the centerpiece of their marketing efforts, but in this early period (1980s) it was instead the vague concept of improved cigarette "quality" that they generally played up.[22]

Fear can focus thought. And by 2000, the State Tobacco Monopoly Administration (STMA, aka China Tobacco) was fearful that it was in a perilous situation. Not only had nationwide cigarettes sales softened in the late 1990s, but also by 2000 Beijing was on the cusp of committing China to two international pacts, both of which STMA's leaders dreaded. The first pact was the World Trade Organization, which China went on to join in 2001, and the second was the United Nations' Framework Convention on Tobacco Control, which Beijing went on to sign in 2003. The STMA worried that entry into these pacts could fundamentally hurt domestic cigarette producers, exposing them to renewed competition from foreign Big Tobacco as well as systemic public health criticism. To defend itself, the STMA decided to make "tar" a key element in a new "Chinese-style cigarette" (中式卷烟) strategy.[23] In close coordination with domestic tobacco enterprises, the STMA ramped up a massive public relations and marketing campaign, the aim of which was to convince everyone that cigarettes produced in China had become as sophisticated and as safe as any made abroad. Messaging went out across new and old media platforms of the

People's Republic, extolling technological improvements in harm reduction. Many domestic cigarette factories, which had been quietly cutting back on the amount of tobacco put into cigarettes for years, now began bragging that these exact same cigarettes were "low-tar, low-harm" wonders. Also repurposed was the flimflam of filtration. No longer were factories simply hyping that their cigarettes were higher quality because of specially formulated tows. They were now marketing these same tows as indispensable to improved safety.

One remarkable fact in this story is how similarly tar has come to be measured—and marketed—in China and elsewhere in the world. Especially notable is that Chinese manufacturers adopted virtually whole hog the robot method of measuring tar and nicotine values from foreign manufacturers, something that public health scholars now recognize as fraudulent and deceptive.[24] The machines used to measure tar and nicotine quantities do not capture how people actually smoke—because of compensation. Compensation is when an addicted smoker switches to a low-tar cigarette brand and "compensates" by taking bigger puffs, drawing smoke deeper into the lungs, smoking more puffs per cigarette and/or further down on the butt, or consuming more cigarettes. It is part of the larger phenomenon of titration, meaning that smokers addicted to a particular level of nicotine will adjust the intensity of their smoking behavior to obtain a constant—and consistent—intake of nicotine. Manufacturers in China and elsewhere have never publicized any of these flaws in the methods used to determine tar and nicotine deliveries. Instead, the advertised message (overt or implied) has been that low-tar cigarettes are safer—when in fact they are not.

Such deceptive tactics have been widely exposed not just through rigorous scholarship, but also through legal proceedings. For instance, courts in the United States have ruled that "light" and low-tar cigarettes are one of the greatest frauds ever perpetrated on consumers. Judge Gladys Kessler of the United States District Court for the District of Columbia in 2006 ruled that cigarettes using descriptors such as "low-tar," "mild," and "light" are dishonest and cannot be allowed in advertising or on packaging.[25]

In compliance with the World Health Organization's Framework Convention on Tobacco Control (FCTC), numerous nations in the last decade have come to ban such descriptors, on the grounds that terms like "light," "mild," and "low tar" are deceptive and misleading. Under FCTC pressure, even the STMA agreed in 2007 to direct all manufacturers across China to remove a number of these terms from cigarette packaging or marketing. In that same decision, however, the STMA reaffirmed its broader strategy, stating categorically that the industry would continue to display tar and nicotine levels on all cigarette packs.[26] Why? Because for the industry the "low tar, less harmful" mythology remains fundamental to its core business strategy.

"Study and Reflect"

In 2004, the State Tobacco Monopoly Administration held a symposium in the seaside city of Xiamen, titled "Developing Chinese-Style Reduced Tar and Harm Cigarettes." There, the deputy director general of STMA, Zhang Baozhen, reiterated that low-tar cigarettes were central to the long-term future of the domestic tobacco trade. He also emphasized something else: "We need deep study and reflection on . . . reducing tar and harm, developing Chinese-style cigarettes, and the survival and advancement of China Tobacco."[27]

Previously, "study and reflection" had not been a particularly important mandate of the Chinese tobacco industry. But in the aughts, industry funding for tobacco research surged under the STMA's "Science and Technology Development Plan." In 2009 alone, the STMA spent 1.7 billion yuan (around US$250 million) on that plan, a 27 percent increase over 2008.[28] Supported by that funding, from 2001 through 2008 almost a thousand scientific papers on "low-tar" and "modified risk tobacco products" were published in Chinese technical journals.[29] A common claim found in these publications is that research shows that low-tar cigarettes are safer than conventional cigarettes, and that these can be made safer still. Noticeably absent in this literature, though, is rigorous use of internationally recognized health science research methods, such as those employed in epidemiological studies or investigations of how much poison humans inhale.[30] By contrast, independent researchers working without any ties to the industry have shown that irrespective of national origin, low tars pose no less of a threat— and may even pose more of a threat—than regular cigarettes.[31] Two recent studies in China compared the urine metabolites of nicotine and tobacco carcinogens in smokers of regular cigarettes and those who smoked cigarettes advertised as "less harmful." Both revealed that the low-tar cigarettes manufactured in China pose just as much of a threat as regular cigarettes.[32] And at least one study conducted by industry-funded researchers disclosed not only that the carcinogenic potency of nine leading Chinese brands fail to correlate with any robot-measured tar deliveries, but also that levels of benzpyrene and nitrosamine in brands advertised as "low tar" were higher than in cigarettes labeled as having higher tar levels.[33]

Nonetheless, researchers from the Chinese tobacco industry have won six national scientific awards for their studies of harm reduction during the last decade. Receiving three of these awards has been Xie Jianping, deputy director of the Zhengzhou Tobacco Research Institute, an organization closely affiliated with and financed by the STMA/CNTC. Mr. Xie graduated from the Chemistry Department of Nanjing Normal College, receiving a bachelor of science in 1982, and then studied at the industry's Tobacco Research Institute in Zhengzhou, where in 1985 he took a master of science degree in engineering.

Xie's most celebrated research—a purported "hazard index" to rank "low-tar, less-harmful" cigarettes—is highly problematic. Xie has insisted that his indexing studies show a significant improvement in the safety of Chinese cigarettes: "If we set the risk index of cigarettes in China in 2008 at 10, then the risk indices in 2009 and 2010 are 9.7 and 9.3, respectively. The overall trend is clear: we are making progress in harm reduction."[34] This, despite the fact that public health statistics make it clear that death and disease have only grown since the introduction of low-tar gimmicks in China. What props up Xie's claim of "progress"? To rank cigarettes as more or less toxic, he utilizes a form of chemical analysis called the ISO/FTC method. This uses robot smoking machines to evaluate fumes sucked from the very tip of a cigarette's filter. Because it only uses robots, while entirely ignoring how people actually smoke (people typically inhale smoke from "low yield" cigarettes deeper into their lungs), the ISO/FTC method has been widely discredited, with study after study since 1981 showing that it dramatically underestimates the true toxicity of low-tar tobacco products.[35] Many critics, as a result, now actually bar the use of ISO/FTC measurements.

Xie's subterfuge made it relatively easy for him to garner accolades within China's scientific circles in the early 2000s. So too did the degree to which many in the scientific community across the country had been intellectually overrun by the industry's "low-tar, less harm" public relations campaign. Both help explain why, between 2003 and 2010, Xie received no less than three National Scientific and Technological Progress Awards from China's

Ministry of Science and Technology: one for researching improvements to burley tobacco quality for low-tar cigarettes, another for researching the reduction of toxic components in cigarette smoke, and a third for devising a hazards evaluation system for cigarettes.[36]

Then, in December 2011, media outlets announced that Xie had been inducted into the Chinese Academy of Engineering (CAE), one of the highest honors for a scholar in China. The tobacco industry was thrilled and once again wasted no time using Xie's latest scientific accolade for marketing purposes (see Figure 8.3). But some domestic scholars were irate, notably those with strong public health bona fides and ties to tobacco-control advocacy. Controversy quickly ensued, involving waves of Chinese- and English-language news stories. By May 2012, nearly one hundred of China's most prestigious scholars had petitioned the Chinese Academy of Engineering to have Xie's research re-reviewed and his induction into the Academy revoked.[37] Some of Xie's strongest critics dubbed him the "Tobacco Academician."[38] Others vigorously challenged the legitimacy

FIGURE 8.3.
Scientific fraud as marketing tool: National Scientific and Technological Progress Award Certificate for Bio-Reducing Cigarette Technology. On the Wuyeshen cigarettes website. Reproduced from Gonghuan Yang, "Marketing 'Less Harmful, Low-Tar' Cigarettes Is a Key Strategy of the Industry to Counter Tobacco Control in China," *Tobacco Control*, 23 (2014): 168. Gonghuan Yang, ©2013, with permission from BMJ Publishing Group Ltd.

of the screening process leading to his induction, noting that although Xie's research deals with matters crucial to public health, China's Ministry of Health was never asked to review his nomination file. In fact, all the sponsorship for his nomination came from the STMA and Xie's file was reviewed only by members of the academy's Division of Environment and Textiles, none of whom have medical or public health training. As the controversy surrounding Xie grew through 2012, the scientific awards he had received previously were also called into question as those, too, were initiated by the STMA/CNTC without review by the Ministry of Health or credible health experts.[39]

Presumably it was because of this swirling backlash that the newly inducted Xie Jianping was not invited to attend the Eleventh Congress of the CAE in June 2012. But conferees there did not vacate his induction, as requested by petitioners. One news report describes Xie's supporters at the conference as insisting that "the rules of the CAE must be strictly observed. The procedure of electing the new academician is complete; it cannot be changed arbitrarily." So at present, Xie remains a member of the Chinese Academy of Engineering.[40]

Gauging the Efficacy of the "Low-Tar, Less-Harmful" Fraud

How effective has the industry's "low-tar, low-harm" program been at confounding the public? Consider some findings from the 2010 Global Adult Tobacco Survey in China conducted by scholars working with the World Health Organization. One in three respondents to that study said that they agree that low-tar means less harmful.[41] The survey also shows that the industry has been especially effective at targeting individuals of high social status. The higher someone's education, the more likely they are to believe the industry's claims that low-tar cigarettes are safer. Over 45 percent of those with at least a college education agree with the industry's claims, whereas 21 percent of those with an elementary school education or less agree. More troubling patterns appear when it comes to occupation, with half of office workers and 55 persent of medical professionals expressing confidence in the notion that low-tar means less harmful. These data indicate that the industry's "low-tar, less-harmful" strategy has paid off handsomely in terms of shaping the views of people across the country, and especially the views of some of nation's most influential citizens.

FIGURE 8.4.
Bottom of this Zhongnanhai Lights ad states: "Low-harm cigarettes give you more loving care! Cigarettes contain conflicting elements of pleasure and harm. Zhongnanhai has always focused on research and development of low-harm cigarette technology and products. Each [Zhongnanhai] product melds the world's most advanced low-harm cigarette technologies, offering a guarantee of health for your smoking life." (*Zhongnanhai World*, September, 2006).

Another way we must take stock of the industry's "low-tar, low-harm" program is sales. Aggregate cigarette sales were actually declining during the late 1990s—until the industry launched its "low-tar, less-harmful" strategy. Then, following the deception, sales took off again.[42] By 2014, overall cigarette sales nationwide reached a record 2.54 trillion sticks, an increase of nearly 50 percent from 2002.[43] Production and sale of cigarettes advertised as "low-tar" were especially hot during this period. Over the first ten months of 2011, low-tar cigarette production and sales in China hit 2.89 million cases, a year-to-year increase of over 400 percent. For several of the years between 2000 and 2014, the low-tar market was growing nearly ten times faster than the rest of China's cigarette market.[44]

Looking to the Future

There is much to be done and much to be undone. The State Council must immediately empower the State Food and Drug Administration (SFDA) to

FIGURE 8.5.
Numeric representations of "tar content" used as brand marketing on the front of cigarette packs in China. Reproduced from Gonghuan Yang, "Marketing 'Less Harmful, Low-Tar' Cigarettes Is a Key Strategy of the Industry to Counter Tobacco Control in China," *Tobacco Control*, 23 (2014): 170. Gonghuan Yang, ©2013, with permission from BMJ Publishing Group Ltd.

regulate all tobacco products, including low-tar offerings and anything else falling under the burgeoning rubric of (purportedly) "modified risk tobacco products" (MRTPs). Not only should the authority to review and approve tobacco products of all kinds, before and after they come to market, be transferred to the SFDA, but also the State Administration for Industry and

Commerce and the General Administration of Quality Supervision, Inspection, and Quarantine must ban all misleading safety claims and gimmicks being made by the STMA/CNTC and their subsidiaries. Cigarettes advertised as "low tar, less harmful" are no safer than conventional cigarettes, even when prettied up with pastel colors or infused with Chinese medicinal herbs.

But there is more to be done. Article 5 of the Law of the People's Republic of China on Tobacco Monopoly should be revised, as it obviously conflicts with the WHO's Framework Convention. The government should also support research into the role of the STMA/CNTC in disseminating health and safety claims about cigarettes, and it should require that internal archival records of the industry be made available for public inspection.

We also need to know more about how ordinary Chinese perceive the health benefits (or harms) of filters and smoking more generally. We need to know what types of internal policing there has been within the companies, whether CNTC researchers actually believe the propaganda being spewed, and what kinds of research or data have been suppressed. We need to know more about how color, imagery, and symbols have been used to suggest a semblance of safety for certain kinds of cigarettes, and what role psychologists or marketers have played in that deception. We need to better understand how to encourage whistle-blowers within the industry, how to empower a courageous few (or many) to challenge the industry's lock-step uniformity, to pull back some of the curtains hiding the truth. There is a need for action from above and from below: the Chinese government should not permit a replay of the "low-tar, less-harmful" deception that has cost so many millions of lives in other parts of the world. But public health activists must also become less complacent, less complicit; they must become more involved in bringing truth to the populace. What could be of greater importance to the health of the nation and its people?

Notes

1. USDHHS, *The Health Consequences of Smoking: Fifty Years of Progress. A Report of the Surgeon General* (Washington, DC: US Government Printing Office, 2014).

2. Robert N. Proctor, *Golden Holocaust: Origins of the Cigarette Catastrophe and the Case for Abolition* (Berkeley: University of California Press, 2011).

3. Lei Zhangquan et al., "China's Progress on Tar Reduction in Cigarettes: Past, Present and Future," *Tobacco Science and Technology*, issue 5 (2003): 29–31. (Throughout the Notes, all works from the journal *Tobacco Science and Technology* are in Chinese.)

4. The amount of tobacco in Chinese cigarettes dropped from over 56 kg/case in 1981 to 52 kg/case in 1990, and by 1995 had been further reduced to only 44 kg/case. Reductions in leaf per cigarette mean that for the same quantity of leaf, it is possible to produce greater numbers of cigarettes. See State Tobacco Monopoly Administration, *China Tobacco Yearbook 1981–1990* (in Chinese) (Beijing: Economic Daily Press, 1991), p. 37; also State Tobacco Monopoly Administration, *China Tobacco Yearbook 1991–1995* (in Chinese) (Beijing: Economic Daily Press, 1996), p. 26.

5. State Tobacco Monopoly Administration, *China Tobacco Yearbook 1981–1990*, p. 50; State Tobacco Monopoly Administration, *China Tobacco Yearbook 1991–1995*, p. 25; T. W. Hu and Z. Mao, "Effects of Cigarette Tax on Cigarette Consumption and the Chinese Economy," *Tobacco Control* 11 (2002): 105, http://tobaccocontrol .bmj.com/content/tobaccocontrol/11/2/108.full.pdf.

6. For a discussion of how this occurred in one province starting in the early 1980s, see Shandong Province Local History Annals Editing Committee, *Shandong Province Tobacco Annals* (in Chinese), vol. 27 (Ji'nan: Shandong People's Press, 1993), pp. 314–15.

7. Hunan Province Local Annals Editing Committee, *Hunan Provincial Annals* (in Chinese), vol. 9 of *Industrial-Mineral Annals Tobacco Industry* (Changsha: Hunan Press, 1997), p. 155. It should also be noted that some cigarette factories had tried to make their own filters previously. According to oral histories preserved via news reports, factories at Jiangxi, Fujian, and a few other localities manufactured small quantities of filters, affixing them to their cigarettes, even during the latter stages of the Cultural Revolution. See Lin Junrong, "The First Filter-Tipped Cigarette in Fujian" (in Chinese), *East Tobacco Press*, September 23, 2005, http:// www.eastobacco.com/ReadNews.asp?NewsID=40868. In the late 1980s, when filter materials were in short supply, a factory in Henan tried using paper filters. See Henan Provincial Tobacco Tiancai Industrial Science Research Institute, "Report on Attempts to Manufacture Paper Cigarette Filters," *Tobacco Science and Technology*, issue 3 (1973): 4–6; also Hangzhou Paper Plant, "Summary of Experiments on Paper Cigarette Filters," *Tobacco Science and Technology*, issue 1 (1975): 27–29; and "No. 6 People's Paper Plant, Tianjin: Report of Experiment on Wet Handmade Paper Cigarette Filters," published by the Tianjin Cigarette Factory in *Tobacco Science and Technology*, issue 3 (1977): 1–7.

8. Jiang Ming, "The Tobacco Industry Must Adopt Polypropylene Cigarette Tows" (in Chinese), *China Tobacco*, issue 11 (1989), http://www.echinatobacco.com /101588/102220/102403/102414/35489.html.

9. Based on extrapolations of national cigarette tow production capacity by factory in 1999. See Zheng Baoshan, "The State of the Cigarette Tow Industry in China, and Its Future" (in Chinese), *Chemical Commodities Science and Technology*, issue 2 (1992): Table 2: Cigarette tow manufacturers.

10. State Tobacco Monopoly Administration, *China Tobacco Yearbook 1991–1995*, pp. 37–38.

11. S. Mittler, S. Nicholson, and Gu Xikun, "Carcinogenicity of Atmospheric Pollutants," *Journal of Wuhan Medical College*, issue 1 (1958): 22, http://www.cnki.com.cn/Article/CJFDTotal-TJYX195801008.htm; Wang Yangzong, "Post-Trauma Primary Lung Cancer" (in Chinese), *Lanzhou Medical College Journal*, issue 4 (1959): 33–35.

12. Surgeon General, *Smoking and Health: Report of the Advisory Committee to the Surgeon General of the Public Health Service* (Washington, DC: U.S. Department of Health, Education, and Welfare, 1964).

13. Edwin L. Rothfeld et al., "The Acute Effect of Cigarette Smoking on Pulmonary Function Studies" (in Chinese, transl. by Song Lizhang), *Tianjin Medical Journal*, issue 10 (1963): 639. Rothfeld's study was originally published (with D. Biber and A. Bernstein) in *Diseases of the Chest*, 40 (1961): 284–90, claiming that there was no way to determine experimentally the acute effect of smoking on pulmonary function.

14. Ni Qixian, "Relations between Judgments," *Qianxian* (Frontline), issue 16 (1962): 18. In this brief statement found in a journal produced by the Beijing Municipal Party Committee, the author states, "Some people believe that 'smoking is bad for you,' while others believe that 'smoking is not bad for you.' In order to establish which of these opinions is correct, we need experiments and science. But could formal logic also be of use to us in finding the answer to this type of question?" http://www.ixueshu.com/document/bbaa202fc6a4cdf3318947a18e7f9386.html.

15. "Smoking and Health," *Tobacco Science and Technology*, issue 3 (1972): 21–24.

16. Christine P. W. Wong, "Fiscal Reform and Local Industrialization: The Problematic Sequencing of Reform in Post-Mao China," *Modern China*, vol. 18, no. 2 (1992): 197–227.

17. To learn more about these contacts, see the Truth Tobacco Industry Documents archive, at https://www.industrydocumentslibrary.ucsf.edu/tobacco/.

18. "A Canadian Expert Discusses Tobacco Curing," and "A Japanese Expert Comes to China to Discuss Tobacco Production in His Homeland," *Tobacco Science and Technology*, issue 4 (1972): 35–36.

19. "Philip Morris Company Overview," *Tobacco Science and Technology*, issue 3 (1978): 33; and "West German Tobacco Manufacturer Visits China," *Tobacco Science and Technology*, issue 4 (1978): 97.

20. "85 mm Filter Loading Machine Is Successfully Refitted," *Tobacco Science and Technology*, issue 4 (1973): 23.

21. "July 1, China Bans Cigarettes with Excessive Tar," *Beijing Youth Daily*, June 22, 2004, http://www.china.com.cn/chinese/2004/Jun/592384.htm (last accessed on September 7, 2017).

22. See Wang Hanlong, "Change the Structure of Filter-Tipped Cigarettes to Improve Their Safety and Profitability," *Tobacco Science and Technology*, issue 2 (1987): 24–26.

23. "China Tobacco's Dilemma and Hope," Sina, May 9, 2006, http://finance .sina.com.cn/review/observe/20060509/18562553659.shtml (last accessed on September 7, 2017); Peng Jialing, "People's Special Feature: Cut the Focus Triggering Tobacco Industry Changes," *People's Daily*, July 5, 2004, http://www.people.com .cn/GB/jingji/1045/2616246.html (last accessed on September 7, 2017).

24. In 2008, the U.S. Federal Trade Commission disavowed this method of measuring tar and nicotine, labeling it one of the industry's "deceptive marketing practices." Federal Trade Commission, "FTC Rescinds Guidance from 1966 on Statements Concerning Tar and Nicotine Yields," press release, November 26, 2008, http://www .ftc.gov/opa/2008/11/cigarettetesting.shtm (last accessed on September 7, 2017).

25. Judge Kessler, "Final Opinion," *United States v. Philip Morris*, Civil Action Number 99–2496 (GK), 2006, http://www.tobaccolawcenter.org/documents/Final Opinion.pdf (last accessed January 31, 2013).

26. "Rules on Cigarette Package Labeling in the Jurisdiction of the People's Republic of China," STMA, 2007, http://www.tobaccocontrollaws.org/files/live/ China/China%20-%20Rules%20on%20Cigarette%20Package%20Labeling%20 %20-%20national.pdf (last accessed on September 7, 2017).

27. Zhang Baozhen, "Speech at the Forum on the Development of Chinese-Style Cigarettes with Low Tar and Less Harm: Paying Attention to Public Health, Promoting Harmony" (in Chinese), April 27, 2010, http://www.tobaccoinfo.com .cn/ztxw/2010/04/33312.shtml (last accessed January 31, 2013).

28. Jiang Chengkang, *Report on the 2009 National Tobacco Working Conference* (in Chinese), January 13, 2009, http://www.tobacco.gov.cn/history_filesystem/ 2009gzh/news1.html (accessed January 31, 2013).

29. Liu Xiaozhou, "The Influence of Chinese Tobacco Enterprises' 'Harm Reduction' Activities on Tobacco Control" (in Chinese), http://cdmd.cnki.com.cn/ Article/CDMD-84501-2009203572.htm (last accessed March 20, 2012).

30. Zhu Maoxiang et al., "Cell Biological Evaluation for Sheng Nong Extraction on Reducing Harmfulness of Smoking" (in Chinese), Chinese Tobacco Academic Annual Meeting, 2002, http://wenku.baidu.com/view/c65f5124bcd126fff7050bd3 .html (accessed January 31, 2013); Xie Jianping et al., "A Study of the Hazards Indices of Cigarette Smoke," *Tobacco Science and Technology*, issue 2 (2009), http://www .cnki.com.cn/Article/CJFDTotal-YCKJ200902001.htm (accessed January 31, 2013).

31. That is the conclusion of the 2014 U.S. "Surgeon General's Report on Smoking and Tobacco Use," https://www.cdc.gov/tobacco/data_statistics/sgr/index.htm (last accessed on September 7, 2017).

32. Quan Gan et al., "Chinese 'Low-Tar' Cigarettes Do Not Deliver Lower Levels of Nicotine and Carcinogens," *Tobacco Control*, 19 (October 2010): 374–79; Quan Gan et al., "Chinese 'Herbal' Cigarettes Are as Carcinogenic and Addictive as Regular Cigarettes," *Cancer Epidemiol Biomarkers and Prevention*, 18 (December 2009): 3497–501.

33. Du Yongmei, Xiao Xiezhong, and Wang Yunbai, "Smoke Tar and Cigarette Safety" (in Chinese), *Chinese Tobacco Science*, 2 (2002): 31–44, http://mall.cnki.net/magazine/Article/ZGYV200202009.htm (accessed January 31, 2013).

34. Wang Chengcheng, "A New Exploration of Harm and Chinese-Style Cigarettes" (in Chinese), *China Tobacco*, no. 3 (2011), http://www.echinatobacco.com/zhongguoyancao/2011-02/01/content_250361.htm (last accessed January 31, 2013).

35. World Health Organization, Scientific Advisory Committee on Tobacco Product Regulation, *SACTob Conclusions on Health Claims Derived from ISO/FTC Method to Measure Cigarette Yield* (Geneva: WHO, 2003), http://www.who.int/tobacco/sactob/recommendations/en/iso_ftc_en.pdf (last accessed March 20, 2012).

36. Ministry of Science and Technology, "List of National Scientific and Technological Progress Awards," 2003: No. J-211-2-03, "Research on Improving Burley Tobacco Quality and Its Application in Low-Tar Cigarettes," http://www.most.gov.cn/cxfw/kjjlcx/kjjl2003/200802/t20080214_59048.htm (accessed March 20, 2012); ibid., 2004: No. J-211-2-03, "Technology Research and Application on Reducing Harmful Ingredients," http://www.360docs.net/doc/info-101538fed 15abe23482f4db9-7.html (accessed August 23, 2017); ibid., 2010: No. J-211-2-01, "Establishment and Application of a Hazard Assessment and Control System for Cigarettes," http://www.most.gov.cn/ztzl/gjkxjs jldh/jldh2010/jldh10jlgg/201101/t20110115_84315.htm (accessed March 20, 2012).

37. "One Hundred Academicians Ask to Review and Reconsider Xie's Validation as a Qualified Academician" (in Chinese), *Beijing News*, http://news.163.com/12/0530/02/82NHNTV000014AED.html (accessed January 31, 2013).

38. "Tobacco Research Scholar Becomes an Academician, Leading to a Dispute over the Network about the So-called 'Tobacco Academician'" (in Chinese), *Southern Daily*, http://china.nfdaily.cn/content/2011-12/09/content_34672668.htm (accessed March 20, 2012).

39. Ministry of Health, press release (in Chinese), April 12, 2012, http://www.moh.gov.cn/publicfiles/business/htmlfiles/mohbgt/s3582/201204/54488.htm (accessed January 31, 2013).

40. "'Tobacco Academician' Was Not Invited to Attend the 11th Academician Congress of CAE, CAE Will Continue to Discuss His Qualifications" (in Chinese),

Southern Metropolis Daily, June 12, 2012, https://goo.gl/KdecıA (accessed August 24, 2017); "CAE's Response, Will Not Dismiss the 'Tobacco Academician'" (in Chinese), *China Youth Daily*, March 8, 2013, http://zqb.cyol.com/html/2013-03/08/nw.D110000zgqnb_20130308_5-T01.htm (accessed September 5, 2017).

41. Chinese Center for Disease Control and Prevention, *Global Adult Tobacco Survey (GATS): China 2010 Country Report* (in Chinese) (Beijing: Sanxia Press, 2011).

42. See Figure I.1 in Matthew Kohrman's introductory chapter to this volume.

43. Euromonitor, "Big Cigarette Sales Rise in 2008 for China," 2008; Euromonitor, "Tobacco in China," 2017. Both items accessed via Euromonitor's Passport database (accessed January 31, 2013).

44. Zhang Yu, "Marketing Low-Tar Cigarettes to Start New Era of Digging Gold Nuggets" (in Chinese), *New Tobacco* 21 (2011), http://www.echinatobacco.com/xinyancao/2011-11/01/content_292532.htm (accessed January 31, 2013).

CHAPTER NINE

Aiding Tobacco
Academic-Industry Collaboration in China

Gan Quan and Stanton A. Glantz

To protect their markets and profits, multinationals from Philip Morris to British American Tobacco and R.J. Reynolds have sponsored research in universities as part of systematic efforts to cast doubt about the dangers of smoking and exposure to secondhand smoke and undermine the need for tobacco control. This campaign dates back to the 1950s, taking root in a variety of academic institutions based in Europe, the United States, and other Western countries.[1] Scientists and physicians willing to take money from the multinationals in exchange for "cigarette friendly" research have been central to the campaign.[2] This pattern of misbehavior was a central element in the ruling, upheld on appeal, by U.S. federal judge Gladys Kessler that the major cigarette companies and their research organizations created an illegal "enterprise" to defraud the public in violation of the Racketeer Influenced and Corrupt Organizations Act.[3]

This manipulation of science has led many academic institutions to adopt formal policies of refusing to accept money from the tobacco industry.[4] For similar reasons, several funding agencies have adopted policies of not awarding grants to institutions that accept tobacco industry funding, and several scholarly journals now have policies of refusing to even consider publications authored by researchers funded by the industry.[5]

Multinational tobacco companies also used deceptive strategies in Thailand, Hong Kong, and China in the late 1980s and 1990s.[6] As part of its effort to coordinate strategies to fight smoke-free legislation worldwide, in 1996 Philip Morris contracted with state tobacco monopolies in Asia, including the China National Tobacco Corporation (CNTC), to establish the Asian Regional Tobacco Industry Science Team (ARTIST), which later developed into an industry organization of scientific representatives.[7] Many researchers from the CNTC as well as researchers from Chinese academic institutions were involved in ARTIST, which included a network to develop allegedly "safer" cigarettes.[8]

Even though China is the world's largest tobacco market and home to the largest tobacco company, little is known about the relationship between the China National Tobacco Corporation and university and other academic researchers. The CNTC oversees nearly all aspects of tobacco in China, proudly asserting that its system continues to repel foreign competitors, leaving them with less than 1 percent of the country's formal cigarette market.[9] The CNTC is part of the central government. Under the umbrella of the CNTC, each province and many cities and towns have their own CNTC branch companies. This massive network monopolizes not only the production and sale of cigarettes, but also the growing and purchase of all tobacco leaf. As efforts to reduce the burden of tobacco-induced death and disease have developed in China, particularly in response to the World Health Organization's Framework Convention on Tobacco Control (FCTC), the CNTC has organized affiliated research institutions to examine the impact of the FCTC and to develop countermeasures to blunt its impact.[10]

China is following global trends as it develops the cigarette market in an environment of increasing public understanding of the dangers of smoking, following a similar course as happened in the West decades ago, with growing public concern about the dangers of smoking and pressure to protect people from exposure to secondhand smoke. This growing awareness has created an urgent need for the CNTC to develop products to present to the public as "safer" and to maintain its position as a legitimate business. To do so, the CNTC is relying more than ever on academic institutions to meet its R&D and social normalization requirements.

R&D Sponsored by the World's Largest Tobacco Company

At the national level, there are currently three main Chinese tobacco research institutes, in the cities of Zhengzhou, Beijing, and Qingzhou. All three are owned by the CNTC, which also owns a number of smaller branch corporations, each with their own institutes (Figure 9.1 and Table 9.1).

The largest of these is the Zhengzhou Tobacco Research Institute (ZTRI), founded in northern Henan Province just south of the Yellow River in the early 1950s.[11] In 1953, four years after the founding of the People's Republic of China, the Communist government nationalized Chunghwa Tobacco, previously owned by the Kuomintang government, and Yizhong Tobacco, previously owned by British American Tobacco. The tobacco research divisions of both companies were merged and placed under the newly created Shanghai Tobacco Cigarette Factory. The new institute, called the Technology Research Division, began erecting research buildings in Zhengzhou City during the late 1950s. In the mid-1980s it was renamed the Zhengzhou Tobacco Research Institute after merging with the China National Tobacco Corporation.[12] In 2015 it employed a staff of over 280, including over 117 research professionals with advanced degrees.[13]

In addition to these national-level institutions, the CNTC has branch corporations in each province and in many cities and towns. Many of these have their own tobacco research institutes to support local tobacco farming

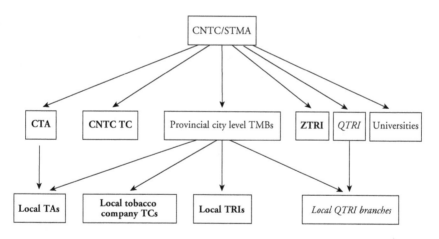

FIGURE 9.1.
Hierarchy of CNTC's research capacities and relationship with academic institutions. Reproduced from Quan Gan and Stanton A. Glantz, "Relationship between the Chinese Tobacco Industry and Academic Institutions in China," *Tobacco Control*, vol. 20, issue 1 (January 2011), ©2011, with permission from BMJ Publishing Group Ltd.

NOTE: Tobacco-company-owned research institutions are in **bold** and academic institutions are in *italics*. CNTC: China National Tobacco Corporation; STMA: State Tobacco Monopoly Administration; CTA: China Tobacco Association; CNTC TC: China National Tobacco Corporation Training Center (located in Zhengzhou); TMBs: Tobacco Monopoly Bureaus; ZTRI: Zhengzhou Tobacco Research Institute; QTRI: Qingzhou Tobacco Research Institute; TAs: tobacco associations; TCs: training centers; TRIs: tobacco research institutes.

TABLE 9.1
Some of CNTC's affiliated research and training institutions

Tobacco research institute (TRI)	Name of institute	Relationship with tobacco companies
Research institutions directly affiliated with CNTC	Zhengzhou TRI[1]	The only TRI owned by CNTC at the national level.
	Hubei TRI	Provincial-level TRI, affiliated with Hubei TMB. China Burley Tobacco Research Center (directly affiliated with CNTC) is housed in Hubei TRI.
	Shaanxi TRI	Provincial-level TRI, affiliated with Shaanxi TMB.
	Jiangxi TRI	Provincial-level TRI, affiliated with Jiangxi TMB.
	Yunnan TRI[2]	Provincial-level TRI, affiliated with Yunnan TMB. China Burley Tobacco Research (Southern) Center (directly affiliated with CNTC) is housed within Yunnan TRI.
	Guizhou TRI[3]	Provincial-level TRI, affiliated with Guizhou TMB. China Tobacco Southwest Agricultural Test Center (directly affiliated with CNTC) is housed in Guizhou TRI.
	Heilongjiang TRI[4]	Provincial-level TRI, affiliated with Heilongjiang TMB.
	Sanming TRI	City-level TRI, affiliated with Sanming TMB, Fujian Province.
	Shaotong TRI	City-level TRI, affiliated with Shaotong TMB, Yunnan Province.
	Nanxiong TRI	City-level TRI, affiliated with Nanxiong TMB, Guangdong Province.
	Qujing TRI	City-level TRI, affiliated with Qujing TMB, Yunnan Province.
	Chuxiong TRI	City-level TRI, affiliated with Chuxiong TMB, Yunnan Province.
	Tongren TRI	City-level TRI, affiliated with Tongren TMB, Guizhou Province.
CNTC training centers	Zhengzhou Tobacco School[5]	National-level training center, also a zhongzhuan, affiliated with CNTC, located in Zhengzhou, Henan Province.
	Yunnan Tobacco School[6]	Provincial-level training center, affiliated with Yunnan TMB.
	Shandong Tobacco School[7]	Provincial-level training center, also a zhongzhuan, affiliated with Shandong TMB. Collaborates with Shandong University and Shandong Agricultural University in tobacco training.
	Heilongjiang Tobacco School[8]	Provincial-level training center, also a zhongzhuan, affiliated with Heilongjiang TMB.
	Xiangtan Tobacco School[9]	Provincial-level training center, also a zhongzhuan, affiliated with Hunan TMB.
	Anhui Tobacco Training Center[10]	Provincial-level training center, affiliated with Anhui TMB.

(continued)

Tobacco research institute (TRI)	Name of institute	Relationship with tobacco companies
	Jilin Tobacco Training Center[11]	Provincial-level training center, affiliated with Jilin TMB. Jointly set up by Jilin TMB and Changchun Tax School.
	Fujian Tobacco Training Center[12]	Provincial-level training center, affiliated with Fujian TMB.
	Inner Mongolia Tobacco Training Center[13]	Provincial-level training center, affiliated with Inner Mongolia TMB.
	Jiangxi Tobacco Training Center[14]	Provincial-level training center, affiliated with Jiangxi TMB.
Tobacco associations	China Tobacco Association[15]	Affiliated with CNTC.
	Local tobacco associations	Affiliated with CNTC branch agencies at the corresponding level of the tobacco association (provincial, city, town).
Academic research institutions	Qingzhou Tobacco Research Institute[16]	A branch institute of the Chinese Academy of Agricultural Sciences, under the joint direction of CNTC. Among the top 10 academic institutions in number of tobacco publications.
	Anhui Institute of Tobacco Research[17]	Provincial-level TRI, affiliated with Anhui Academy of Agricultural Sciences, strong ties with Anhui Tobacco Monopoly Bureau.
	Henan Institute of Tobacco Research[18]	Provincial-level TRI, affiliated with Henan Academy of Agricultural Sciences, under strong influence from Henan Tobacco Monopoly Bureau. Among the top 10 academic institutions in number of tobacco publications.
	Yunnan Agricultural Institute[19]	Among the top 10 academic institutions in number of tobacco publications.
	Ganzhou TRI	City-level TRI, affiliated with Ganzhou Agricultural Sciences Research Institute, under the supervision of Ganzhou TMB, Jiangxi Province.
Universities	Henan Agricultural University[20]	CNTC established the National Tobacco Research Center (NTRC) in Henan Agricultural University. NTRC is directly affiliated with CNTC. Among the top 10 academic institutions in number of tobacco publications.
	Hunan Agricultural University[21]	China Tobacco South-Central Agricultural Experiment Station, established by Hunan TMB and Hunan Agricultural University, is situated in Hunan Agricultural University. Among the top 10 academic institutions in number of tobacco publications.
	University of Science and Technology of China	Tobacco and Health Research Center[22] closely tied to CNTC, conducts joint education programs with CNTC.[23] Among the top 10 academic institutions in number of tobacco publications.

(continued)

Tobacco research institute (TRI)	Name of institute	Relationship with tobacco companies
	Chinese Academy of Sciences[24]	Joint PhD program with CNTC. Among the top 10 academic institutions in number of tobacco publications.
	Dongnan University[25]	Joint PhD program with CNTC.
	Yunnan University[26]	Among the top 10 academic institutions in number of tobacco publications.
	Shandong Agricultural University[27]	Among the top 10 academic institutions in number of tobacco publications.
	Yunnan Agricultural University[28]	Among the top 10 academic institutions in number of tobacco publications.

NOTE: TMB: Tobacco Monopoly Bureau; TRI: Tobacco Research Institute; zhongzhuan: vocational high school. The list is not comprehensive and only includes institutions that have websites.

SOURCE: Reproduced from Quan Gan and Stanton A. Glantz, "Relationship between the Chinese Tobacco Industry and Academic Institutions in China," Tobacco Control, vol. 20, issue 1 (January 2011), ©2011, with permission from BMJ Publishing Group Ltd.

[1] http://www.ztri.com.cn/ (access date: July 13, 2013)

[2] http://www.yntsti.com/ (access date: July 13, 2013)

[3] http://www.gzyks.cn (access date:July 13, 2013)

[4] http://www.hljyczb.com/index.html (access date: July 13, 2013)

[5] http://www.ctt.cn/elms/newportal/index-8.jsp?parentType=2000 (access date: July 13, 2013)

[6] http://www.ctt.cn/elms/portal/more.jsp?parentType=10&type=10&company=yn (access date: July 13, 2013)

[7] http://www.cnsdjxw.com/school_brows.asp?id=3906 (access date: July 13, 2013)

[8] http://www.ctt.cn/elms/portal/more.jsp?parentType=10&type=10&company=hlj (access date: July 13, 2013)

[9] http://www.xtyx.com/ (access date: July 13, 2013)

[10] http://www.ctt.cn/elms/portal/more.jsp?parentType=10&type=10&company=ah (access date: July 13, 2013)

[11] http://www.ctt.cn/elms/portal/more.jsp?parentType=10&type=10&company=jl (access date: July 13, 2013)

[12] http://www.ctt.cn/elms/portal/more.jsp?parentType=10&type=10&company=fj (access date: July 13, 2013)

[13] http://www.ctt.cn/elms/portal/more.jsp?parentType=10&type=10&company=nmg (access date: July 13, 2013)

[14] http://www.ctt.cn/elms/portal/more.jsp?parentType=10&type=10&company=jx (access date: July 13, 2013)

[15] http://www.tobacco.org.cn/html/index.html (access date: July 13, 2013)

[16] http://www.caas.net.cn/caasnew/jg/yzgsw/51195.shtml (access date: July 13, 2013)

[17] http://www.ati.org.cn/showjgsz.asp?art_id=2&cat_id=16 (access date: July 13, 2013)

[18] http://baike.baidu.com/view/1477252.html?fromTaglist (access date: July 13, 2013)

[19] http://www.yaas.org.cn (access date: July 13, 2013)

[20] http://baike.baidu.com/view/299689.html (access date: July 13, 2013)

[21] http://hnndxb.cuepa.cn/show_more.php?doc_id=19930 (access date: July 13, 2013)

[22] http://www.tobaccocollege.com/tcads/tccenter.htm (access date: July 13, 2013)

[23] http://www.tobacco.gov.cn/html/21/2101/67728_n.html (access date: July 13, 2013)

[24] http://www.gsc.dicp.ac.cn/zsxx/lhpybsgg.htm (access date: July 13, 2013)

[25] http://kaoyan.eol.cn/yuan_xiao_xin_xi_3988/20061212/t20061212_209166.shtml (access date: July 13, 2013)

[26] http://www.ynu.edu.cn (access date: July 13, 2013)

[27] http://www.sdau.edu.cn (access date: July 13, 2013)

[28] http://www.ynau.edu.cn (access date: July 13, 2013)

and product development (see Table 9.1). Many of the research laboratories affiliated with the CNTC are housed in these local research institutes. Because the CNTC is part of the central government—under the auspices of the State Tobacco Monopoly Administration—the CNTC and its branch corporations, as well as their affiliated tobacco research institutes, are all supported by government funding.

CNTC's Relationship with Academic Institutions

In addition to overseeing research institutes that sit administratively within the tobacco company system, the CNTC also maintains a close relationship with many academic institutions (Figure 9.1 and Table 9.1). Most academic research institutions and universities in China and all of those listed in Table 9.1 are government owned. The Chinese Academy of Agricultural Sciences (CAAS), the most prestigious public agricultural research unit in China, established its tobacco research institute in 1958 in Qingzhou City, Shandong Province.[14] In 1987 the CNTC and CAAS began to co-administer this institute and added another name—"China Tobacco Qingzhou Tobacco Research Institute"—to its official title. The Qingzhou Research Institute (QTRI) boasts the second largest number of journal publications on tobacco between 1983 and 2012 (683 articles), second only to the Yunnan Tobacco Research Institute (with 809 articles), owned by the Yunnan Tobacco Monopoly Bureau.[15]

For decades, the CNTC has also maintained a close relationship with a number of different universities, some of which now offer degrees in tobacco research. Henan Agricultural University established the first tobacco science major in China in 1975. In 1984, the CNTC began to support Henan Agricultural University, helping to establish tobacco farming degree programs that granted undergraduate, master's, and PhD degrees as well as coursework in continuing education.[16] In 1997, the CNTC established a National Tobacco Research Center (NTRC) within Henan University operating under the direct administration of the CNTC. The NTRC is a research and education-oriented institute with the goals of promoting innovations in tobacco farming and cigarette manufacturing, and training tobacco researchers.[17] The QTRI and NTRC have both become major tobacco research centers at the national level along with the ZTRI.

In 2004 Changde Cigarette Factory, a CNTC subsidiary in Hunan Province, established a Tobacco Engineering and Technology Research and Development Center and a program for master's and PhD students and post-doctoral fellows at Hunan Agricultural University.[18] Three years later the CNTC established its China Tobacco South-Central Agricultural Experiment Station in Hunan Agricultural University, with a focus on breeding and cultivation techniques.[19]

According to Ministry of Education regulations, only universities and government-affiliated research institutions can grant bachelor's, master's, and PhD degrees. Because the CNTC is part of the central government, however, and since the ZTRI is affiliated with the CNTC, this means that the ZTRI in Zhengzhou can have its own master's programs dedicated to tobacco chemistry, cigarette manufacturing, and tobacco farming. The ZTRI also has a joint PhD program with the Chinese Academy of Sciences (on tobacco chemistry) and another joint PhD program with Dongnan University (on cigarette manufacturing).[20] It might seem strange to outsiders that one can get a doctoral degree in cigarette manufacturing, but such is the state of affairs in China in 2017.

In 1999 the Hefei Institute of Economics and Technology, established by the CNTC in 1989 and under the direction of the CNTC ever since,[21] was merged into the University of Science and Technology of China (USTC), one of China's most prestigious universities, and a Tobacco and Health Research Center was established at that university.[22] The director of the Tobacco and Health Research Center is a member of the CNTC's Science and Technology Committee, which is responsible for scientific evaluation, including grant evaluation, within the CNTC. Beginning in 2003 the CNTC and USTC established a tele-continuing education tobacco program that confers bachelor of science degrees in tobacco farming and cigarette manufacturing on CNTC employees.[23] In 2007, the CNTC expanded its collaboration with USTC by establishing a joint master of business administration program and a mechanical engineering master's program for CNTC employees.[24]

Another top university in China, Renmin University in Beijing, did not until 2012 have strong ties with the tobacco industry. In December 2012, the deputy director of the CNTC, Zhao Hongshun, was elected to the board of Renmin University. During the ceremony honoring that appointment, the president of Renmin University expressed his hope that Zhao's election would facilitate collaboration between the university and the industry.

The CNTC and its local corporations have also established training centers for the continuing education of their employees (Table 9.1). Although training is the primary focus, investigators from these centers participate in a broad range of tobacco research, including studies into the health effects of tobacco use, either by themselves or in collaboration with researchers from the industry. Five of these training centers were also established within *zhuanke* (vocational training, or junior college level) schools, which are part of the higher education system just like universities, except one level lower.

The Chinese tobacco industry has also become involved in the education of school-aged children. According to a 2010 report by the Tobacco Control Office at China CDC, more than a hundred elementary schools nationwide are sponsored by tobacco companies, with the schools renamed after the tobacco companies. And according to a CNTC spokesperson, the industry's sponsorship of these schools is a "contribution to social welfare."[25]

Research Productivity and the Focus of the CNTC

The number of papers published in China on tobacco has increased dramatically over the past thirty years since the founding of the CNTC (see Figure 9.2).[26] Tobacco farming and cigarette manufacturing dominated this work by the CNTC, but fell from 79 percent of all the research papers in 1983–1987 to only 64 percent in 2008–2013. Publications on quality assessment and quality control of tobacco leaf and cigarettes and tobacco company management grew over this same time frame, reflecting the fact that the CNTC has put more resources into developing a more sophisticated product and improving the managerial efficiency of the industry.

Health research has never been a major focus of Chinese cigarette manufacturers, but what we have seen is a sizable increase in research into "low-tar" cigarettes (Figure 9.2), especially during the period between 2008 and 2012. This increase suggests that the CNTC is transitioning from a focus on increasing productivity to a focus more on product development and managerial refinement. During the 2010 National Tobacco Working Meeting, CNTC director Jiang Chengkang reported that developing "low-tar, less-harmful cigarettes" had been set as one of the CNTC's major objectives. The report also set the goal of lowering the maximum level of tar to below 12 mg/cigarette by January 1, 2011, and to below 10 mg/cigarette by

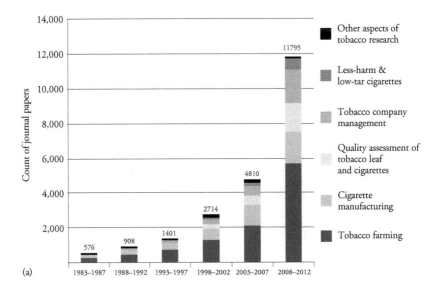

(a)

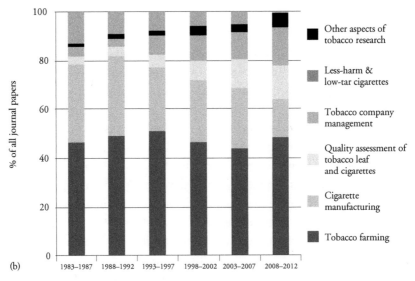

(b)

FIGURE 9.2.

(a) The number of research papers published by tobacco companies or sponsored by tobacco companies in six areas of tobacco research between 1983 and 2012. (b) Mix of topics of research papers published or sponsored by tobacco companies in six areas of tobacco research between 1983 and 2012.

NOTE: The data have been obtained from a search of online databases of journal articles published in both Chinese and English for academic institutions in China conducting research with or sponsored by Chinese tobacco companies. The websites of tobacco companies, their affiliated institutions, and academic institutions were also searched for reports of collaborations. For details on the methods, see Quan Gan and Stanton A. Glantz, "Relationship between the Chinese Tobacco Industry and Academic Institutions in China," *Tobacco Control*, vol. 20, issue 1 (January 2).

January 1, 2015—as measured by the industry's deceptive smoking robots. The report also stated that "for major cigarette brands in China, developing low-tar, less-harmful cigarettes is not only needed for development, but for survival."[27]

In late 2011, Xie Jianping, the deputy director of the Zhengzhou Tobacco Research Institute, owned by the China National Tobacco Corporation, was elected to the Chinese Academy of Engineering (CAE), one of the most prestigious honors a scholar can receive in China. Xie's main research is on developing low-tar and herbal cigarettes that supposedly reduce the harms of smoking. The election of Xie to the CAE gave the industry self-justification for its "less-harm, low-tar" campaign and more resources are expected to be put into research and development for such misleading products in the future.

Collaborations between the CNTC and Academic Institutions in Published Research Papers

Academic institutions are heavily involved in tobacco companies' research. Forty-two percent of all the papers published by tobacco company researchers or sponsored by tobacco companies involve academic collaborations. The percentage was only 6 percent in the mid-1980s but increased to nearly half in the first decade of the new millennium—and then dropped slightly (to 45 percent) during 2008–2012 (see Figure 9.3). In the thirty years be-

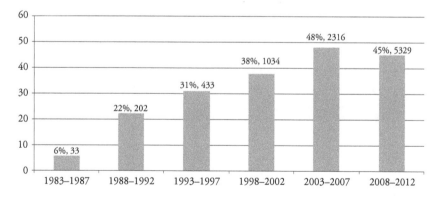

FIGURE 9.3.
Percentages of academic involvement in papers published or funded by tobacco companies over the years as reflected in joint authorship in journal publications.

NOTE: The denominator for the percentages is the number of papers published or funded by the Chinese tobacco companies. For the source of the data, see the Note in Figure 9.2.

tween the founding of the CNTC and 2012, the CNTC collaborated with or sponsored tobacco research in 337 universities and 160 public research institutes, as evidenced by joint authorship or disclosures of company sponsorship. One hundred and fifty-four universities and 68 public research institutions conducted tobacco research with declared tobacco company sponsorship, and the remainder collaborated with the companies through joint authorship.[28]

The extent of collaboration with the CNTC varies considerably among academic institutions. The ten academic institutions with the most collaboration (Table 9.1) account for 64 percent of all the coauthored research papers with industry researchers, while three-fourths of the academic institutions have published fewer than five research papers coauthored with the tobacco companies.

Academic institutions are most actively involved in three segments of tobacco research: tobacco farming, quality assessment of leaf and cigarettes, and research into "low-tar, less-harmful" cigarettes (Figure 9.4). From 2008 to 2012, for example, 60 percent of the papers published on tobacco farming have academic researchers as coauthors. Academic researchers are coauthors of 54 percent and 43 percent of the papers on quality assessment and on "low-tar, less-harmful" cigarettes.

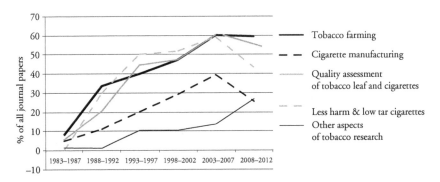

FIGURE 9.4.
The increasing involvement of academic researchers in tobacco companies' research over the years in different segments of tobacco research, as reflected in the percentage of joint authorship of published research papers out of all papers published or sponsored by tobacco companies.
NOTE: For the source of the data, see the Note in Figure 9.2.

Implications of the CNTC's Research for Tobacco Control

The CNTC maintains an extensive network of tobacco research institutions owned by the industry. Exploiting its official role as a government agency, the CNTC has set up research centers throughout China to train its employees and to advance its research agenda, here again involving academic scholars. Increasingly over time the industry has come to rely on academic investigators in every aspect of tobacco research, with the important exception of research into the actual harms caused by smoking. There is little evidence that the Chinese tobacco industry has ever been involved in research—internal or extramural sponsored—into the health dangers of smoking.

In publications we surveyed, the industry did not seem to fund research to create a controversy over the link between smoking and disease. This is probably because the evidence of the dangers of smoking has been so conclusive in both Western and Chinese medical literatures. Chinese cigarette makers *have* shown increasing interest in the development of (purported) "harm-reduction" techniques, however. Hundreds of research papers have been published on low-tar and herbal cigarettes, both of which have been claimed by CNTC to be less harmful.[29] The tobacco industry has also used academic authorities as spokespersons to justify the "less-harmful, low-tar" strategy.[30] The CNTC promotes "low-tar, less-harmful" research and products in the name of protecting the public's health, but there is no evidence that these products actually make smoking any less hazardous.

In contrast, independent research has shown that low-tar and herbal cigarettes do not deliver lower doses of nicotine or carcinogens—not in China nor anywhere else.[31] Because access to internal CNTC documents is very limited, it is hard to find evidence that the industry is promoting "low-tar, less-harmful" cigarettes as part of a deliberate campaign of deception, like in some Western countries such as the United States.[32] But a paper published by Xie Jianping, China's premier defender of "low-tar, less-harmful" cigarettes, revealed his awareness (and presumably that of other industry researchers as well) of the defects of the "ISO" or "FTC method" in measuring the intake of smokers from low-tar cigarettes as early as 2006.[33] Xie nonetheless has continued to promote his "ISO method"–based "less harmful" research and used the defective evaluation method in all his research on low-tar and herbal cigarettes. Serious questions have been raised about Xie's credibility as a researcher, especially since his election into the Chinese

Academy of Engineering. Neither Xie nor the CNTC has ever responded to such criticism in public.

In light of the globalization of the tobacco market and increasing communication between the CNTC and the large transnational cigarette manufacturers,[34] the CNTC may develop and adopt more sophisticated promotion strategies, including conducting research and sponsoring academic research to confuse the public about the health consequences of smoking and secondhand smoke.[35] Existing evidence, while limited, suggests that the Chinese tobacco industry in certain respects is acting much as the transnational tobacco companies have acted in the past, using popular athletes to promote cigarettes, for example, and also making unjustified claims about low-tar and herbal cigarettes.[36] In September 2009, a Chinese tobacco industry official openly questioned the science linking secondhand smoke with disease during a public hearing on smoke-free legislation in Shanghai.[37] To foster debate around tobacco, though, it would seem that the industry knows it needs to deploy voices that appear more scholarly and thus authoritative. Oreskes and Conway laid out in *Merchants of Doubt* how leading scientists were hired in the United States to disseminate opinions contrary to conclusions reached by the mainstream scientific community to confuse the public.[38] Similarly, the Chinese tobacco industry has been keen to support their own researchers, like Xie Jianping, to be elected to prestigious posts. Xie's academic research on light and mild cigarettes, though under serious question by the public health community, and his comments in media about the issue, have undoubtedly helped the legitimacy and the promotion of light and mild cigarettes by the Chinese tobacco industry in the past decade.

Implications of China's Ratification of the Framework Convention on Tobacco Control

That the CNTC is a government agency legitimizes tobacco sponsorship among academic researchers and their institutions. Several academic institutions openly take pride in the great number of research projects sponsored by the CNTC and in being allowed to contribute to the company's research and development agenda. As mentioned above, the CNTC also maintains administrative authority over the tobacco research centers in several universities. Article 5.3 of the Framework Convention on Tobacco Control, ratified by China in 2005, clearly states that a country's tobacco control policies should be protected from tobacco industry influence and manipulations.[39] Tobacco sponsorship of academic research and tobacco industry involvement in the administration of academic research centers can easily subject academic research to industry influence.

While there is no direct evidence of the kind of systematic manipulation of the scientific process to protect the CNTC's interests known to have been common among the multinational companies, closer links to the multinationals have been forged since Philip Morris's ARTIST program in 1996 when the multinationals first reached out to the CNTC to involve it in their global efforts to manipulate science to defend the global tobacco industry's interests.[40] To the extent that the CNTC's involvement with academic institutions provides an avenue for influencing tobacco control policy making, these connections violate Article 5.3 of the FCTC.

In addition to violating FCTC Article 5.3, CNTC sponsorship of elementary schools violates FCTC Article 13, which clearly bans sponsorship from the tobacco industry in any form, including donations to educational institutions.[41] Such behavior of the CNTC likely promotes tobacco use and normalizes the tobacco industry and its involvement in education.[42] Chinese academic institutions should also consider the fact that engagement with the tobacco industry, particularly on issues related to health or the promotion of tobacco products, could damage their reputation, a concern that has led many Western universities to eschew relationships with the industry.

Limitations of This Work

Although more and more scientific journals in China require disclosure of funding sources for publication, many still do not. This could well lead to an underestimate of the extent of tobacco company sponsorship. It should also be recognized that collaborations between the industry and academic researchers is not restricted to scientific publications, which is what we have examined in this chapter. While all the research funds examined here came from the tobacco industry, in some parts of China where tobacco tax contributes a considerable portion of local revenue, provincial and city governments sometimes support research into tobacco through other departments—such as the Department of Technology or the Department of Agriculture. These funds are beyond the scope of examination of this chapter, yet it should be noted that there are other sources of support besides the industry for academic researchers to conduct research on tobacco.

In contrast to the United States, the UK, and some other countries for which there are extensive internal documents from the transnational tobacco companies available as a result of litigation in the United States (and accessible through the UCSF Legacy Tobacco Documents Library, http://legacy.library.ucsf.edu), few CNTC internal documents are available. This has limited the depth of our understanding of the ties between the Chinese tobacco industry and academic researchers. For instance, our analysis included one hundred publications of Professor Zhou Jiheng from Hunan Agricultural University, and 60 percent of these publications are disclosed as being funded by the tobacco industry. A notorious lobbyist for the tobacco industry, Professor Zhou has signed many research contracts with the CNTC. However, because of the lack of access to such confidential information, our understanding of the true nature of the ties is limited.

Conclusions

Besides maintaining a vast research network of its own, the Chinese tobacco industry has also fostered collaboration with public universities and research institutions in every research area of tobacco from cultivation to manufacturing. Such collaboration has increased over the years and now accounts for nearly half of all tobacco publications in China. The involvement of public universities and public research institutions in tobacco companies' research boosts the competitiveness of the industry through increasing its efficiency and helping it develop more consumer-appealing products, one notable example being low-tar and herbal cigarettes, which are heavily promoted by the tobacco industry as less harmful alternatives.

The intimate connection between public universities and research institutions with the tobacco industry complicates tobacco control policy making and violates the FCTC and its Article 5.3 guidelines. It contributes to the legitimization of an industry that has been selling a lethal product for decades and continues to do so under the new disguise of harm reduction.

Notes

1. Norbert Hirschhorn, "Shameful Science: Four Decades of the German Tobacco Industry's Hidden Research on Smoking and Health," *Tobacco Control*

9(2) (2000): 242–48; Robert N. Proctor, *The Nazi War on Cancer* (Princeton, NJ: Princeton University Press, 1999); Monique E. Muggli et al., "The Smoke You Don't See: Uncovering Tobacco Industry Scientific Strategies Aimed against Environmental Tobacco Smoke Policies," *American Journal of Public Health* 91 (2001): 1419–23; Lisa A. Bero, "Tobacco Industry Manipulation of Research," *Public Health Report* 120 (2005): 200–208; Stanton A. Glantz, "Tobacco Money at the University of California," *American Journal of Respiratory and Critical Care Medicine* 171(10) (2005): 1067–69; J. Barnoya and S. Glantz, "Tobacco Industry Success in Preventing Regulation of Secondhand Smoke in Latin America: The 'Latin Project,'" *Tobacco Control* 11 (2002): 305–14; Joaquin Barnoya and Stanton A. Glantz, "The Tobacco Industry's Worldwide ETS Consultants Project: European and Asian Components," *European Journal of Public Health* 16 (2006): 69–77.

2. Hirschhorn, "Shameful Science"; Muggli et al., "The Smoke You Don't See"; Robert N. Proctor, *Golden Holocaust: Origins of the Cigarette Catastrophe and the Case for Abolition* (Berkeley: University of California Press, 2011).

3. United States District Court for the District of Columbia, Plaintiff, and Tobacco-Free Kids Fund, American Cancer Society, American Heart Association, American Lung Association, Americans for Nonsmokers' Rights, and National African American Tobacco Prevention Network, Intervenors v. Philip Morris Incorporated, et al., Defendants, Civil Action No. 99–CV-02496 (GK), United States District Court for the District of Columbia, 2006: i2454.

4. Joanna E. Cohen, "Universities and Tobacco Money," *BMJ* 323(7303) (2001): 1–2; Glantz, "Tobacco Money at the University of California"; David Grimm, "Is Tobacco Research Turning Over a New Leaf?" *Science* 307 (2005): 36–37.

5. Susan Mayor, "UK Universities Agree Protocol for Tobacco Company Funding," *BMJ* 329 (2004): 9; Fiona Godlee et al., "Journal Policy on Research Funded by the Tobacco Industry," BMJ Editorial, *BMJ* 347 (2013), http://www.bmj.com/content/347/bmj.f5193.

6. Ross Mackenzie and Jeff Collin, "'A Good Personal Scientific Relationship': Philip Morris Scientists and the Chulabhorn Research Institute, Bangkok," *PLoS Medicine* 5 (2008): 1737–48; Belinda O'Sullivan and Simon Chapman, "Eyes on the Prize: Transnational Tobacco Companies in China 1976–1997," *Tobacco Control* 9 (2000): 292–302; Monique E. Muggli et al., "'Efforts to Reprioritise the Agenda' in China: British American Tobacco's Efforts to Influence Public Policy on Secondhand Smoke in China," *PLoS Medicine* 5 (2008): 1729–69.

7. E. K. Tong and S. A. Glantz, "ARTIST (Asian Regional Tobacco Industry Scientist Team): Philip Morris' Attempt to Exert a Scientific and Regulatory Agenda on Asia," *Tobacco Control* 13 Suppl 2 (2004): ii118–24.

8. "Summary of Artist Mini-Symposium and 8th Meeting," April 17, 2000, Luxury Hall, Minzu Hotel, Beijing, http://legacy.library.ucsf.edu/tid/lth92g00;

"Summary of the 10th Artist Meeting," Four Seasons Hotel, Singapore, May 10–11, 2001, http://legacy.library.ucsf.edu/tid/fbt34a00.

9. China Tobacco in 2014 reported that imported cigarettes had dropped to as little as 0.17 percent of the market. See State Tobacco Monopoly Administration, *China Tobacco Yearbook* (in Chinese) (Beijing: China Economic Publishing House, 2014).

10. Zhou Ruizeng and Cheng Yongzhao, ed., *Research on Counterproposals to the WHO Framework Convention on Tobacco Control and Countermeasures to Address Its Impacts on the Chinese Tobacco Industry* (in Chinese) (Beijing, Economic Science Press, 2006).

11. ZTRI, "The History of Zhengzhou Tobacco Research Institute" (in Chinese), *China Tobacco*, 2009, http://www.ztri.com.cn/zzygk/2007/06/55331.shtml.

12. "Chunghwa Cigarettes" (in Chinese), *Hudong Encyclopedia*, 2009, http://www.hudong.com/wiki/中华香烟 (accessed October 27, 2009).

13. "Zhengzhou Tobacco Research Institute" (in Chinese), Zhongshan Century Elasic Lock Co., December 25, 2012, http://www.elasic.cn/eg/aboutus/465/3134.html.

14. Chinese Academy of Agricultural Sciences, "Chinese Academy of Agricultural Sciences" (in Chinese), 2009, http://www.caas.net.cn/caas/ (accessed October 27, 2009).

15. Quan Gan and Stanton A. Glantz, "Relationship between the Chinese Tobacco Industry and Academic Institutions in China," *Tobacco Control* 20(1) (2011): 12–19.

16. Zhao Chuanxing and Zhang Lijun, "The College of Tobacco Science at Henan Agricultural University: A Better School Developed in the Reform" (in Chinese), *Dahe Daily*, September 2, 2009, http://newpaper.dahe.cn/hnrbncb/html/2009-09/02/content_218745.htm.

17. "China National Tobacco Research Center" (in Chinese), *Baidu Baike*, http://baike.baidu.com/view/299689.html?fromTaglist (accessed October 27, 2009).

18. "A Key Laboratory for Tobacco Science and Health" (in Chinese), *Baidu Zhidao*, http://zhidao.baidu.com/question/60406500.html (accessed October 27, 2009).

19. Liu Yibin, Li Miao, and Zhang Yiyang, "China Tobacco South-Central Agricultural Experiment Station Is Unveiled" (in Chinese), Red Net, October 23, 2007, http://hn.rednet.cn/c/2007/10/23/1353313.htm (accessed August 19, 2017).

20. Graduate Education at the Zhengzhou Tobacco Research Institute, "Joint PhD Program of Dongnan University and the Zhengzhou Tobacco Research Institute" (in Chinese), 2009, http://www.ztri.com.cn/yjsjyweb/ArticleShow.asp?ID=1232 (accessed October 27, 2009).

21. "Hefei Institute of Economics and Technology" (in Chinese), *Wikipedia*,

http://zh.wikipedia.org/zh-cn/%E5%90%88%E8%82%A5%E7%BB%8F%E6%
B5%8E%E6%8A%80%E6%9C%AF%E5%AD%A6 (accessed October 27, 2009).

22. Ibid.; "Center for Tobacco and Health Research, University of Science and Technology of China" (in Chinese), 2009, http://www.tobaccocollege.com/tcads/tccenter.htm (accessed October 27, 2009).

23. "CNTC Tobacco Training Center and USTC Collaborate on a Tele-education Program" (in Chinese), March 17, 2003, *China Tobacco*, http://www.tobacco.gov.cn/html/21/2101/67728_n.html (accessed Octobr 27, 2009).

24. CNTC Tobacco Training Center, "CNTC Tobacco Training Center Establishes Master's Education Program" (in Chinese), July 18, 2008, *China Tobacco*, http://www.tobacco.gov.cn/html/31/3103/640957_n.html.

25. "Special Issue on the National People's Congress and the Chinese People's Political Consultative Conference (March 2010)" (in Chinese), *China News*, 2010, http://www.tcrc.org.cn/html/zy/cbw/jc/1583.html (accessed April 10, 2010); Glen Loveland, "Company Posts Pro-Tobacco Messages in Sichuan School," *San Francisco Examiner*, December 29, 2009, http://www.examiner.com/x-15615-Asia -Headlines-Examinery2009m12d20-Company-posts-protobacco-messages-in-Sich uan-school (accessed April 10, 2010).

26. This section and the next draw on Gan and Glantz, "Relationship between the Chinese Tobacco Industry and Academic Institutions in China."

27. Jiang Chengkang, "Comprehensively Promote the 'Better Cigarettes' Strategy to Maintain Sustained and Healthy Development of the Industry: Report on the 2010 National Tobacco Work Conference" (in Chinese), January 19, 2010, *China Tobacco*, http://www.tobacco.gov.cn/history_filesystem/2010ychy/hybg1.html (accessed April 10, 2010).

28. Our data come from a search of online databases of journal articles published in both Chinese and English for academic institutions in China conducting research with or sponsored by Chinese tobacco companies. We also searched the websites of tobacco companies, their affiliated institutions, and academic institutions for reports of collaborations. For more on our methodology, see Gan and Glantz, "Relationship between the Chinese Tobacco Industry and Academic Institutions in China."

29. Huang Huangui, Zhu Maoxiang, and Zhao Mingyue, "The Application of Shennong Extract in Reducing Harms from Smoking" (in Chinese), *Proceedings of the Symposium on the Harmonious Development of Tobacco Production, Human Health, and Environmental Protection* (Shanghai: Chinese Tobacco Association, 2003); Zhu Maoxiang et al., "The Molecular Biological Assessment of Shennong Extract in Reducing Harms Caused by Smoking," in *Proceedings of the 5th Food Toxicology Conference and Bioactives Symposium* (2004); Weng Junbin, "Shennong

Extract Reduces TSNAs in Mainstream Tobacco Smoke" (in Chinese), *Neijiang Technologies* 10 (2008): 127.

30. Zhu et al., "The Molecular Biological Assessment of Shennong Extract in Reducing Harms Caused by Smoking"; Zhu, Zunquan, "Chinese-Style Cigarettes—From the Perspective of the History of Cigarettes" (in Chinese), February 2, 2008, *Sina Blog*, http://blog.sina.com.cn/s/blog_4fe5dfff01008dvj.html (accessed August 20, 2017).

31. Quan Gan et al., "Chinese Herbal Cigarettes Are as Carcinogenic and Addictive as Regular Cigarettes," *Cancer Epidemiology, Biomarkers & Prevention* 18 (2009): 3497–3501; Quan Gan et al., "Chinese 'Light' Cigarettes Do Not Deliver Lower Levels of Carcinogens," *Tobacco Control* 19(5) (October 2010): 374–79.

32. Silvy Peeters and Anna B. Gilmore, "Understanding the Emergence of the Tobacco Industry's Use of the Term Tobacco Harm Reduction in Order to Inform Public Health Policy," *Tobacco Control* 24(2) (2015): 182–89.

33. Xie Jianping, "Priority Research Topics from CORESTA," *Tobacco Smoke and Chemistry* 12(1) (2006): 13–16.

34. CNTC Information Center, "Hongta and Imperial Tobacco Collaboration Project Signed in Beijing" (in Chinese), *TobaccoChina Online*, August 11, 2003, http://www.tobaccochina.com/news/China/highlight/20038/2003811143048 _99680.shtml (accessed April 10, 2010); Hu Xianquan and Shi Jinglei, "First Cigar Collaboration Project Signed in Beijing" (in Chinese), *TobaccoChina Online*, September 19, 2008, http://www.tobaccochina.com/news/China/highlight /20089/200891812158_324163.shtml (accessed April 10, 2010); Liao Zhenyu, "First Marlboro Made in China off Production Line" (in Chinese), *TobaccoChina Online*, July 22, 2008, http://www.tobaccochina.com/news/China/industry/20087 /200872112466_313892.shtml (accessed April 10, 2010).

35. O'Sullivan and Chapman, "Eyes on the Prize"; Tong and Glantz, "ARTIST (Asian Regional Tobacco Industry Scientist Team)."

36. "Baisha's Tobacco Advertising Involving Liu Xiang Is Illegal and Banned" (in Chinese), *Xinhua.net*, November 3, 2004, http://news.xinhuanet.com/sports /2004-11/03/content_2171088.htm (accessed October 27, 2009); Gan et al., "Chinese Herbal Cigarettes Are as Carcinogenic and Addictive as Regular Cigarettes."

37. "Tobacco Company Representative Debated with the Public over Health Effects of Passive Smoking during Public Hearing in Shanghai on Smoke-free Legislation" (in Chinese), Tobacco China, October 9, 2009, http://www.tobacco china.com/news/China/society/200910/200910622916_379532.shtml (accessed August 20, 2017).

38. Naomi Oreskes and Erik M. Conway, *Merchants of Doubt: How a Handful of Scientists Obscured the Truth on Issues from Tobacco Smoke to Global Warming* (London: Bloomsbury Press, 2010).

39. WHO Framework Convention on Tobacco Control (WHO FCTC); and "Guidelines for Implementation of Article 5.3 of the WHO Framework Convention on Tobacco Control," http://www.who.int/fctc/protocol/guidelines/adopted/article_5_3/en/index.html.

40. On the ARTIST program, see Tong and Glantz, "ARTIST (Asian Regional Tobacco Industry Scientist Team)."

41. "Guidelines for Implementation of Article 13" of the WHO Framework Convention on Tobacco Control, http://www.who.int/fctc/guidelines/adopted/article_13/en/.

42. Simon Chapman, "Advocacy in Action: Extreme Corporate Makeover Interruptus: Denormalising Tobacco Industry Corporate Schmoozing," *Tobacco Control* 13 (2004): 445–47; Gerard Hastings and Jonathan Liberman, "Tobacco Corporate Social Responsibility and Fairy Godmothers: The Framework Convention on Tobacco Control Slays a Modern Myth," *Tobacco Control* 18 (2009): 73–74.

CHAPTER TEN

Manuals of Obstruction
China Tobacco Blueprints Its Resistance to the WHO's Framework Convention on Tobacco Control

Wu Yiqun, Li Jinkui, and Pang Yingfa

Readers of this volume should by now be well aware that China is a party to the World Health Organization's Framework Convention on Tobacco Control (FCTC). Over 160 of UN member, non-member, and observer states have become parties to the treaty. But with membership comes responsibilities. The FCTC in its preamble states that participating parties, on whatever continent, must be vigilant against efforts by the tobacco industry to thwart the treaty. Parties "need to be alert to any efforts by the tobacco industry to undermine or subvert tobacco control efforts." Crucial also is that signatories "be informed of activities of the tobacco industry that have a negative impact on tobacco control."[1] These imperatives figure prominently in the treaty's preamble, because history has shown that progress in tobacco control can only occur once we have a good understanding of the tactics and strategies of the industry. This is not an easy task, nor one for the faint of heart. From country to country, Big Tobacco and its agents have been remorseless in devising programs of delay, denial, and distraction—and obstruction.

Within the past decade, two hefty books outlining plans to neutralize the FCTC have come to the attention of public health advocates in China. The most important of these was published in Chinese in 2006 with the ungainly title *Research on Counterproposals to the WHO Framework Convention on Tobacco Control and Countermeasures to Address Its Impacts on the Chinese Tobacco Industry* (hereafter referred to as *Research on Counterproposals and Countermeasures*).[2] A second volume was released in 2011, titled *Global Tobacco Control Outlook* (hereafter *Global Outlook*). Both were published in Beijing by respectable presses.[3]

What is remarkable about these two books is how clearly they set forth the Chinese tobacco industry's efforts to weaken the FCTC. That these books have been released for public consumption suggests that cigarette makers must have determined there was little need to conceal their efforts to undermine either the Framework Convention in particular, or tobacco control more generally. In this chapter, we explore how the first of these volumes came into existence and how it has influenced the FCTC's implementation in China. We then offer some critical reflections, including comments on how the second book, *Global Outlook*, reveals some of the evolving tactics of the industry.

Background

China became a signatory to the FCTC on November 10, 2003, but the treaty which China signed was not entirely innocent of industry influence. Metaphorically speaking, Beijing and the World Health Organization did not just suddenly jump into bed together under a finished canopy called the FCTC. A number of preliminary steps were taken, during which the industry was able to exercise its influence. In October 2000, for example, the director general of the WHO inaugurated an Intergovernmental Negotiating Body, opening it to all WHO member states while charging it with drafting the FCTC. It was around this time that the wheels that would eventually generate the industry's *Research on Counterproposals and Countermeasures* began to turn. In July 2001—shortly after the WHO's Fifty-fourth World Health Assembly adopted a resolution emphasizing the importance of transparency and non-interference from the industry in matters of tobacco-control, and just as the Intergovernmental Negotiating Body for the FCTC was about to reconvene—high-level leaders of China's State Tobacco Monopoly Administration (STMA) shifted into high gear. They established the FCTC Counterproposals Research Work Group (hereafter the "Counterproposals Group"), led by two major figures in the Chinese tobacco industry: Zhou Ruizeng, director general of the Beijing Tobacco Monopoly Administration, and Cheng Yongzhao, vice president of the Yunnan Academy of Tobacco Science. Zhou and Cheng had clear marching orders. The STMA ordered their Counterproposals Group "to conduct proactive research, facilitating decision making, serving the needs of the industry."[4]

From that point on, the Counterproposal Group worked closely alongside and with China's delegates to the FCTC Intergovernmental Negotiating Body. Whereas this latter body presumably saw its mission to be that
of negotiating a strong and effective treaty, the Counterproposals Group
began an effort to weaken the still embryonic FCTC. Substantial human
and financial resources were allocated for this more corrosive mission. The
Counterproposals Group held meetings in July 2001, February 2002, August 2002, and January 2003 to draft counterproposals to texts from the
third, fourth, fifth and sixth Intergovernmental Negotiation Body meetings.
Members of the Counterproposals Group also travelled with the Chinese
delegation to all four rounds of intergovernmental meetings.[5]

The Counterproposals Group studied carefully all drafts of texts released
by the intergovernmental chairman before each round of FCTC negotiations and produced preliminary, intermediate, and advanced action-plan
counterproposal scenarios. A total of 128 different suggestions and recommendations were discussed and agreed to by the STMA, reported as special
study findings to the Chinese government delegation involved in negotiating the treaty. Fifty-one of these recommendations were eventually adopted
by the Chinese delegation and incorporated into China's position documents. These recommendations—mostly aimed at weakening the treaty and
the conditions of its implementation—significantly diminished the force of
the FCTC as applied to the world's largest producer of cigarettes.[6]

In May 2003, the WHO's Fifty-sixth World Health Assembly adopted
resolution WHA56.1, creating the FCTC. Three months later, as China
was about to sign the treaty, the STMA Counterproposals Research Group
formed a new "FCTC Countermeasures Research Group," holding its first
meeting in August of that year. The Chinese government signed the FCTC
on November 10 and then, in March and August of the following year, the
Countermeasures Research Group held its second and third meetings (in
Haikou, Hainan Province, and in Hohhot, Inner Mongolia, respectively).
The STMA Countermeasures Research Group was subsequently renamed
the STMA FCTC Implementation Work Group.[7]

The group also generated a large number of reports, special communications, and newsletters, all of which were designed to help the industry
prepare for—and neutralize—threats posed to the industry by the FCTC.
The mission of the FCTC Countermeasures Group was, simply put, safeguarding the tobacco industry's interests by undermining the treaty, even if

that meant undermining public health. And, if nothing else, one can applaud the group for being prolific, having produced over a hundred different countermeasures or proposals designed to hinder the treaty. We shall describe some of these in a moment.

For the purpose of shoring up relationships crucial for their work, the Counterproposals Group hosted a variety of Chinese government officials during March 2001 and June 2002 in tobacco growing and manufacturing regions. Over the next four years, the Counterproposals Group organized dozens of lectures, published scores of research papers, and disseminated industry-friendly booklets. By one industry estimate, more than ten thousand man-hours were devoted to designing and promoting the group's FCTC counterproposals and countermeasures.[8]

The net effect was a weakening of the language of the FCTC treaty. The summary report of the industry's *Research on Counterproposals and Countermeasures* actually credits the FCTC Counterproposals and Countermeasures Group with success in this regard, ensuring that "some strict provisions of the FCTC were modified."[9] Translation (from English into Chinese) was a key instrument of such modifications. Recall that a primary task of the PRC's intergovernmental delegation was to negotiate and approve the Chinese-language version of the treaty. As part of that process, members of the industry's Counterproposals and Countermeasures Group worked hand-in-glove with the STMA's Resource and Translation Subgroup to review everything that would end up in the treaty. Joined at the hip, the group and subgroup made every effort to convert strong English-language terms coming out of Geneva into softer Chinese-language terms. For instance, they repeatedly suggested that Chinese-language terms denoting "may," "at discretion of," "recommended that," and "when appropriate" be swapped in for stronger English-language words like "should" and "shall." Many of the industry's edits were accepted by the Chinese government delegation negotiating the treaty. And today, more than a few of those very proposals constitute the language governing "tobacco-control" objectives of the government of China. So happy was the STMA with its success in getting industry-friendly language into the Chinese-language version of the treaty that the STMA showered group/subgroup members with an award.[10]

Other accolades jump off the pages of *Research on Counterproposals and Countermeasures*, especially in its opening remarks. The front matter of this 445-page book is full of praise from media outlets and academic groups.

One also finds a glowing testimonial from the National Development and Planning Commission of the STMA. Perhaps most significant is the preface, penned by none other than Jiang Chengkang, general manager of the China National Tobacco Corporation. Jiang praises everyone involved in producing the book, thanking them for serving "leaders' decision-making and industry needs." His message is clear: the book has been produced from within the Chinese government, in support of the Chinese government, and with its full endorsement.

Establishing Governing Logics, or, How the Fox Came to Guard the Henhouse

Once established, bureaucratic thinking has a way of becoming routinized. Contributors to *Research on Counterproposals and Countermeasures* clearly understood it as their job to establish logics for the FCTC that will be beneficial to the industry. Throughout the book, we see these authors articulating principles that have gone on to become hallmarks of tobacco control in China. One thing they posit, for example, is that China's tobacco situation is special, insofar as "our industry is state-owned, not private."[11] And since it is state-owned, the industry can only be effectively regulated and controlled from within—by its very own state agency. It follows, therefore, that there was no need for the FCTC to be rejected altogether; indeed, the industry should be "open to tobacco control."[12] The Supervisory State Tobacco Monopoly Administration would not be weakened by the FCTC; on the contrary, it will be "strengthened and protected."[13]

Of course the FCTC's original authors, most of whom were based outside of China, cannot have imagined a situation where the tobacco industry and the treaty would be anything but fundamentally adversarial. But the Counterproposals Group clearly envisioned something else, a more mutually supportive relationship, a "coordinating mechanism" whereby the STMA would play a key role in creating and implementing the treaty.[14]

Based on this logic, the inclusion of industry representatives in China's delegation to the FCTC makes perfect sense. So too, does the fact that Beijing would ensure that the industry would work closely with the treaty's implementation office after the treaty came into effect. In 2007, the State Council created an office inside the central government called the Inter-Agency FCTC Implementation Coordination Mechanism. The Ministry of

Health was not called upon to run this new office. Instead, the State Council tucked the office within the Ministry of Industry and Information Technology (MOIIT), a more powerful government unit. And what other branch of the Chinese government falls under the auspices of the MOIIT? The State Tobacco Monopoly Administration, which in 2007 was generating nearly 400 billion RMB in annual profits and taxes for the Chinese government. In other words, under one tent, a small new regulatory body and a fabulously rich cash cow have come to sit together, side by side. The one is charged with implementing the world's first public health treaty, the other is a sprawling manufacturing entity, responsible for making and selling the very product the new treaty is designed to regulate. A more gigantic and consequential conflict of interest could not be imagined. And all of this flows from the logic mapped out in *Research on Counterproposals and Countermeasures.*

. . .

Publication of the industry's *Research on Counterproposals and Countermeasures* took place in 2006, with the editors assigning that task to Beijing's stately Economic Science Press. Throughout the text, the editors and authors take pains to portray themselves as practical and conscientious people. Emphasizing terms like "China's actual situation," "fairness and objectivity," and "realistic suggestions," they insist that everyone involved with the FCTC "needs to be fully aware of the dependence of China's national economy on the tobacco industry." There is also an insistence on a need to avoid "partial, subjective, or even aggressive actions."[15] As such, contributors to the volume insist that everyone involved in tobacco must understand the importance of limiting the job at hand: "promoting China's image as a responsible and developing country, we must try to fulfill only the minimum requirements of FCTC provisions."[16]

And how should this minimum be achieved? Let us look at some of these Counterproposals and Countermeasures, classified by strategy.

Denying the Science and Downplaying the Harm

Management of tobacco-related science is one such procedure. Perhaps it is not surprising, but *Research on Counterproposals and Countermeasures* invokes many of the same denialist strategies deployed by cigarette makers in the United States and Europe since the 1950s.[17] The book encourages creating the illusion of the industry as a fair arbiter of science, but also broadcasting false claims, agitating for more research, and denigrating the scientific methods used by public health scholars. As such, nowhere in the volume is it admitted that cigarettes can actually cause disease or death, or that hundreds of thousands of Chinese die every year from smoking. Instead, the editors make the astonishing claim that "most scientists agree that, among over 4,850 components identified in mainstream tobacco smoke, 99.4 percent are not harmful to the human body."[18] That is like defending the safety of war by saying that most of the things that enter your body will not be bullets. The book also promotes the ruses that ill effects of smoking depend on "differences in individual constitutions"; that "limitations of epidemiological research is well known" (e.g., "containing only statistical relations and hypothetical assumptions, not definite and final answers"); and that "only comprehensive and more targeted research will lead to scientific and fair results."[19]

Challenging the science with regard to tobacco is central to *Research on Counterproposals and Countermeasures*. No one today with any serious medical credentials can doubt that exposure to tobacco smoke causes death and disability; that is as true as the earth going round the sun, or that vaccines can prevent disease. The editors of *Research on Counterproposals and Countermeasures* have a very different agenda, however. They call for a campaign to "reduce or minimize the negative impact caused by this viewpoint" (i.e., the science implicating harms), a campaign that will "create a scientific scholarly environment" pushing back against "incorrect and biased views." Their call is for a campaign to "correctly publicize the issue of smoking and health and create a positive climate of opinion."[20]

The editors of *Research on Counterproposals and Countermeasures* do not see their job as simply fomenting a campaign of misinformation, however. They also hope to pressure the WHO to make changes to how the FCTC communicates the science of cigarette harms. Here is what they suggest should be done to Article 4 of the treaty, *Guiding Principles*:

> We suggest deleting "the health consequences, addictive nature and mortal threat." Our reasoning: It is impossible to determine the addictiveness of smoking, and "deadly risk" is even more groundless. We also suggest deleting "the incidence of diseases, premature disability and mortality." Our reasoning: it is impossible to establish that diseases, premature disability, and mortality are caused by tobacco consumption.[21]

A Safer Cigarette?

No less central to the editors' program of countermeasures are rhetorics of "harm reduction." Cigarette manufacturers outside of China began deceptively marketing "light" and "low-tar" cigarettes in the mid-twentieth century, ignoring their own internal research showing that such products are no less deadly than regular cigarettes.[22] The STMA took up this same playbook at the turn of the millennium, several years before the 2006 publication of *Research on Counterproposals and Countermeasures.* In 2003, STMA released *The Development Outline for China's Cigarette Science and Technology,* giving highest priority to the development of "high-aroma, low-tar and low-harm" cigarettes.

Members of the Counterproposals Group were big and early advocates of this new STMA strategy. The editors recommended that China's industry vigorously reassure everyone, both smokers and non-smokers alike, that everything is being done to produce a less harmful cigarette. We must "respond proactively, turn pressure into a driving force, turn challenges into opportunities, take the initiative and strive for survival." We must "reduce harmful components in tobacco smoke, and manufacture high-quality 'high-aroma, low-tar and low-harm' cigarettes."[23] The disingenuous nature of this program was hardly lost on the Counterproposals Group, which by then knew full well that the international tobacco-control establishment had already come to expose "light" cigarettes as utterly fraudulent, as gimmicks that harm people even more than conventional cigarettes. However much the medical and public health establishment "disapproves of the development direction of 'low-tar and low-harm' cigarettes," that is simply irrelevant, because that public health position runs "counter to tobacco industry efforts."[24]

Safeguarding the Economy

Economic fearmongering is a favored trick in *Research on Counterproposals and Countermeasures.* The book insists that "we still need to depend on tobacco to accumulate national wealth at present in China"[25] and that "if we borrow tobacco-control experience directly from other countries, or follow to the letter provisions in the first draft of the FCTC, there will be major impacts on national economic development in China."[26] The cigarette industry "is very important to China's economic development," which means that "strict restrictions on tobacco product manufacturing and business operations mandated by the FCTC will certainly have an impact on China's tobacco industry." Indeed, "as the impact deepens, China's tobacco economic development will slow down."[27]

In deploying these scare tactics, the editors make it clear that their goal is not just to shore up "national fiscal revenues, local economies, the interests of smokers, and the interests of tobacco workers."[28] Theirs is not an agenda of the status quo but rather of expansion. The fiscal security of the industry, as they see it, can only be sustained through increases in cigarette production.

And thus *Research on Counterproposals and Countermeasures* has no love for health experts' desires to change tax codes. The book provides a litany of arguments why tobacco taxes should never be raised, from stimulating smuggling and counterfeiting to being unfair. Our industry "should enjoy the same treatment as other industries. There should be a relatively lax environment for its survival and development to ensure steady growth."[29] It even suggests that tax rates should remain low in order to protect smokers—since higher taxes would negatively "affect the profitability of tobacco companies, causing a reduction in investments in science and technology, thereby delaying tar and harm reduction."[30]

Instead, the book encourages three main countermeasures. First, the tobacco industry should coordinate more closely with government agencies, including those responsible for finance and taxation. Second, there should be more research into the effects of taxation on tobacco product costs and consumer demand. And lastly, the FCTC should be watered down when it comes to taxation. In place of strong wording in the original text about taxation, the Chinese translation of the treaty should employ terms like "it is recommended," "consider," and "at the discretion of" in order to "limit the binding force of the FCTC."[31]

Thwarting Denormalization

A core goal of the FCTC is to denormalize tobacco use. By contrast, the editors of *Research on Counterproposals and Countermeasures* hold that a common mission of the tobacco industry must be "to cultivate a perception among our consumers that smoking is a normal behavior."[32] The editors are not shy about suggesting ways to characterize cigarette smoking as normal. They paint it as a reasonable and "basic source of pleasure." They define it as a "fundamental right," even a "human right."[33] They depict smoking as "a social habit" and a matter of "free choice."[34]

As much as normalizing smoking is a mission, so too is tarring as unreasonable any health organization (versus the industry itself) seeking to implement the FCTC. And the editors of *Research on Counterproposals and Countermeasures* are quite open in suggesting how to do just that. The imperative is to depict organizations allied with the FCTC as blind to the nation's local conditions. The plan is to call them out for acting counter to the People's interest, and to represent them as behaving irresponsibly. Tobacco-control advocates were to be besmirched as failing to "seek truth from facts" and as choosing to parrot what others say.[35]

Warning Labels

Like elsewhere, the tobacco industry in China has *vociferously* resisted laws requiring the strengthening of warning labels on cigarette packs. Perhaps to limit future liability, the STMA has agreed to small but anemic labels—stating, "Smoking is harmful to health"—first placed on the sides of packs in the closing years of the twentieth century. Since then, it has fought public health efforts to strengthen warnings, permitting only trivial changes to labels in 2008, 2012, and 2016.

Substantial portions of *Research on Counterproposals and Countermeasures* address the issue of warning labels. The book's authors outline how implementation of the FCTC's articles governing "Packaging and Labeling of Tobacco Products" and "Tobacco Advertising, Promotion and Sponsorship" would result in substantial changes to warning labels in China, including the addition of graphic images. The authors are adamant that the industry must do all it can to thwart these FCTC provisions.[36]

One crucial consideration, the editors of *Research on Counterproposals and Countermeasures* emphasize, is the future of "high-end cigarettes" (*gaoduan juanyan*), a rapidly growing product category over the last two decades. The profit margins of high-end cigarettes have been so large that the industry has come to see them as indispensable for its ability to keep posting annual double-digit upticks in revenue. FCTC provisions regarding warning labels could devastate "the fortunes of the companies that depend on high-end cigarettes," the editors admonish. Especially perilous for high-end cigarettes would be the implementation of FCTC requirements that packs carry graphic warning labels. Such warnings "could cause high-end cigarette prices to fall, causing tobacco industry profits to suffer a dramatic decline."[37] Since cigarettes are traditionally "a must-have consumer product on special occasions such as festivals, holidays, social gatherings, ceremonies and wedding banquets," placement of large and conspicuous warnings on the packs would have "a direct" and negative impact on the industry, "one that merits our great attention."[38]

Regarding implementation of FCTC Article 11 on "Packaging and Labeling of Tobacco Products," the authors of *Research on Counterproposals and Countermeasures* conclude that large and graphic warnings "would completely destroy original package designs." So what do they suggest in response? The industry should welcome new warnings that are "easy to accept" for the average adult male smoker, such as "Smoking affects fetus development" and "Smoking is harmful to children's health."[39] Cigarette makers should permit rotating warning labels, few in number, with long periods between rotation—to help consumers distinguish real from counterfeit cigarettes. Stronger warnings should be rejected, on the grounds that they would be inappropriate or disrespect Chinese local conditions. Graphic warnings in particular should be rejected as "aesthetic monstrosities" that would "completely destroy original package designs."[40]

Guided by these principles, the STMA has successfully managed to fend off stronger warnings. It continues to insist that warnings be inoffensive, little changed from what was first introduced at the end of the 1990s, absent any graphic imagery, and with infrequently rotating textual warnings guaranteed to attract little attention.

Current rules governing Chinese cigarette labeling are contained in the Regulations on Cigarette Package Labels in the Territories of People's Republic of China, issued by the STMA and General Administration of Quality Supervision, Inspection, and Quarantine. Many public health experts were angered when these regulations were first circulated in 2008. They wrote to government agencies calling for a strengthening of the regulations, demanding large, clear, and graphic warnings. They also asked that warnings be created and approved by health authorities to avoid the dishonesty of the fox being asked to guard the henhouse. Their recommendations have always been rejected.

Curiously, and coinciding with such rejections, mainland cigarette manufacturerers have been quietly packaging some of their top brands embla-

China's current text-only warning

FIGURE 10.1.
Comparison of a pack of Chunghwa brand cigarettes sold in China with two packs of the same brand sold elsewhere. Collected and provided by the author Wu Yiqun.

zoned with graphic warnings. Most citizens of the PRC have never seen these products, though. That is because they are all designed for export, going to countries and territories where local laws mandate graphic warnings, including nearby locales such as Thailand, Taiwan, and Hong Kong. The contrast between such exports and domestic offerings is striking (see Figure 10.1).

Advertising, Promotion, and Sponsorship

Product packaging is not the only form of cigarette marketing. Equally central are advertising, promotion, and sponsorship of sports or cultural events. On those fronts, contributors to *Research on Counterproposals and Countermeasures* have been no less outspoken. Their prodding began with the negotiations that defined the very text of the FCTC. As already described above, the Counterproposals Group lobbied successfully to have key language of the treaty's Chinese-language version watered down. Perhaps most significant was its softening of Article 13 of the FCTC, which covers tobacco marketing. Today, whereas the English-language version of that article calls for a "comprehensive ban" (全面禁止, *quanmian jinzhi*) on all tobacco advertising, promotion, and sponsorship, the Chinese-language version only calls for a "wide-ranging ban" (广泛禁止, *guangfan jinzhi*).[41]

The Counterproposal Group's activities related to marketing have extended beyond wordsmithing, though. After the FCTC was ratified by Beijing, the group advised that the industry adopt specific strategies regarding advertising and promotion. Important here have been the strategies of invoking local conditions as limiting factors and trumpeting that the FCTC has already been sufficently implemented. "In light of China's local conditions, we should stress 'limiting' rather than 'extensively banning' tobacco advertising, promotion and sponsorship."[42] Whenever possible, the industry should claim that Chinese laws regarding cigarette advertising and promotion, thanks to the treaty, are now "already very strict," and that since FCTC requirements have already been met, "there is no need for additional measures."[43]

The Counterproposals Group has likewise advised the industry to champion sponsorship of "public interest causes" as a way to get around restrictions on advertising.[44] The plan has been to "enhance the image of tobacco companies by giving back to society." This includes a recommendation to use the media to keep cigarette brand and factory names in circulation: "As tobacco advertising faces increasing restrictions, hold some debates and donate, naming the events after tobacco companies."[45] The industry has followed this advice, with countless causes and events receiving cigarette sponsorship, from campaigns to combat poverty to causes supporting health, education, and disaster relief.

Particularly well rewarded, for instance, have been Chinese branches of Project HOPE, a humanitarian organization founded during the 1950s in the United States that gained a foothold in China in the 1980s. In the early 2000s, the Beijing Cigarette Factory established the Zhongnanhai Love Foundation, following which packs of Zhongnanhai cigarettes were printed with the words, "For every packet of cigarettes you consume, you are contributing your share of love to Project HOPE." It was also during this period that tobacco sponsorship of primary schools took off across the country—via Project HOPE. Hundreds of these schools were sponsored by cigarette factories, with many of these also named after them! For years now, on the rooftop of eponymous HOPE primary schools in Sichuan province, billboards have been emblazoned with the logo of the China National Tobacco Corporation and the words writ large, in Chinese characters: "Tobacco helps you succeed."

Global Tobacco Control Outlook: *A Second Tobacco Industry Text*

The second volume to be discussed here, albeit briefly, is *Global Tobacco Control Outlook*, compiled by one of the chief editors of *Research on Counterproposals and Countermeasures*, Cheng Yongzhao, with financial support and text contributed by the industry. Cheng began assembling *Global Tobacco Control Outlook* in 2010, and it was published by the Economic Daily Press a year later. This large tome claims to be the first Chinese monograph to review and forecast tobacco control globally, and it brandishes the conceit of independent thinking throughout. Contributors try to downplay their tobacco industry connections, suggesting that they are either unaffiliated experts interested only in tobacco control or that their views in no way represent those of their employers. This contrivance may be in response to criticisms leveled against the earlier *Research on Counterproposals and Countermeasures* for being so overtly a tool of the STMA. Cheng Yongzhao would certainly have been aware of that criticism since, again, he had been an editor of that first volume.

Also, by January 2011, health advocates in Beijing had already enjoyed five years of FCTC cover under which to press an anti-tobacco agenda. By then, the drumbeat of tobacco control was clearly on the rise, despite strenuous efforts at industry foot dragging. Opinion leaders, experts, journalists, and diverse NGOs were becoming more and more aggressive in educating the public on the need for tobacco control and the tactics and tricks used by the industry to undermine it. In such an environment, outright opposition to the FCTC, such as that found in *Research on Counterproposals and Countermeasures*, risked being dismissed as reactionary and unethical. A softer, subtler tone involving more complex strategies needed to be struck. Which is what *Global Outlook* offers.

But no matter how much softer its prose or convoluted its thinking, the intent of *Global Outlook* remains the same as its predecessor: to obstruct effective FCTC implementation.[46] This should come as no surprise, given that *Research on Counterproposals and Countermeasures* and *Global Outlook* were written by the same group of high-level tobacco industry insiders.

The first two-thirds of *Global Tobacco Control Outlook* is ostensibly an objective stocktaking. It describes in relatively neutral language the prevalence of tobacco use, tobacco control progress and legislation, the current status of advertising and promotion, tobacco packaging and labeling, and questions surrounding tobacco taxation. The last third of the book presents, in more overtly tendentious language, outlooks on tobacco control, including the view that the "debate" about smoking and health "is not over."[47] Here, the authors also advocate more research into harm reduction, claiming that increasing tobacco taxation will only fuel smuggling and that tobacco control will impair national economic security. In the remaining portion of our chapter, we outline some of these views and provide refutations.

A. One of the claims made in *Global Outlook* is that, as a developing country, China needn't be over-zealous in pursuing tobacco control, because there is a natural correspondence between how strictly tobacco policies are enforced in a country and the level of economic development to be found there: "Developed countries tend to have very strict tobacco-control policies, and smoking rates tend to decline."[48]

Refutation: Experiences of tobacco control in Asia tell a different story. Development, as defined by metrics like GDP, does not closely correlate with how earnestly tobacco-control policies have been pursued. Thailand, for example, does not yet have a highly developed economy, but it does have robust and strictly enforced tobacco-control policies. The level of development in many cities of China, too, is near that found in Hong Kong, Macao, and Taiwan, but tobacco control in wealthy mainland cities is far looser today than in those other Chinese cultural contexts.

B. Another claim made in *Global Outlook* is that "policy makers must keep in mind two duties—protecting national economic security and people's health—when making decisions on what parts of the FCTC are to be implemented and how rigorously: "While not violating our duties under the FCTC, we should adopt only beneficial measures and avoid harmful measures to safeguard national interests. International organizations should respect the different situations and choices of different countries with regard to how to approach tobacco control, its proper scope and reach."[49]

Refutation: Nowhere in the FCTC are such dual responsibilities stated. The principal aim of the FCTC is to "protect public health" by responding to "the devastating worldwide health, social, economic and environmental consequences of tobacco consumption and exposure to tobacco smoke."[50] Signing and ratifying the FCTC are decisions made by each member state. Making those decisions means that a country recognizes and agrees to meet the terms of the treaty. But if each party to the treaty is free to follow its own "approach, scope and reach" during implementation, that would make the whole treaty meaningless.

C. Two overlapping assumptions in *Global Outlook* are that smoking is a basic human right, and that prohibition is unreasonable: "Tobacco control is a good thing, which I raise both hands to support. But prohibition of smoking is impossible. . . . No country, government or organization can issue a decree that says that people are barred from smoking from a certain hour of a certain day, month and year. . . . You cannot ban smoking. . . . Based on provisions that respect human rights in the United Nations' Universal Declaration of Human Rights and the International Covenant on Civil and Political Rights, smoking is a fundamental right of adults and must be respected."[51]

Refutation: The purpose of the Framework Convention on Tobacco Control is to *control* harms caused by tobacco use, not to ban the sale of cigarettes or to eradicate tobacco from the face of the earth. No part of the FCTC calls for a *moratorium* on smoking. The treaty does require bans on smoking in public places—to protect nonsmokers from harms caused by being forced to breathe other people's smoke. The United Nations' Universal Declaration of Human Rights does not guarantee the right to smoke. But its Article 3 does state that "Everyone has the right to life, liberty and security of person," and Article 29 specifies that that "In the exercise of his rights and freedoms, everyone shall be subject only to such limitations as are determined by law solely for the purpose of securing due recognition and respect for the rights and freedoms of others." Banning smoking in public places clearly embraces the spirit of the Universal Declaration of Human Rights.

D. *Global Outlook* likewise claims that there is a conspiracy, fomented by foreigners, to unfairly target tobacco in China, as evidenced by a recent study about the presence of heavy metals in Chinese cigarettes: "Globalized tobacco control creates opportunities for some organizations hoping to destroy a country's tobacco fiscal system and to grab its wealth, profiting from tobacco-control schemes. The latest incident involves publicity surrounding the finding of heavy metals in some tobacco products. We need to be scientific, rational and objective with regard to behaviors intended to stir up intrigues and cause incidents by certain organizations and individuals who attack with one argument but ignore the rest, especially those who consider themselves important by virtue of support from foreigners and US dollars."[52]

Refutation: Scholars from a Chinese research institute and a foreign university in 2006 measured the heavy metals in thirteen different brands of Chinese cigarettes and in 2010 reported that the cadmium, arsenic, and lead in Chinese cigarettes were more than three times higher than in Canadian cigarettes.[53] The Chinese media reported these findings, causing some readers to become concerned about the safety of their smokes. This is a common pattern in science—and hardly grounds for suspicions of a foreign conspiracy or ill-will. Why do the authors of *Global Outlook* turn a routine research finding into an international plot? Political paranoia should play no part in science or public policy.

Concluding Remarks

Research on Counterproposals and Countermeasures is clearly a product of proactive planning by the State Tobacco Monopoly Administration, and *Global Outlook* is a follow-up book written by tobacco industry friendlies. Both publications reveal tobacco industry tactics to manipulate the FCTC, with the goal of continuing the expansion of China's tobacco trade and weakening the FCTC. The authors of both volumes claim their books to be major "scientific achievements" safeguarding "national" and "consumer interests."

In light of this, it is important to return again to the Preamble of the Framework Convention, which acknowledges "the need to be alert to any efforts by the tobacco industry to undermine or subvert tobacco control efforts." In the case of China, we find that an industry-friendly FCTC has been negotiated and implemented as a result of dedicated efforts by the STMA Countermeasures Research Group. Since China has a tobacco regime mingling governmental and commercial operations, and since the STMA is de facto also the China National Tobacco Corporation, two legal entities that are really the same group of people work from very strong positions of power. Under such a regime, the government agency responsible for regulating the tobacco industry is not really in a position to limit tobacco industry conduct. Indeed, the combination of state administrative power and financial strength makes it possible for Chinese cigarette manufacturers to effectively (and openly!) oppose tobacco control and FCTC implementation. The defects in such a regime have become the principal obstacle to effective tobacco control in China.

Tobacco production in the PRC has grown in the years following Beijing's ratification of the FCTC, and smoking rates remain very high. Under this treaty, cigarettes have become the leading preventable cause of death in China. By 2011, China had been a party to the FCTC for five years but still scored lowest on treaty-implementation rankings among all but a few of the one hundred plus parties to the FCTC. And more recent evaluation scores of FCTC implementation in China continue to be egregiously low.[54]

When a country's tobacco-control policy is managed under the same tent with tobacco corporations that have governmental functions, it is like negotiating with a tiger to obtain its fur. The other image that comes to mind is the fox guarding the henhouse. Whatever the metaphor, China must remove the tobacco industry from its position of authority in all matters of tobacco policy if the country is to implement the FCTC treaty with any honesty and effectiveness.

Profit is the ultimate goal of cigarette makers. But that goal comes at a very high price to public health. Human health and tobacco industry profits are, and will always remain, irreconcilable.

Dr. Margaret Chan, director general of the World Health Organization, in her speech at the Conference of Parties held in Uruguay in November 2010 noted that even countries with the best of will and good intentions face obstacles, and that "unquestionably the biggest obstacle is fierce opposition from the tobacco industry. . . . This is an epic battle between the protection of public health and the pursuit of corporate wealth."[55]

Notes

1. World Health Organization, *WHO Framework Convention on Tobacco Control* (Geneva: World Health Organization, 2003), 2.

2. Zhou Ruizeng and Cheng Yongzhao, ed., *WHO yancao kongzhi kuangjia gongyue duian ji dui Zhongguo yancao yingxiang duice yanjiu* [Research on Counterproposals to the WHO Framework Convention on Tobacco Control and Countermeasures to Address Its Impacts on the Chinese Tobacco Industry] (Beijing: Economic Science Press, 2006) (hereafter cited as *Counterproposals*).

3. Cheng Yongzhao, *Quanqiu kongyan liaowang baogao* [Global Tobacco Control Outlook] (Beijing: Economic Daily Press, 2011).

4. STMA Research Group, "Guanyu WHO yancao kongzhi kuangjia gongyue duian ji dui Zhongguo yancao yingxiang duice yanjiu de zongjie baogao" [Summary Report on Research on Counterproposals to the WHO Framework Convention

on Tobacco Control and Countermeasures to Address Its Impacts on Chinese Tobacco], in *Counterproposals*, 3–20.

5. Zhao Baidong, "Shijie weisheng zuzhi kuangjia gongyue gailan" [Overview of the WHO Framework Convention], in *Counterproposals*, 78–84.

6. STMA Research Group, "Guanyu WHO yancao kongzhi kuangjia gongyue duian ji dui Zhongguo yancao yingxiang duice yanjiu de zongjie baogao," 8.

7. Zhao, "Shijie weisheng zuzhi kuangjia gongyue gailan," 84.

8. STMA Research Group, "Guanyu WHO yancao kongzhi kuangjia gongyue duian ji dui Zhongguo yancao yingxiang duice yanjiu de zongjie baogao," 17.

9. Ibid., 8.

10. STMA Research Group, "Shouji fanyi he zhengli youyong ziliao que bao gongyue yanjiu gongzuo shunli kaizhan" [Collecting, Translating and Organizing Useful Materials to Ensure Smooth Research Work], in *Counterproposals*, 220.

11. STMA Research Group, "Dui FCTC juti tiaokuan de jiben renshi ji duice jianyi" [Our Understanding of the FCTC Articles and Policy Recommendations], in *Counterproposals*, 263.

12. Zhao Baidong, "Zhuanmai youliyu kongyan lüyue kongyan geng xuyao zhuanmai" [A Monopoly Regime Is Conducive to Tobacco Control, and FCTC Implementation and Tobacco Control Require a Monopoly Regime], in *Counterproposals*, 358.

13. Zhou Ruizeng, "Tigao renshi cai qu cuoshi youxiao yingdui yancao kongzhi kuangjia gongyue zai gongyue duice yanjiu gongzuo xiaozu erci huiyi shang de jianghua" [Improve Awareness and Take Steps to Effectively Deal with the Framework Convention on Tobacco Control], speech presented at the second meeting of the FCTC Countermeasures Research Group, in *Counterproposals*, 228.

14. STMA Research Group, "Dui FCTC juti tiaokuan de jiben renshi ji duice jianyi," 263.

15. STMA Research Group, "Guanyu WHO yancao kongzhi kuangjia gongyue duian ji dui Zhongguo yancao yingxiang duice yanjiu de zongjie baogao," 3.

16. Zhou, "Tigao renshi cai qu cuoshi youxiao yingdui yancao kongzhi kuangjia gongyue zai gongyue duice yanjiu gongzu xiaozu erci huiyi shang de jianghua," 230.

17. Robert N. Proctor, *Golden Holocaust: Origins of the Cigarette Catastrophe and the Case for Abolition* (Berkeley: University of California Press, 2011).

18. Zheng Fugang, "Yancao kongzhi yu gongzhong jiankang yishi de jiaoyu ji jiaoliu yanjiu" [Research on Tobacco Control and Education and Exchanges on Public Health Awareness], in *Counterproposals*, 318.

19. Zhao Mingyue, "Xiyan yu jiankang de zhenglun yu fazhan" [Debates on Smoking and Health], in *Counterproposals*, 312.

20. STMA Research Group, "Dui FCTC juti tiaokuan de jiben renshi ji duice jianyi," 262–78.

21. STMA Research Group, "Dui INB6 zhuxi wenben de xiugai jianyi" [Suggested Revisions to the Chairman's Text for INB6], in *Counterproposals*, 207.

22. U.S. District Judge Gladys Kessler on August 17, 2006, issued a final opinion in the U.S. government's landmark lawsuit *United States v. Philip Morris* against U.S. cigarette manufacturers, finding them to have "falsely marketed and promoted low-tar/light cigarettes as less harmful than full-flavor cigarettes."

23. Cheng Yongzhao et al., "Zuohao shuangdui yanjiu yingdui kongyan tiaozhan" [Do Good Research on Counterproposals and Countermeasures to Address Challenges from Tobacco Control], in *Counterproposals*, 62.

24. STMA Research Group, "Guanyu lüxing yancao kongzhi kongjia gongyue dui Zhongguo yancao jingji yingxiang de libi fenxi yanjiu baogao" [Report on Positive and Negative Impacts of Implementing the FCTC on China's Tobacco Economy], in *Counterproposals*, 36.

25. Cheng Yongzhao et al., "Guanyu xiyan yu jiankang wenti yanjiu lanpishu" [Blue Book on Smoking and Health], in *Counterproposals*, 369.

26. STMA Research Group, "Guanyu WHO yancao kongzhi kuangjia gongyue duian ji dui Zhongguo yancao yingxiang duice yanjiu de zongjie baogao," 3.

27. STMA Research Group, "Yancao kongzhi kuangjia gongyu dui Zhongguo yancao de zhuyao yingxiang ji Zhongguo yancao ying caiqu de zhuyao cuoshi jianyi zhongqi baogao" [Main FCTC Impacts on Chinese Tobacco and Main Policy Recommendations for Chinese Tobacco (Mid-term Report)], in *Counterproposals*, 251.

28. Cheng Yongzhao, "Disici quanqiu kongyan langchao de xingqi yu fazhan yancao kongzhi kuangjia gongyue tongguo yizhounian shuping" [Rise and Development of the Fourth Global Tobacco Control Movement: Review One Year after the Adoption of the FCTC], in *Counterproposals*, 47.

29. STMA Research Group, "Yancao kongzhi kuangjia gongyue dui Zhongguo yancao yingxiang yanjiu de duice baogao" [Report on Countermeasures to Address FCTC Impacts on Chinese Tobacco], in *Counterproposals*, 282.

30. Hao Heguo, "Jiashui zhengce tiaozheng dui woguo yancao hangye yingxiang de fenxi" [Analysis of Taxation and Pricing Policy Adjustments on the Chinese Tobacco Industry], in *Counterproposals*, 341.

31. STMA Research Group, "Yancao kongzhi kuangjia gongyue dui Zhongguo yancao yingxiang yanjiu de duice baogao," 265.

32. Cheng Yongzhao, "Yi ren wei ben guan'ai jiankang Zhongguo juanyan chanpin de shehui zeren" [People Centered, Health Concerned: The Social Responsibility of Chinese Cigarettes], in *Counterproposals*, 58.

33. Cheng Yongzhao et al., "Zhongguo yancao yu yancao kongzhi kuangjia gongyu" [Chinese Tobacco and the FCTC], in *Counterproposals*, 377–88.

34. Zhou, "Tigao renshi cai qu cuoshi youxiao yingdui yancao kongzhi kuangjia gongyue zai gongyue duice yanjiu gongzuo xiaozu erci huiyi shang de jianghua," 229.

35. Cheng et al., "Zhongguo yancao yu yancao kongzhi kuangjia gongyue," 376.

36. Zhao Baidong, "Yancao kongzhi kuangjia gongyue yanjiu" [Research on the FCTC], in *Counterproposals*, 242.

37. Wang Yulin et al., "Yancao kongzhi kuangjia gongyue" [FCTC Impacts on Chinese Tobacco and Our Countermeasures], in *Counterproposals*, 246.

38. Zhou, "Tigao renshi cai qu cuoshi youxiao yingdui yancao kongzhi kuangjia gongyue zai gongyue duice yanjiu gongzuo xiaozu erci huiyi shang de jianghua," 228.

39. Ibid.

40. Zhao Baidong, "Gongyue tanpan zhong de jiaodian wenti fenxi" [Analysis of Key Issues in FCTC Negotiations], in *Counterproposals*, 87.

41. Ibid.

42. STMA Research Group, "Yancao kongzhi kuangjia gongyue dui Zhongguo yancao yingxiang yanjiu de duice baogao," 285.

43. STMA Research Group, "Dui FCTC juti tiaokuan de jiben renshi ji duice jianyi," 268.

44. STMA Research Group, "Guanyu kaizhan yancao kongzhi kuangjia gongyue duian ji dui Zhongguo yancao yingxiang duice yanjiu keti diaoyan de huibao" [Report on Surveys for Research on Counterproposals and Countermeasures], in *Counterproposals*, 64.

45. STMA Research Group, "Guanyu Yunnan bufen yancao qiye diaoyan qingkuang de huibao" [Report on a Survey of Some Tobacco Companies in Yunnan], in *Counterproposals*, 68.

46. Cheng, *Outlook*, 4.

47. Ibid., 6.

48. Ibid., 55–56.

49. Ibid., 5.

50. World Health Organization, *WHO Framework Convention on Tobacco Control*, 1.

51. Ibid., 3.

52. Ibid., 312

53. Richard J. O'Connor et al., "Cigarettes Sold in China: Design, Emissions and Metals," *Tobacco Control*, 19 (2010): 147–153.

54. Yang Gonghuan and Hu Angang, ed., *Kongyan yu Zhongguo weilai—Zhongwai zhuanjia Zhongguo yancao shiyong yu yancao kongzhi lianhe pinggu baogao* [Tobacco Control and China's Future: A Joint Review by Chinese and Foreign

Experts on Tobacco Use and Tobacco Control in China] (Beijing: Economic Daily Press, 2010), 67 and 139.

55. Margaret Chan, "Address by Dr Margaret Chan, Director-General of WHO" (speech, Punta del Este, Uruguay, November 15, 2010), WHO Institutional Repository for Information Sharing.

Afterword

Robert N. Proctor

From one point of view, nothing could be more natural. Every morning, like clockwork, 350 million Chinese light up a cigarette—and then another and another. Farmers grow and cure leaf, factories roll it into tubes using super-thin paper, and retailers display and sell the finished product. And the state taxes it.

This is hardly something about which we can be complacent. Tobacco kills an estimated 1.2 million Chinese every year, a figure that will grow before it declines. Cigarette death is caused by the massive quantities of poisons inhaled with cigarette smoke: millions of tons of blackening soot and tar are delivered directly into the lungs of Chinese smokers every year—along with thousands of tons delivered into the lungs of nonsmokers. Few parts of the body remain unscathed: the lungs contract cancer of course, but cigarettes also cause gangrene of the feet, macular degeneration, premature sexual senescence, and dozens of other maladies.

China is in the grip of the deadliest epidemic in the history of human civilization. And as with other human-caused calamities, there is plenty of blame to go around. Cigarettes cause disease in China because smokers smoke them, retailers sell them, factories roll them, and farmers grow the leaf. Cigarettes also cause death, though, because the Chinese government encourages the cigarette trade; indeed it is the Chinese state that owns and controls all tobacco manufacturing in China. All of these are causes of the cigarette calamity, parts of a complex chain or web of causality, any one link of which could be broken, and cigarette death would diminish.

It is important to understand these causal links historically. One purpose of history is to understand how the present came into being, but another is to understand how things might have been (and still might be) different. The world that is, is not the world that has to be. We are subject to historical forces, but not in such a way that these are beyond our control.

The Malignant Catastrophe

In China, what is remarkable about the cigarette epidemic is how recently it has emerged. In 1949, the year of China's Communist Revolution, only about eighty billion cigarettes were smoked in the People's Republic. Today that number is larger by a factor of over thirty. This is only partly to be explained by growing wealth and population; it also has to be understood against the backdrop of the monopolization of the tobacco trade by the state and the pharmacologic grip of nicotine. It has to be understood in terms of the isolation of China from the rest of the world, the personal habits of Chinese leaders (notably Mao Zedong and Deng Xiaoping), and the insatiable desire of government for tax revenues. It also has to be understood in terms of the ignorance of ordinary people, which in turn can be traced to the failure of Chinese manufacturers, educators, physicians, and the media leaders to properly warn the public.

It is a convenient myth that "everyone already knows" about the hazards of smoking. Indeed in the United States, the idea of "common knowledge" serves as the cigarette industry's chief exculpatory myth. When the industry is sued for hiding the truth or for selling a defective product, the argument is made that since knowledge of harms has long been "common," smokers have only themselves to blame for whatever injuries they have suffered. Lawyers call this the "assumption of risk" defense—but it has a broader appeal in notions of "personal choice" and "personal responsibility."

Even in the United States, where cigarette sales have been declining for over thirty years, there is much that educated elites do not know about smoking. I teach a lecture course at Stanford, and when I ask my students whether they are *convinced* that smoking is *the leading cause* of cancers of the lung, I find only about two-thirds of the class responding in the affirmative. Surveys from different parts of the world show that smokers are less well informed than nonsmokers, and the poor less informed than the rich. Smoking in most parts of the world has become a habit of vulnerable populations, on whom the companies prey to capture their fidelity.

R.J. Reynolds already in the 1980s expressed these sentiments when asked whether its executives smoke: "Are you kidding? We reserve that right for the poor, the young, the black and the stupid."[1]

Public opinion polls show a poor understanding of the nature and magnitude of tobacco harms. In 2012, a report by the World Heart Association found that only half of all Chinese smokers knew that smoking caused heart disease. "Significant gaps" were also found in the public's understanding of risks from secondhand smoke.[2] And myths about Chinese cigarettes circulate widely. One common myth is that Chinese-style cigarettes are substantially different from foreign brands, despite the total lack of evidence supporting such a view. Chinese cigarettes deliver a similar mix of arsenic, nicotine, cyanide, formaldehyde, carbon monoxide, and radioactive isotopes into a smoker's lungs. Chinese cigarettes are smoked the same way, are just as addictive, and generate cancers and death at about the same rate. Chinese cigarettes cause about one death for every million smoked—as cigarettes do in virtually every corner of the globe. Which means that the 2.6 trillion cigarettes smoked in China this year will cause more than two million deaths a couple of decades from now.

Of course there are some differences. The price elasticity of cigarettes is lower in China (−0.15 vs. −0.4), because Chinese smokers can and do often switch to cheaper brands when taxes go up. Chinese cigarettes also vary much more in price than elsewhere in the world: luxury brands can cost as much as $35 a pack, for example, whereas a cheap pack might cost only 35 cents. On March 28, 2011, the day after the conference that generated this book, I bought a carton of Cold Dew cigarettes at a duty-free shop in Beijing for only 26 renminbi, which is not even 40 cents US per pack. Chinese cigarettes have become significantly more affordable over time: in the ten years from 1996 to 2006, for example, Chinese cigarettes became about 72 percent more affordable, by contrast with the trend in most other Asian nations, where cigarettes have become less affordable.[3]

A Perfect Storm of Neglect?

Cigarette use has to be understood against the backdrop of broader trends. China has become rich in cigarette ritual and romance; cigarettes are used to affirm all manner of human connection and feature regularly in films. Consider the movie *A Big Deal* (2011), where the heroine at one point opens her coat to her lover to shelter him from the wind, allowing him to light his cigarette. The timing of the discovery of cigarette harms is also crucial. Recall that the most important dangers of smoking were discovered in Germany, Argentina, England, and the United States from 1939 to 1954, a period when China was hard pressed to pay attention to medical literature coming out of those countries. The Japanese occupation would not end until 1945, but the postwar years were equally turbulent, and cigarette harms cannot have been high on anyone's list of concerns. The Chinese also smoked only about eighty *billion* cigarettes in 1950, meaning that there cannot have been many people suffering from diseases caused by smoking—especially given the other, more immediate concerns (like starvation). To repeat: 2.6 *trillion* cigarettes are now smoked in China every year, roughly thirty times the number smoked in the year of the Communist Revolution.

Recall also the political climate of the early 1950s, when the key epidemiology and animal experiments were being published in Britain and the United States. Can we really expect the Chinese people to have paid much attention, while still struggling to overcome years of foreign occupation and impoverishment? Would people in Shanghai or Beijing have been reading English language journals like *JAMA* and *Cancer Research* and the *British Medical Journal* during these years? Recall also how trivial cigarette maladies must have seemed in 1959–1960, when the Great Leap famine cost the lives of tens of millions. (Some sources suggest the number could be as high as forty-five million.)[4] At the height of such sufferings, can we expect much significance to have been given to the 1962 report of Britain's Royal College of Physicians, or the 1964 report of the U.S. Surgeon General?[5]

Cigarettes cannot also have been much of a concern in the 1960s or '70s, when the Cultural Revolution shuttered many universities and schools and millions of urbanites were forced to resettle in the countryside. And we should not forget that per capita consumption of cigarettes then was still only about a tenth what it was in Europe or America.[6]

These and other forces led to a "perfect storm of neglect," and make it easier to understand how long it has taken for China to give serious attention to its cigarette epidemic. There is more to this story, however, given the long-standing appeal of cigarettes as a source of governmental income. Tobacco was recognized as a cash cow from the earliest years of its introduction (from the Americas) in the Ming dynasty. Little changed in this regard with the birth of the PRC; indeed, as opportunities for unimpeded commerce shrank, the Chinese government quietly stepped in to take over cigarette manufacturing. The strength of the current monopoly is largely a consequence of the massive tax revenues generated by the golden leaf—over $100 billion in 2013 alone, plus another $20+ billion in profits—and we may not see China's leaders turn seriously against cigarettes until the cost of cigarette-generated illness and lost labor productivity start visibly draining the Chinese economy.

Crucial also to appreciate is the myth-making that surrounds cigarettes. Several essays in this volume have mentioned the myth of "Chinese-style cigarettes," but there is also the myth that filters actually filter (they really don't) and that "low tar" or "light" cigarettes are safer (they are not). Cigarette filters aren't really filters at all, since there is no such thing as "clean smoke." The dirty part is what smokers crave. Filter-tipped cigarettes reassure the public and may be cheaper to produce than regular cigarettes, but they certainly aren't any safer. Indeed there is evidence they are even more dangerous, since filters force the smoker to inhale more deeply, allowing smoke particles to travel deeper into the lungs, where maladies are more difficult to diagnose and to treat.[7] Filters have caused a new wave of adenocarcinomas in the lungs, which is why we sometimes hear such tumors called "filter cancers." Filters also falsely reassure smokers, keeping some at least from quitting. The secret documents from the American tobacco industry are explicit on this: filtered and "low tar" cigarettes were promoted as a "psychological crutch" to keep smokers smoking.[8] As early as 1953, the world's largest cigarette company called filters nothing but "a merchandising and sales promotion proposition."[9] A filter on a cigarette is like a seatbelt made of wet noodles.

Filters, though, are only one of several ways smokers have been led to think of cigarettes as being safe, or at least safer. "Low tar" has become a big push since the 1990s, and Chinese cigarettes are now sold with labels prominently boasting levels of "tar" supposedly delivered by different brands (see Chapter 8 for illustrations). Such numbers are meaningless—and should not be regarded as measures of relative safety. And if this is not widely known in China this should come as no surprise, since it was not widely appreciated by scholars elsewhere until the new millennium. Distinguished Chinese academicians have fallen for the ruse, as the world saw in 2011, when Xie Jianping was elected to the People's Republic's prestigious Academy of Engineering. The award cited Xie's accomplishments in developing "low-tar" cigarettes (he is deputy director of the Zhengzhou Tobacco Research Institute, owned by the China National Tobacco Corporation), when it is well known in the global scientific community that low-tar claims are fraudulent. One might as well have given a prize to a leader of the Flat Earth Society or a denier of Darwin's theory of evolution—or some celebrated practitioner of dragon bone divination.

Chinese manufacturers have often suggested that cigarettes containing "herbal" ingredients like ginseng or ginkgo or jiaogulan are safer than Western smokes. Scientific studies have shown, however, that smokers of herbal cigarettes inhale just as many poisons as smokers of regulars.[10] Ideas about health developed long ago in China may also have made it harder for people in the PRC to realize how dangerous cigarettes really are. Chinese medical practitioners began using smoke (or fire) for therapeutic purposes ages ago: moxibustion dates back thousands of years, for example. And smoke has long been used to cure meats and (more recently) to sterilize medical instruments in many parts of the world, which is also, of course, why it took so long globally to grasp that inhaling cigarette smoke could be deadly: tobacco had been listed in the official pharmacopeia of many nations, and smoke was often used to treat maladies from asthma to the plague.

Compounding the epidemic has been the constant drumbeat of advertising. Tobacco ads were technically banned even before China's ratification of the WHO's Framework Convention on Tobacco Control in 2005, but advertising has continued, albeit in more subtle or surreptitious forms. Sports and cultural event sponsorship has become an insidious form of advertising, allowing the name of a particular brand of cigarette (or cigarette factory!) to remain in circulation simply by naming (or broadcasting) a sponsored event. The prominent display of cigarette packs in stores is another form of advertising, since the pack itself serves as a colorful micro-ad. Package advertising is crucial for brand differentiation, and can be more important than the cigarettes inside. In blind taste tests, smokers are generally unable to distinguish different brands. The cigarette in this sense is very much about images, impressions, and imaginative associations; preferences for different kinds of cigarettes are literally superficial: the packaging is essentially dressing for the nicotine fix inside. Which also helps explain why cigarette companies are so adamant in their opposition to plain packaging, as we now (finally) have in Australia, England, France, and a number of other nations. Smokers purchasing the new packs, festooned with graphic images of diseased feet, teeth, and lungs, report the new cigarettes as "tasting worse," even though all that has really changed is the pack art. Big Tobacco will continue its fight against plain packaging, but that is a battle it is likely to keep losing.

China's cigarette future is by no means clear. By some indications, the country has already become the world's cigarette superpower. It already produces nearly half the world's cigarettes—about 2.6 trillion per year—and that could rise further before it goes lower. Such fabulous volumes are made possible by complex automated machinery, much of which is fashioned abroad but more and more is starting to come from domestic ingenuity. The cigarette-making machines now deployed in China's most advanced factories produce upwards of *20,000 cigarettes per minute*, at extremely low cost. Factories such as the Yuxi Cigarette Factory in Yunnan can now crank out 90 billion cigarettes per year, and since one person is killed for every million cigarettes smoked, this means that a single factory can cause the death of about ninety thousand Chinese every year. The Kunming Cigarette Factory likewise produces seventy-one billion cigarettes per year, killing about seventy-one thousand per annum. China has several dozen such factories, among the deadliest in the history of human civilization.[11]

One glimmer of hope is that China's cigarette industry is owned by the state; the China National Tobacco Company is a state-owned monopoly. Governmental control of the industry could arguably be an asset, insofar as it could make it possible for the state to take strong measures that might not otherwise be possible. China in the 1990s banned the sale or import of (highly polluting) two-stroke engines, for example, a bold step that would have been difficult elsewhere. For this reason I am hopeful that China might actually become one of the first countries to ban the sale of cigarettes.[12] If China were to do this, it would have an enormous and indeed unprecedented impact. Tens of millions of lives, or even hundreds of millions, would be saved. China would become a global public health hero.

Research Opportunities for the Future

The goal of this book has been to stimulate inquiry; it is a beginning, not an end. There are in fact many areas of needed research.

We need to know more about what ordinary Chinese think about cigarettes—whether smokers know that cigarettes contain radioactive polonium, for example, or that smoking can cause gangrene of the feet and erectile dysfunction. We need to know how many Chinese realize that smoke from your neighbor can cause fatal lung cancer, or that millions of Chinese have died from breathing other people's smoke. We need to know what kinds of messages could be given to smokers and potential smokers to make them more likely to quit or less likely to start, whether that be statistics about lung disease or images of facial wrinkles, sexual impotence, or heart attacks and strokes.

We also need to better understand the history of Chinese cigarette designs—what kinds of chemicals have been added, for example, whether by design or by accident (from pesticides or fertilizers). Hundreds of different compounds have been added to cigarettes elsewhere, and the Chinese are likely to have done the same. Elsewhere, cigarette additives have included cough suppressants like menthol but also bronchodilators like theobromine (from chocolate), compounds designed to increase the potency of the nicotine molecule (like ammonia), and chemicals designed to make it easier for nicotine to bind in the brain (like levulinic acid). They have also included castoreum, a secretion from the anal gland of the Siberian beaver, and similar extracts from the civet cat. Have Chinese cigarette makers been putting such compounds into their cigarettes?

And what about burn accelerants—like potassium or sodium citrate or polyvinyl acetate? How often are these found in cigarettes made in China? Elsewhere, many different sugars are added to cigarettes—to stimulate certain physical sensations, of course, but also to lower smoke pH to make the resulting smoke more inhalable. Are similar compounds added to Chinese cigarettes? And what about sugar alcohols like glycerin or flavorants like chocolate or licorice? American manufacturers add millions of pounds of such chemicals to cigarettes every year; what kinds of compounds have been added to Chinese cigarettes, and for what purpose? And what chemicals make their way into cigarettes by accident—insecticides sprayed onto the leaf, for example, or contaminants from the factory or fertilizers used to promote growth?

We also need to know more about the extent to which tobacco industry money has penetrated Chinese academic institutions. Are Chinese cigarette makers using third-party strategies to obscure tobacco hazards—paying scientists to carry water for them? How many professors at universities in China are taking money from cigarette manufacturers? Universities elsewhere have a long history of collaborating with the industry—and at least twenty-five Nobel laureates have taken tobacco money. Are Chinese universities comparably compromised? And to what extent can we talk about scholars being corrupted by such monies?

Another question: What has the Chinese military done to encourage or discourage smoking? Are cigarettes given free to soldiers? When did that practice begin, and when did it end? Some factories used to be run by the People's Liberation Army (PLA)—has this made it difficult to create a smoke-free fighting force? We need a history of cigarettes and cigarette use in the PLA and in other branches of the military, and how cigarette practices, pricing, and policies have changed over time.

We also need to know more generally about how tobacco came to be regarded as an acceptable health catastrophe—by contrast with, say, polio or smallpox. It is strange when you think about it: Chinese public health authorities have done an excellent job eradicating polio, smallpox, and malaria through aggressive preventive measures dating from the Mao era; and even today there is tight border control when it comes to contagious epidemics like SARS or swine flu.

But think about how different this is with tobacco! Tobacco kills far more than polio or smallpox ever did—over a million people every year just in China—so why the soft gloves approach? Is it just that there is no powerful government apparatus making money from the polio virus or malarial mosquito? Is it just that SARS or the swine flu virus do not generate billions of dollars in revenue for the Chinese state? The tobacco epidemic has a distinctly different mechanism of transmission; the principal disease vector is not a mindless virus or some bacterium, but rather a powerful state enterprise generating billions of dollars in tax revenue and profits for the Chinese government. Tobacco is a cash cow, and if "tobacco exceptionalism" is the rule here as elsewhere, this cash flow ("the second addiction") would surely seem to be one plausible explanation.

Sociopolitical Research Challenges

It would be good to know more about how cigarettes might be challenged in the Chinese legal system. Is there any hope for filing lawsuits against the industry, as has been done in the United States? Is there room in Chinese legal doctrines to punish companies claiming that lights, low tars, or filters are safer? Several countries have successfully sued the industry; is there room for a legal action on behalf of Chinese insurance companies burdened with paying for illnesses caused by smoking? What about a lawsuit on behalf of employees forced to inhale secondhand smoke, or smokers suffering from illnesses caused by their habit?

One of the most important outcomes from litigation in the United States has been the release of secret business records; much of what we know about how cigarettes are made and how they have been marketed comes from the documents that have been released through litigation. Is there any way to liberate Chinese cigarette company documents? When did such companies first realize that lights or low tars or herbal cigarettes were no safer, for example, and what steps have been taken to make cigarettes more or less addictive? And if archives are not available, what can we learn from cigarette insiders? Is it possible to set up a website, perhaps a kind of Tobacco Wikileaks, where whistle-blowers could tell what they know without fear of recrimination?

We also need to know more about traditional Chinese notions of blame and responsibility—how Communist or Confucian or Taoist or Buddhist ethics might help us understand whom to blame for the suffering caused by cigarettes, and what should be done. Is the smoker alone to blame for his or her illness? How much should we blame the manufacturers, or governmental elites? And if cigarettes harm the people to such a degree, then why are they still tolerated? What parts of cigarette manufacture can be harmonized with Communist, capitalist, or Confucian ethics, or modern notions of social and corporate responsibility? Tobacco is not just a medical problem; it is also a moral and a political problem, and we need to know more about how different philosophical systems can be harnessed to grapple with this history. And how do Chinese government leaders today regard the sustaining (and exporting) of this epidemic? Is there room in China for considering the global cigarette a violation of human rights, or a crime against humanity?

In the United States, tobacco use is now regarded as a pediatric disease: most smokers start in their teenage years and quickly become addicted. What opportunities are there for regarding Chinese cigarette use as a pediatric disease? And how do children in China get their cigarettes? The Chinese government in 2014 barred cigarette ads, sales, and smoking in schools— but what evidence do we have that cigarette makers still target youth? What is the history of such targeting, and of brand segmentation more generally? And is it still true in China, as in the United States, that no one starts smoking to look younger?

We also need to know more about the history of Chinese conceptions of addiction. Pharmacologists now recognize the nicotine molecule as being as addictive as heroin and cocaine—and we say that while the 1964 Surgeon General's report showed that smoking *causes* disease, the 1988 Surgeon General's report showed that smoking *is* a disease. But how widely is this appreciated in China? And how, precisely, has addiction been understood in Chinese medical and philosophical traditions? China has powerful cultural memories of suffering from imperialistic opium wars, but how fair is any comparison between nicotine addiction and the country's experience with opium? And why has there been so little focus on the addictive powers of cigarettes in China—is this because nicotine is not regarded as hampering manual or intellectual labor? What can we say about Marxist or Maoist conceptions of addiction, or addiction as it has been understood in older Confucian, Taoist, or Buddhist traditions? And how can traditional concepts of addiction (or dependence, or slavery, or liberation) be adapted to the modern situation in ways that would promote the health and well-being of the people?

We need to know more about whether Chinese movies are starting to include product placement—there is a long history of Hollywood films containing ads for particular cigarette brands, but what kind of arrangements have been made in China? Cigarettes are now being glamorized and romanticized in Chinese cinema and television, and we need to know what kinds of quid pro quos may be involved.

We need to know more about when and where Chinese have been allowed to smoke, and why smoking was not barred in Chinese hospitals sooner. And why even today nearly half of all physicians still smoke! We need histories of resistance to cigarettes, and how arguments against their use have changed over time. We need explorations of the "material culture" of tobacco and cigarette paraphernalia: histories of Chinese ashtrays and matches and lighters, for example, and of Chinese retail displays; we need histories of Chinese smoking gestures and iconography and smoking etiquette—and histories of Chinese tobacco trade associations. And histories of specific brands and factories. And again, we need insiders to come forward and tell their stories.

We also need creative research into how ordinary smokers understand the diseases they contract from smoking. Whom do the Chinese blame when they contract cancer? Do they blame themselves, or their cigarettes, or no one at all? Why don't they blame the manufacturer, or the government that profits so much from such products?[13] And what kinds of educational or media campaigns might make them more likely to blame someone other than themselves?

We also need more research into the history of individual cigarette factories and the kinds of propaganda they have issued—internally or to the public at large—to sell cigarettes. For how long has there been an effort to deny the reality of harms linked to smoking? And when and from whom did Chinese cigarette makers learn their techniques of creating ignorance? From foreign manufacturers? Is there evidence of such links in the American documents?

We need to know more about the extent to which rhetorics of trivialization, moderation, and distraction have been deployed. All of these rhetorics are familiar in Western tobacco denialism ("anything can be considered harmful . . . applesauce is harmful if you get too much of it");[14] but we also need to know how techniques used to create ignorance with regard to cigarettes may differ from those used, say, to suppress information about the Tangshan earthquake of 1976 (which killed hundreds of thousands) or the massacre at Tiananmen Square (1989), or high levels of Chinese air and water pollution. Asymmetries in media reporting should be examined: why did the poisoning of a few thousand people with infant formula (with melamine in 2008) become such a scandal, while the poisoning of millions by cigarettes is so easily tolerated? To what can we trace this ongoing state of radical tobacco apathy and radical tobacco exceptionalism?

One last point: we need to better understand the history of Chinese cigarette manufacturing in the broader context of efforts to combat corruption. President Xi Jinping has launched an aggressive campaign against corruption, a campaign targeting both large and small, "tigers and flies." This could well create another opportunity to see the cigarette as more than a consumed object, an opportunity to link the tobacco catastrophe with the broader history of corruption and pollution. The cigarette corrupts the body, the way corruption as we normally regard it corrupts the body politic. It could well be that the campaign against corruption may start to expose cracks in the cigarette behemoth, and gain strength from the better publicized and more loudly vocalized need to clean up China's urban air. Worries about pollution are weakened, though, if nothing is done to rein in a multibillion dollar industry dedicated solely to delivering deadly poisons directly into the lungs of addicted cigarette smokers. Similar concerns—and a similarly critical historiography—have been crucial to opening eyes and clearing lungs in many nations, and we can hope that similar efforts may have similar impacts in China. What is needed, again, is an effort to go upstream, to identify "the causes of causes." So not just what causes cancer or lung or heart disease or a slavish devotion to an inhaled alkaloid, but what can be done to break the complacent attitude we find with regard to the world's leading preventable cause of death.

. . .

However much appearing ferocious, those inside the cigarette industry of all countries are paper tigers. Even so, it is probably best to use a long stick in waking them. Critical historiography can help us sculpt such a long stick, one with a suitably pointed end.

Notes

1. Bob Herbert, "Tobacco Dollars," *New York Times*, Nov. 28, 1993, http://legacy.library.ucsf.edu/tid/ojv68aoo.

2. World Heart Federation, "Global Ignorance of Tobacco's Harm to Cardiovascular Health Costing Lives," April 20, 2012, http://www.world-heart-federation.org/press/releases/detail/article/global-ignorance-of-tobaccos-harm-to-cardiovascular-health-costing-lives.

3. Teh-wei Hu et al., "Tobacco Taxation and Its Potential Impact in China," summarized in "Tobacco Taxes in China," http://www.worldlungfoundation.org/ht/a/GetDocumentAction/i/6558.

4. Frank Dikötter, "Mao's Great Leap to Famine," *New York Times*, Dec. 15, 2010, http://www.nytimes.com/2010/12/16/opinion/16iht-eddikotter16.html?_r=1&.

5. Royal College of Physicians of London, *Smoking and Health* (London: Pitman, 1962); U.S. Department of Health, Education and Welfare, *Report of the Advisory Committee of the Surgeon General* (Washington, DC: U.S. Government Printing Office, 1964).

6. In 1960, 680 million Chinese smoked about 200 billion cigarettes, or about 290 cigarettes per person. That same year 180 million Americans smoked about 480 billion cigarettes, or about 2,700 per person. Thus per capita consumption was roughly nine times higher in the United States than in China.

7. U.S. Department of Health and Human Services, *The Health Consequences of Smoking—50 Years of Progress: A Report of the Surgeon General* (Washington, DC: U.S. Government Printing Office, 2014).

8. George Weissman to Joseph F. Cullman, III, "Surgeon General's Report," Jan. 29, 1964, http://legacyllibrary.ucsf.edu/tid/byg56boo.

9. Hiram Hanmer's assessment is memorialized in a memo from November 17, 1953, http://legacy.library.ucsf.edu/tid/wti54foo, p. 4.

10. Quan Gan et al., "Chinese 'Herbal' Cigarettes Are as Carcinogenic and Addictive as Regular Cigarettes," *Cancer Epidemiology, Biomarkers & Prevention*, 18 (2009): 3497–3501.

11. For maps and production data on these and 480 other global cigarette factories, see the *Cigarette Citadels* website maintained by Matthew Kohrman at: http://www.stanford.edu/group/tobaccoprv/cgi-bin/wordpress/, and http://www.stanford.edu/group/tobaoccoprv/cgi-bin/map/; also Robert N. Proctor, "The History of the Discovery of the Cigarette–Lung Cancer Link: Evidentiary Traditions, Corporate Denial, Global Toll," *Tobacco Control*, 21 (2012): 97–91.

12. By "cigarettes" I mean combustible tobacco products rolled in paper which deliver nicotine with a smoke pH less than 8. E-cigarettes are not cigarettes in this sense, nor are cigars. "Small cigars" are often de facto cigarettes—because they are designed to be inhaled and are wrapped in a kind of paper made from reconstituted tobacco. Different tobacco products have radically different health consequences and radically different ethical or political assessments. In China, conventional cigarettes now generate roughly 98 percent of the negatives linked to tobacco use.

13. Matthew Kohrman, "Depoliticizing Tobacco's Exceptionality: Male Sociality, Death, and Memory-Making among Chinese Cigarette Smokers," *China Journal*, 58 (2007): 85–109.

14. The applesauce comparison is by Helmut Wakeham, Philip Morris's powerful vice president for research, in an interview for the 1976 Thames Television documentary *Death and the West*; see my *Golden Holocaust: Origins of the Cigarette Catastrophe and the Case for Abolition* (Berkeley: University of California Press, 2011), pp. 301–4. And for ignorance creation more generally, see Robert N. Proctor and Londa Schiebinger, eds., *Agnotology: The Making and Unmaking of Ignorance* (Stanford, CA: Stanford University Press, 2007).

Contributors

Carol Benedict is professor of history at the Edmund Walsh School of Foreign Service and the Department of History, Georgetown University. Her
research focuses on the social history of medicine and disease in China,
gender, and the history of Chinese consumer culture. Her most recent book
is *Golden-Silk Smoke: A History of Tobacco in China, 1550–2010*.

Gan Quan is the director of Tobacco Control of the International Union
Against Tuberculosis and Lung Disease. His research tackles various topics
pertaining to tobacco control in China. He has been investigating the burden of disease wrought by secondhand smoke, tobacco industry sponsorship in Chinese universities, and the deception of light, mild, and herbal
cigarettes.

Stanton Glantz is one of the world's leading tobacco-control advocates and
researchers. Professor of medicine at the University of California at San
Francisco, he directs the UCSF Center for Tobacco Control Research and
Education and conducts research on a wide range of topics ranging from
the health effects of secondhand smoke to the efficacy of different tobacco
control policies. He is the author of four books and over 350 scientific papers, including the first major review that identified involuntary smoking as
a cause of heart disease and the landmark July 19, 1995, issue of *JAMA* on
the Brown and Williamson documents.

Teh-wei Hu, professor emeritus of the University of California at Berkeley, is the director of the Public Health Institute's Center for International
Tobacco Control. Professor Hu's areas of expertise are the application of

econometrics to health care services research, mental health economics, and the economics of tobacco control. He has authored more than two hundred publications, with special focus on tobacco tax policy. He has served as a consultant to the World Bank, the World Health Organization, and the governments of Hong Kong and Taiwan, and as a senior policy advisor to the Chinese Ministry of Health.

Huangfu Qiushi is a lecturer in the history of modern China at Fudan University. Her scholarly work focuses on China's economic development in both indigenous and international contexts. She is the author of the book *The Choices in Crisis: The Chinese Cigarette Market during the Nanjing Decade.*

Matthew Kohrman is an associate professor in Stanford's Department of Anthropology and senior fellow at the Stanford Medical School. His research brings anthropological methods to bear on the ways health, culture, and politics are interrelated, as seen in his book, *Bodies of Difference: Experiences of Disability and Institutional Advocacy in the Making of Modern China.* He has published widely on the biopolitics of tobacco in Chinese contexts, co-founded Pioneers for Health (China's first tobacco-control NGO), and created the *Cigarette Citadels* mapping project.

Cheng Li directs the Brookings Institution's John L. Thornton China Center. Informed by his youth in China during the Cultural Revolution and his PhD in political science from Princeton, Dr. Li's research examines the transformation of Chinese political leaders, generational change, and technological development. He has authored and edited numerous books, including *China's Emerging Middle Class: Beyond Economic Transformation, The Political Mapping of China's Tobacco Industry and Anti-Smoking Campaign,* and *Chinese Politics in the Xi Jinping Era: Reassessing Collective Leadership.*

Li Jinkui received a master degree in epidemiology and health statistics from Hebei Medical University. He previously worked for the Tangshan CDC and is now clinical deputy director at the Beijing-based ThinkTank Research Center for Health Development, where he focuses on disease prevention and treatment, with special emphasis given to tobacco-related issues.

Liu Wennan is associate researcher at the Institute of Modern History, Chinese Academy of Social Sciences. Her primary research interests focus on the history of everyday life in twentieth-century China, with particular emphasis on interactions between politics and people's daily life. In addition to anti-cigarette campaigns, she studies nuisance management in nineteenth-century Shanghai and the New Life Movement in the 1930s. She is the author of *The Anti-Cigarette Campaigns in Modern China.*

Pang Yingfa worked for 35 years at the Chinese Academy of Preventive Medicine (renamed the Chinese Center for Disease Control and Prevention in 2001), where, for a decade, he directed the Department of Health Standards. Since then, he has been affiliated with the Beijing-based ThinkTank Research Center for Health Development, working on tobacco-related issues.

Robert N. Proctor is professor of the history of science at Stanford University, where he is also professor, by courtesy, of pulmonary medicine. He works on the political history of knowledge and ignorance, ranging into topics such as Nazi medicine, human origins, and the political history of gems. He is the author of *Golden Holocaust: Origins of the Cigarette Catastrophe and the Case for Abolition.*

Sha Qingqing is a researcher at the Shanghai Library with an academic background in history and philology. His articles have appeared in *Journal of Modern Chinese History* and *Social Sciences in China* as well as *Lishi yanjiu, Jindaishi yanjiu,* and *Zhonggong dangshi yanjiu.* He is a contributor to *Maoism at the Grassroots: Everyday Life in China's Era of High Socialism.*

Ronald Sun received a bachelor of arts degree in history and economics from Fudan University. He then completed a master of arts degree in sociology at Tsinghua University, where he researched relationships between public health, governance, and the market as related to issues such as tobacco control, blood donations, and obesity. He currently lives in Beijing.

Wu Yiqun is executive director of the ThinkTank Research Center for Health Development in Beijing. She has been a professor at the Chinese Academy of Preventive Medicine, where she served as the academy's vice president. For nearly two decades she has been a leading advocate of stronger tobacco-control policies in China. In 2010, she received a WHO Director-General Special Recognition Award.

Yang Gonghuan is a professor in the Chinese Academy of Medical Sciences as well as the School of Basic Medicine, Peking Union Medical College. An epidemiologist of chronic noncommunicable diseases, she has served as vice-director of China's National Center of Disease Control and Prevention.

For much of her career she has focused on tobacco prevention, with her research papers appearing in many of the most prestigious of English- and Chinese-language medical journals. Professor Yang has received numerous awards, including from the World Health Organization and China's Ministries of Health and Education.

Index

academic institutions and tobacco industry, 26–27, 234, 239–46, 281, 284–85
air-cured tobacco, 159, 163
air pollution, 14, 149, 288
Aivaz, Boris, 208
allocation stations, 163, 175nn7–9
American Cancer Society, 14
An Pingsheng, 187, 188, 189
Analects Fortnightly, The (*Lunyu banyuekan*), 100
Analects group, 100
Anhui Institute of Tobacco Research, 237
Anhui Province, 181, 182, 185
Anhui Tobacco School, 236
Anti-Japanese War (1937–45), 17, 25, 37, 38, 39, 43–44, 50, 141
ARTIST. *See* Asian Regional Tobacco Industry Science Team
Aschoff, Karl, 153n25
Asian Regional Tobacco Industry Science Team (ARTIST), 233–34, 247
Australia: plain packaging in, 282

Bai Enpei, 188

Baojiafang, 141
Beijing, 175n1, 201n5, 234; Nanchang Road, 142
Beijing Cigarette Factory, 142, 266
Berlant, Lauren, 150
Big China (*Da Zhongguo*) brand, 8
Big Deal, A, 279–80
biogovernance/biopolitics, 158, 162
Bloomberg Philanthropies, 167
Bonsack, James, 4
branding of cigarettes, 3, 7, 9–10, 41, 147–48, 162, 211, 282; megabrands, 135; relationship to masculinity, 98–99; relationship to normalization, 8, 9; STMA/CNTC policies regarding, 11–13, 149; variants within brand families, 30n28; in Yunnan Province, 185, 187
Brandt, Allan: on the cigarette century, 4
Brazil: cultivation of tobacco in, 3
British American Tobacco (BAT), 51, 54n12, 78, 80, 145, 146, 233, 235; marketing in China, 8, 9, 112; Shanghai factory, 138, 140; vs. STMA, 2, 22
Butler, Judith: on petty sovereigns, 150

Uneasy Partnerships: China's Engagement with Japan, the Koreas, and Russia in the Era of Reform
Edited by Thomas Fingar (2017)

Divergent Memories: Opinion Leaders and the Sino-Japanese War
Gi-Wook Shin and Daniel Sneider (2016)

Contested Embrace: Transborder Membership Politics in Twentieth-Century Korea
Jaeeun Kim (2016)

The New Great Game: China and South and Central Asia in the Era of Reform
Edited by Thomas Fingar (2016)

The Colonial Origins of Ethnic Violence in India
Ajay Verghese (2016)

Rebranding Islam: Piety, Prosperity, and a Self-Help Guru
James Bourk Hoesterey (2015)

Global Talent: Skilled Labor as Social Capital in Korea
Gi-Wook Shin and Joon Nak Choi (2015)

Failed Democratization in Prewar Japan: Breakdown of a Hybrid Regime
Harukata Takenaka (2014)

New Challenges for Maturing Democracies in Korea and Taiwan
Edited by Larry Diamond and Gi-Wook Shin (2014)

Spending Without Taxation: FILP and the Politics of Public Finance in Japan
Gene Park (2011)

The Institutional Imperative: The Politics of Equitable Development in Southeast Asia
Erik Martinez Kuhonta (2011)

One Alliance, Two Lenses: U.S.-Korea Relations in a New Era
Gi-Wook Shin (2010)

Collective Resistance in China: Why Popular Protests Succeed or Fail
Yongshun Cai (2010)